385-846
$14.95

Remembering LEACOCK

Remembering LEACOCK

an oral history by

ALLAN ANDERSON

DENEAU

Canadian Cataloguing in Publication Data

Anderson, Allan, 1915-
Remembering Leacock: an oral biography

ISBN 0-88879-093-7 (bound) - ISBN 0-88879-088-0 (pbk.)

1. Leacock, Stephen, 1869-1944-Biography. 2. Authors,
Canadian (English)—20th century—Biography. 3.
Humorists, Canadian—Biography. I. Title.

PS8523.E15Z56 1983   C818'.5209   C83-090089-6

Design: Ron Greene and Heather Walters
Cover photograph courtesy of the Stephen Leacock Memorial Home

© Allan Anderson, 1983

Deneau Publishers
411 Queen Street
Ottawa, Canada K1R 5A6

Printed in Canada
First Printing

This book is for Stephen Leacock, who remains vividly alive in the minds of all those who knew him. The kindest, the most colourful of men, he was unique in his generation. He was a most beloved teacher, an internationally-known humourist, but, above all, a man of intense intellectual vigour, of abounding wit, a man who was forever young and always curious about life.

Contents

The Storytellers

These are the people whose personal recollections of Stephen Leacock make up this book. They are grouped in categories. For the sake of simplicity, only the year a student graduated is given. Most of the students were in Leacock's classes during their undergraduate years.

Family:
Jean Cain (Stephens), second cousin of
    Leacock's wife Beatrix
George Leacock, brother
Mary Leacock, sister-in-law
Barbara Nimmo (Ulrichsen), niece
Dovie Payne (Leacock), second cousin

Friends and acquaintances:
Douglas C. Abbott
Mrs. Alice Baldwin (Sharples)
Norah Bastedo (Drinkwater)
Fred Carter
Marge Carter (Tudhope)
Catherine Drinkwater
John Drinkwater
Charles Fisher
Marjorie Fisher
Harold Hale
Beth Hatley
Henry Janes
Bob Kilby
Elizabeth Burrows Langdon
Hal Lawrence
Joe McDougall
Louis Melzack

Sue Mulcahy
Dora Noy (Vick)
Hilda Outridge
Paul Phelan
Harold Roland
B.K. Sandwell
Dode Spencer (Tudhope)
Iva Street
Redvers Stubley
Bob Tait
Hélène Tolmie
Wilf Varley

Employees:
Hilda Elsliger
Aubrey Gaudaur
Joe Gaudaur
George Moase
Oscar Olimer
Albanie Pelletier
Fred Perigo
Grace Reynolds
Jennie Mackenzie Smith
Morley Young

Students and colleagues:
Allan Anderson, 1936
Wilson Becket, 1931
F. Munroe Bourne, 1931
Bob Bowman, 1932
Bob Campbell, 1930
Prof. John Culliton
Garner Currie, 1933
Brigadier-General Jimmy de Lalanne, 1919

Eileen Flanagan, 1934 (student of Lea-
cock's in 1917)
Senator Eugene Forsey, 1925
Norman H. Friedman, 1921
D. Lorne Gales, 1932
Senator H. Carl Goldenberg, 1928
The Hon. Mr. Justice G. Miller Hyde, 1926
Col. H. Wyatt Johnston, 1921
Judge Harold B. Lande, 1929
Senator Alan A. Macnaughton, 1926
Maysie MacSporran, 1927
Dr. T.R. Matthews
Gladstone Murray, 1912
A. Gordon Nairn, 1926
Frank Nobbs, 1936
John Pemberton, 1927
Col. Charles Petch, 1928
Charlie Peters, 1928
William H. Pugsley, 1934
G. Meredith Rountree, 1931
Phoebe Gutelius Seely, 1931
Trueman Seely, 1931
Margaret Stephen, 1926
Fred Stone, 1931
Frederick Taylor, 1930
Herbert H. Tees, 1933
Laurence Tombs, 1924
Jean Van Vliet, 1932
Philip Vineberg, 1935
The Hon. Mr. Justice Allison Walsh, 1933
Barbara Whitley, 1940

Others:
Grace Annesley
Frank Birbalsingh
Jay Cody
Bill McGill
Pete McGarvey
Karen McKee
S. Morgan-Powell
Jim Nichol

Preface

It is a sweltering July afternoon in southern Ontario. Even under the big red oak and the old maple tree, the heat is intense. The world has been hushed by heat. From the hilltop where our house is, I scan the valley ahead and, beyond that, the undulating ridges of bush, farmland, and farmhouses and the sideroad leading south: nothing moves. The battered wicker furniture near the honeysuckle bush waits in vain for occupants. It seems as if there have always been summer days like this in old Ontario.

There might be a bit of a breeze on Lake Couchiching, out from Orillia. Half a century ago, Stephen Leacock could have been in one of his nondescript boats, falling asleep over his fishing line or talking and drinking with friends (in equal

Birthplace of Stephen Leacock in Swanmore, Hampshire, England. *Courtesy of the Stephen Leacock Memorial Home.*

proportions) as the wind ruffled the water slightly, and the fish ignored them.

Almost fifty years ago, a little later in the summer, he put up a notice concerning his sailboat, the *Selwyn*, saying:

The Yacht Selwyn challenges the Dinghy Shaw
to defend the Kingston Cup won in 1933.
The old Brewery Bay Yacht Club
will place a Quart of Champagne
on the Pier of the Club House,
otherwise the Wharf of the Boat House:
If the Selwyn loses
a New Cup will be given to the Defender.
Race 5:30 P.M.
Course Out and Back Around the New Bay.
God Save the King.

It was a good life, the best life possible for him during those long summer days: writing, fishing, sailing, poking around his garden. Ontario suited him; Orillia was the right place for him.

It's humdrum to say that artists are complicated people. I studied under Stephen Leacock and have never forgotten him in five intervening decades. In certain ways, of course, he was complicated, but basically, he was artless and straight-forward.

Leacock was a genius, as Robertson Davies has pointed out. He was also a country man who looked like a burly teddy bear that had been painstakingly taught to dress itself but had never quite got it right. His appearance, ruddy cheeks and all, was like a farmer whose wife made him put on whatever of his Sunday clothes happened to be hanging in the cupboard and dragged him along on a shopping spree.

J.B. Priestley met him in the 1930s and described him very accurately: "He was a chunky man, with a square face, rumpled grey hair, bristling eyebrows and moustache, and small deep-set eyes: a good physical type. I cannot remember a word of our talk but I know it was easy and companionable and that we laughed a lot . . . his rather loud laugh rang out at his own jokes as well as mine, as we swapped stories and passed the whisky; he was immediately and immensely likeable."

Leacock enjoyed the countryside. He liked fishing and sailing, and he liked growing things. Orillia suited him, and whether the town liked it or not, he suited Orillia. He was a man who was comfortable with small places.

He was born in 1869 in Swanmore, England and, for years, didn't know which Swanmore (since there are two) until he finally got his birth certificate from Swanmore, Hampshire. His boyhood was spent near Sutton, Ontario on a farm. There were eleven children, an incompetent father whom Leacock detested, misery and debt. His beloved mother moved to Orillia in 1895, which then had 4,900 people and was a fast-growing little town, having added 155 people to its population in ten years.

Little towns have very distinct personalities. In 1951, the Canadian historian Arthur Lower (a man who had the bad luck to be born in Barrie) poked fun at Orillia for making a big thing of Champlain and Leacock. Lower said:

Leacock with unknown girl, circa 1890. *Courtesy of the Stephen Leacock Memorial Home.*

"Citizens of Barrie would not erect a monument to the Angel Gabriel, even if a visit from him should actually have taken place. They are their own best monuments and feel no need of support from men like Champlain. Had Leacock lived in Barrie, he would, as a native son, have been ostentatiously ignored."

That's because Barrie was a dull place, not at all like Orillia. Orillia had a high proportion of peculiarly interesting people and when these curious and lovable citizens fell under Leacock's penetrating gaze, they became an integral part of his fertile imagination. It was like blotting paper soaking up ink. Many of the Leacocks were extraordinary themselves so Leacock had a natural affinity for the characters who strolled the streets of Orillia, ran businesses, or got themselves into ridiculous situations. More than anything else, the people he saw around him in Edwardian Orillia delighted him.

Leacock liked the conservatism of rural Ontario, to the easy and natural country life, and a structured existence at Old Brewery Bay, where he was left alone as much as he wanted and could have company when he cared to. He slopped around happily in old clothes like any hobo, and was regarded by some as the town drunk—there were stories of wild

parties at Old Brewery Bay. It's true that Leacock took to Scotch like a camel takes to water after a forty-mile hike across the Sahara, but Leacock was never a drunk. No one ever saw him drunk, and though his face might get beet-red on occasion no one has yet legislated against that.

Leacock went to the University of Toronto in 1887. He claimed he lived in seventeen different boardinghouses during this period and this description of them is one of his classic paragraphs.

I was not alone in the nomadic life that I led. There were hundreds of us drifting about in this fashion from one melancholy

The University of Toronto *Varsity* (student newspaper) staff, 1891. Stephen Leacock, standing, is at the far right in back row. *Courtesy of the Stephen Leacock Memorial Home.*

habitation to another. We dined in the basement. We always had beef, done up in some way after it was dead, and there were always soda biscuits on the table. They used to have a brand of soda biscuits in those days in Toronto boarding houses that I have not seen since. They were better than dog biscuits, but with not so much snap.

Leacock studied under economist Thorstein Veblen at the University of Chicago. That university more than willingly gave him a Ph.D. when an examiner unhappily asked him a question about the very subject on which Leacock had feverishly swotted up. Leacock spouted at him, and the other examiners, hour after hour.

During his period at the University of Chicago, he wooed Beatrix (Trix) Hamilton, an elegant, gracious amateur actress and a niece of Sir Henry Pellatt, who sought to immortalize himself by building Casa Loma. They were married in 1900 and it was, by all reports, an excellent marriage.

Before his Chicago period, he taught at Upper Canada College and hated it. In 1901, he joined the brand-new Department of Economics and Political Science at McGill full-time. In 1906 he published his very serious *Elements of Political Science*. It sold more copies than any of his other books.

Meanwhile he was in and out of Orillia, first settling at Old Brewery Bay in 1908, where he and his brother Charlie threw up a shack called "the cook house." Around then he gathered up a clutch of humourous pieces he'd published in magazines and periodicals over the years and sent them to Houghton Mifflin, the firm that had published his *Elements of Political Science*. They thought he was mad

and told him as much, so he got together with his brother George and published the collection as *Literary Lapses*. The book sold 3,000 copies in Montreal. John Lane published it in England. Leacock, the humourist, was launched.

Beatrix Leacock as a young woman. The photograph is believed to be here graduation picture. *Courtesy of the Stephen Leacock Memorial Home.*

In 1911 *Nonsense Novels* appeared, but his greatest book, *Sunshine Sketches of a Little Town*, came out in 1912. Except for Canon Greene (who was Dean Drone) and one or two others, Orillians were appalled. People in little towns poke their noses into each other's business, but they can't abide outsiders doing it. Even less can they accept a local author, teacher or whoever, ridiculing them in the eyes of the world. In little towns this is not done; there is no other side to the issue.

What is fascinating is that of all the jesters, humourists, satirists, and ironists who ever wrote in the English language, Leacock was the gentlest. He had a mischievous sense of fun, and often took aim at greedy, big-city merchants and shallow, pretentious women. But he was a small-town boy all his life (albeit an intelligent and inventive one) and truly understood small places and their iconoclastic individualism and idiosyncrasies.

Orillia was a small place—by the 1930s its population had only risen to 8,000. Leacock's beloved McGill was also a small place. When I was there, just before Leacock was unceremoniously booted out in 1936 at the age of sixty-five, it had an undergraduate population of 2,400. It was a lively, cosy, friendly university with an unbelievable number of student activities and an assortment of good and weirdly colourful professors. Leacock loved McGill, as did his students; but above all, those who took his classes loved him.

Then there was the University Club in Montreal, to which Leacock and his inseparable buddy, Professor René du Roure (his most unlikely companion), repaired after classes to drink Scotch and sodas and cheat each other at billiards.

So all Leacock's worlds were little ones and, in a way, he always remained an innocent. When he first worked on *Sunshine Sketches*, he could see nothing wrong in using people's real names and, when he was talked out of that, the changes he made in surnames often amounted only to the alteration of a letter or two.

All his life, Leacock had the curiosity of a child. He poked into people's lives in that direct way that is common to children. He was very impetuous: he always wanted things done *right now*, and he was constantly given to reeling off lists of books or quoting paragraphs or pages from books, or making up lists, in the same way that children insist on rattling off their ABCs or counting over and over again, or making little piles of this-and-that.

Gossip goes on all the time. Adam and Eve probably gossiped about each other to the birds and the bees, and Leacock gossiped about Orillia. But it was marvellous fun; he never set out to cut up people. As Frank Birbalsingh points out in this book, Stephen Leacock realized the world would always be imperfect. He wasn't out to change it. He just wanted to record the wonderful foibles of human nature.

Once more, I go back to J.B. Priestley, writing about Leacock's humour: "It is in fact the satirical humour of a very shrewd but essentially good-natured and eupeptic man, anything but an angry reformer."

The essence of Leacock is, indeed, the comic spirit of man at its best. Leacock chuckled his way through life, but he had a sad side too. His wife, whom he deeply loved, died of cancer at the age of forty-six and his only son, Stevie, Jr., was a dwarf. Leacock, whenever he could, lavished love on him, but young Stevie quickly turned into a little fiend and remained so throughout his life.

Fortunately, after the death of Trix, Leacock had a very good friend in Fitz Shaw, an artistic, attractive (though to some an occasionally haughty) Montreal socialite. They were great pals, drinking and talking and laughing in Montreal and Orillia (where she had a summer home next to his). So, while Leacock was down in the dumps at times, he soon got over it and erupted in chuckles.

In certain ways Stephen Leacock was an old-fashioned man, the nineteenth-century man at his best. Never urban, he was always rural and believed in the virtues of hard work, morality and directness. He stared you straight in the eye. He was also an Edwardian man, with the gusto and vitality that characterized that age. Above all, he was a man with the enthusiasm, the sense of puckish fun and the mischievousness of youth. He laughed spontaneously and revelled in his own jokes, as do the young. He was his own man, and said it best:

> *Let me lie down among the daisies, with my*
> *stomach to the sky,*
> *Making poses in the roses, in the middle of*
> *July,*
> *Let me nestle in the nettles, let me there*
> *absorb the dew*
> *On a pair of flannel breeches with the*
> *stitches worked in blue.*

I have done seven books in seven years, the main ones oral histories. I am getting too long in the tooth to be running around Canada with a tape recorder. But before I wrapped up this demanding business of doing books, I promised myself I would do one book that would be a memorial to Stephen Leacock, still so alive in the memories of those who knew him.

It wasn't always easy. He died in 1944, so I set out to find people who knew him before then. I tracked down seventy-six. The other contributors' recollections came from previously published sources. I could have found more, but a writer must know when to stop. I had what I'd gone after. I talked to people in Orillia who worked for him, knew him socially or who, as children, acted in the short plays he used to write for them and their parents at Christmastime and in the summer. I found students of his going back to 1917 and old colleagues. I chatted with men who knew him at the University Club and bought him drink after drink as he entertained a charmed circle with his witty and wonderful talk. In the book there is also material from twelve people who were unavailable to me or are now dead. In all, ninety-one people recall Leacock at first hand; I don't think anyone has done an oral history of a Canadian like this before.

In my interviews, I discovered two or three prevailing themes. Over and over, men and women told me how kind Leacock was to them and others, how thoughtful and considerate. Those who studied under him, and those who knew him in other capacities, all recalled him vividly, and most had their own original stories to tell about him.

Academic historians often think there is only one version of history, which has to be dug out of archives. Such a view, actually, is incompatible with human nature. We all see things differently, even the most casual occurrence. Stephen Leacock was a multifaceted man, even though his basic character was clear.

People saw this absorbing man in different ways and from different angles. You'll find stories here and there in this book that contradict each other. It doesn't happen often, but it happens. Each person is right: that's what was seen and felt. The great Canadian historian, Donald Creighton, told me once that history is "character and circumstance." It is the character of Stephen Leacock and the circumstances that made up his life that you will find here.

ALLAN ANDERSON
R.R. #3, Tottenham, Ont.
July 2, 1983

Portrait of Stephen Leacock, probably taken in the mid-1920s.
Courtesy of J.E. McDougall.

CHAPTER ONE

The Unique and Lovable Stephen Leacock

THE LEACOCK TRAITS   I am very proud of Stephen Leacock. I realize that he was much better known in Europe, and especially in England, than he ever was here, also in the United States, as a matter of fact. I was very proud to be related to him, proud of my maiden name, Dovie Leacock. Our son is named John Leacock Payne.

I am a direct descendant of E.P. Leacock, whom Stephen wrote about so entertainingly in *My Remarkable Uncle*.

Stephen Leacock's hair, as I remember it, was salt-and-pepper grey. His fingers did very well for a comb. I remember his eyes. His eyes were crinkly, they were very friendly, but they almost looked as though they were laughing, laughing at the world, not at you, but laughing at what they saw around them.

I believe they were hazel. By hazel, I mean that they changed. Sometimes they would look bluish, sometimes they might be grey, or they might have a little greeny cast, but I think that is a Leacock eye to tell you the truth. It could be anything that made them change. It could be emotion, colour, what you're wearing. My father's eyes tended to be more greyish, but they were hazel too. This is a Leacock characteristic.

The Leacock eyebrow—one eyebrow seems to go up, if you are thinking. I know that Stephen had it, and my father did, and people said, "Oh, that's the Leacock eyebrow!"

Stephen had quite a ruddy complexion, more like an English complexion, as they call it. A healthy glow. He had a prominent forehead, inset eyes, and high cheekbones. A squarish face. This is a typical Leacock face. I went up with my father to see Stephen's brother, George, whom I had never met. I was just a little girl, and we were in the Royal York Hotel and we came out of the elevator into the lobby, and, right away, I knew that man in front of us was a Leacock, and it had to be George, because it wasn't Stephen. Even our son has that same kind of face.

And I believe that the hands are kind of different. Almost a square hand with tapered fingers, not long fingers, but shortish fingers—a well-shaped hand and a strong hand.

Stephen was careless but he was clean, he was well-groomed. You know he didn't have bad fingernails. He looked after himself that way. But he didn't care anything about clothes, they were incidental, just something to cover him up.

DOVIE PAYNE (LEACOCK)

A SANTA CLAUS FACE   I thought that he had a happy, cheery face, sort of Santa Claus face with crinkly eyes. He always came in with a smile, and he always seemed to have something amusing to say or a little anecdote, a little something that had amused him. I think his eyes were light blue and they twinkled. And there were these wrinkles from constant laughter around his eyes. He had a very nice face. He shambled or shuffled around and walked with a bit of a stoop. I can't ever remember him looking like a "youngish" man. I don't remember how old he was when we first knew him, but he had iron-grey hair.

MARGE CARTER

FOXY GRANDPA   Stephen Leacock, to me, was a rather foxy grandpa type of man. He was rather dishevelled in appearance, with very shaggy hair. He didn't always appear to have had a fresh shave. His moustache was outstanding and prominent. His eyebrows were shaggy.

He was a lovable sort of a person. His countenance was happy, he was enjoying life. He had laughing eyes. They were palish—rather nondescript eyes. There were permanent wrinkles from, I think, his inner feeling of worth. I think they were from his constant laughter. He laughed continually at himself and everybody and everything.

He was a bon vivant type. He exub-

erated joy, laughter in life. A great interest, a great curiosity, a great desire to share his feelings and his exuberance. I think he enjoyed his students very much.

MARGARET STEPHEN

THE MOUSTACHE VIBRATED WHEN HE LAUGHED   He had a dandy moustache. It used to kind of vibrate when he laughed. He had quite a set of eyes; they seemed to be set back in his head quite a ways, but there was always just a real sparkle coming out of them. Sometimes when you'd meet him he looked as if he hadn't shaved for maybe a week or something. He resembled some of these fellows that took off to go deer hunting.

BOB KILBY

HOMELY WITHOUT A MOUSTACHE
He looked a little homely without a moustache, back about 1916. And the next time I seen him, he had one. He looked a lot better with a moustache.

OSCAR OLIMER

A DELIGHTFUL OLD GENTLEMAN
I knew him as a professor at McGill and I attended classes in the early 1930s. I also knew him as a friend of my father, who was principal and vice-chancellor of McGill, General Sir Arthur Currie.

He was a delightful-looking old gentleman to me at my young age. He had iron-grey hair. It was sort of wiry and he had a full moustache.

When talking to you, if something amused him, or he said something amusing, his whole face would light up and his eyes would sort of twinkle. And I remember hearing him and my father in the library in our house, and the two of them just roaring with laughter.

GARNER CURRIE

ALWAYS IN A HURRY   His eyes were usually half shut when he was laughing, so it was very hard to see what they were. He had ruddy cheeks, a very short neck and rather a heavy body. His moustache was sort of untidy and unkempt and we rather felt that he had decided that he was a certain character and he would remain in that character as long as he came before the public and in his teaching.

He was always in a hurry and he was bursting with something to get out, and didn't even care about what he looked like, but he wanted to get what he had outside of himself.

FRANK NOBBS

A RUGGED MAN   Stephen Leacock was a rugged man. His face was well-lined and he had a ruggedness and his hair always looked as though it needed combing badly. He had a wonderful twinkle in his eye. He was a little bit sarcastic in some of his remarks, but there was always a twinkle. He was average height—five feet ten or eleven. I don't remember Stephen as anything but round-shouldered and walking with his head sort of stuck out, you know, going ahead of himself.

He certainly had a masculine look about him. But he wasn't my idea of a handsome man. He was attractive and you looked at him a second time, but I only figured it was his eyes that got you back to him. I think they were light blue. When

you are related, you don't pay attention. His wife Trixie was my father's cousin.

JEAN CAIN

RIGHT OFF THE FARM   He impressed you as being a man who had just come off the farm. He had a ruddy complexion, rugged physique, although he was getting to be stooped by the time he was teaching us. After all, he came from Sutton, where I believe his father was a farmer.

You got the impression that he could very well have been piling hay or cutting logs or doing heavy chores for which he was quite competent. When you saw him in his later days you still had that impression of physical strength.

I can see a very strong resemblance between Hemingway and Dr. Leacock. They both had that same shaped head, a large head that gave you the impression of being a very strong personality. As he spoke he would impress you not only by his physical appearance but he had a deep resonant voice that put over what he was saying very well.

The smile on his face, no matter how serious the conversation or the subject he was discussing, would always add humour to it, clothe it with some form of humour, so that no matter how serious the subject was, he found something humane and interesting about it. Not only that, he seemed to have a universal appeal, no matter whether the person was a super-intellect or just an average person. You couldn't help but listen to the man. You would never think of interrupting him or doodling on the desk, as many students did when Hemmeon was speaking, for example.

JUDGE HAROLD B. LANDE

A LARGE, CUDDLY WOOLLY BEAR

Stephen Leacock was like a large, cuddly, woolly bear. He exuded good humour and was very entertaining. You could call him a great raconteur. He was, of course, all hunched up with his old academic gown wrapped around him and he fiddled with his watch chain which had the odd paper clip holding the parts together. Everyone knows that the gown was draped around his arm and the lower part of it was largely torn off, tattered and battered and torn. I would say that Leacock and combs hadn't had too much contact. His hair was tousled. That part of him, obviously anyone would notice, but that always seemed to me so much window dressing and I really didn't pay too much attention to it.

His face—I think of it as all scrunched up and crinkled with laughter, laughter wrinkles. I don't really remember the colour of his eyes. I would say light blue. His moustache was just cozy-looking, quite heavy. The whole effect was very engaging, endearing and intriguing. I would consider he had a quality that was appealing. I think he did attract women.

Stephen Leacock had a great, what we now call, charisma, charm. I always found him extremely kind, and warm and not at all peppery.

MAYSIE MacSPORRAN

SAFETY PINS AND A COLLAR STUD

I suppose some people would consider him eccentric. But one thing you have to remember about him was that he created an image of himself which he consistently maintained. For example, I don't think he ever had a suit pressed in his life.

In those days, people wore watch chains across their waistcoats and a watch fob too. And he had his watch chain held together by an enormous safety pin which was always in place there.

His tie was never pulled tight, so that you always saw his stud behind the tie, it was always just a little bit loose. I think the collar was probably made of cellulose—a big high collar.

JOHN PEMBERTON

THE KEY TO IT ALL

Hemmeon pointed out to him one time the oddity of his hanging a key on a couple of safety pins on his watch chain and asked him what it was and he said, "That's my house key. If I don't keep it that way I'll get locked out—I'll lose it." And Hemmeon said, "Well, don't you think it looks a bit odd?" And I think Leacock admitted that perhaps it did. And I don't know that he wore it afterwards, but he may have.

SENATOR EUGENE FORSEY

HAT IN THE STACKS

He had an extraordinary way of keeping clothes, he kept them like he did books. He'd fold up a pair of pants and a vest and then a coat and stack them altogether. Then he had another cupboard where he pressed down hats and he might have four or five hats, one on top of another.

I was with him one time in the McGill Library in the stacks, and we were looking for some books that he wanted and he lost his hat. And I managed to find the hat squeezed amongst two of the books he'd been looking at.

He always wore clean shirts and things—he was quite fussy about that. He used to complain about little Stevie. I remember him saying to little Stevie, "For heaven's sakes take a bath—you smell worse than the dogs!"

HENRY JANES

HATS OFF   One evening he was going out for dinner with the Ardaghs, and he was in a big hurry. He had his old tweed coat on, which was full of dust, and so on, so I brushed him off. Then he had one hat on and he had a second hat on top of that. He was on his way 'till I told him you'd better take that hat off. He had both hats on. He had a straw hat and a Panama hat on top of it—that was his best hat.

HILDA ELSLIGER

ONE WAY TO DRESS FOR DINNER
Theoretically, he was fastidious about dressing for dinner, but he was also very absent-minded. He used to insist that, for meetings for the Political Economy Club, all the heads of departments should come to dinner dressed in evening clothes, which Hemmeon detested. I think he used to protest by wearing grey wool socks with his evening clothes.

Well, one evening, a very wet evening in early spring or late winter, Leacock arrived with a stiff boiled shirt, a stiff evening collar, a black tie hanging from it in two strings as it were. I mean there was no kind of a bow; the two sides hung down.

The rest of his costume was a very loud checked suit with the trouser ends

Leacock, seated in wheelbarrow, at Old Brewery Bay, with two unknown women, Mrs. Anna Biener (second from right) and her husband (seated on ground). *Courtesy of the Stephen Leacock Memorial Home.*

turned up. And I am perfectly certain that when he was dressing for dinner, something interrupted him, or his mind went off on some tangent, and that he came there feeling that he was in evening clothes.

He'd got the collar and he'd got the tie, and that's the way he always wore an evening tie—just knotted and hanging down—and he'd got the shirt. And I think he just was simply totally unaware that he was otherwise dressed in a very old, baggy dilapidated checked suit.

SENATOR EUGENE FORSEY

LOOKED LIKE A SACK   Stephen Leacock's general appearance was such that he looked like a sack of something or other, but I really think that he enjoyed looking that way. I think it was almost put on.

Don't you remember when he used to wear the detachable starched collar arrangement? It slid around his neck, but often he didn't wear it. But when the collar was on, it could sort of ride over to one side. He wore linen suits, cotton or linen, white, sort of creamy—unpressed linen suits.

In wintertime, he wore navy blue serge. It was very heavy. He still had the same shirt with the detachable collar, which was always too large. It hung outside his neck. The suit was unpressed. I don't think he had anybody to press it. But I don't think that worried him particularly.

He wore black brogues at Brewery Bay. They were boots, laced black boots. I think he might have worn sneakers occasionally. Old, dirty sort of white ones. He always had a very rumpled look. He wore

hats too; he wore an old fedora, but in the summertime, it was a straw hat.

DODE SPENCER

I'LL TAKE THEM   He was not a fancy dresser. If he needed a pair of trousers, he came in and bought a pair of flannels. And he didn't quibble about the price at all, he just said, "Measure me up for those and I'll take them." They were just flannels off the rack. And he'd buy the odd sweater here and there but he'd wear them 'till they were pretty shoddy, before he came back.

WILF VARLEY

THE KNIGHT OF THE ROAD   If you saw Stephen Leacock walking down Mississaga Street in Orillia, and you didn't know him, you would think that he would be just a knight of the road.

My father was a tailor and he made his clothes for him. As far as his clothes and the quality of them, don't forget that he was an Englishman, and the tweed goes with the English and he would wear a tweed jacket, either a herringbone or a black weave interwoven with grey.

HILDA OUTRIDGE

I THOUGHT HE WAS KINDA QUEER I worked for Mr. Leacock for a number of years when I was about sixteen or seventeen years old.

I didn't consider him at the time intelligent, I thought he was kinda queer. But my father said he's no queerer than anybody else. But, he says, when you get a little older, why, you'll understand that Mr. Leacock has his own method of conveying orders to you, different than somebody else.

He didn't shave too well. He always had a bit of beard in the corner of his mouth I would notice once in a while, unless he was particularly going some place. And he had a big moustache—untrimmed. The moustache was very similar to my father's, which was sometimes trimmed and sometimes untrimmed. I think he was blue-eyed and very sharp eyes. I mean to say by that he didn't miss too much. He had quite heavy eyebrows.

I think his hair, at the time that I recall, was grey and speckled with darker hair, and he had a heavy head of hair that hung down over his forehead. He always had a glass in his hand.

He always wore a white shirt, and of course, at that time, there was no collar attached. It would be undone and he'd have a suit coat on and an old pair of pants and an old pair of shoes. Of course, he was the owner of the "Manor," as you'd say, and the boss—he could dress the way he liked.

He wore a tie for a belt and I had often seen him with a rope, just a chunk of rope, probably from his sailboat, or a chunk of rope that was lying around, for a belt.

MORLEY YOUNG

PANTS TO SPARE   His clothes—you were never sure whether they were going to stay on him or not. They were hanging at half-mast. His trousers—as his mother-in-law always used to say—you never need worry about Stephen losing his trousers, because you'll find he has another pair on underneath. He was apt to wear two pairs of trousers at all times.

JEAN CAIN

VERY HAPHAZARD   The old boy looked exactly like a cabby driver who was standing with the horse-drawn cab below the campus on Sherbrooke Street. Pipe ashes all over his gown, should have been washed or cleaned or thrown away. And he had been put together in a most haphazard manner, but that didn't spoil his charm.

He always had the same gown, I never saw him wear anything different. It was absolutely tattered and soiled; you felt like taking up a collection to buy him a new one. But, he was a real character, in the true spirit and true sense of that word.

PHOEBE GUTELIUS SEELY

SOMETHING OF A PLOY?   His tattered academic gown was something of a ploy, I suppose, or it may have been simply he wasn't aware of it. It really was green with age and bits of cardboard were quite visible. His very shaggy, very ancient raccoon coat was perhaps even more noticeable as he walked through the streets. He was an inveterate walker and one could certainly notice him even if he simply walked to the campus. In those days there weren't many cars. He was shaggy and he just sort of shuffled along.

He was gracious, and the very essence of a gentleman.

LAURENCE TOMBS

THE OLD COON COAT   I recall seeing the old man moving up the campus from the Roddick Gates in his usual bent posture in his coon coat half-open and half-closed, with a button or two missing. And both parts of it would be dragging on the ground, and it certainly had seen better days. He apparently had had it for many years. It was in very bad shape, and, like his gown, the two of them were in a state of obvious neglect.

JUDGE HAROLD B. LANDE

Leacock in his beloved racoon coat, around 1928. *Courtesy of the Stephen Leacock Memorial Home.*

IT WENT BACK TO RIEL   I've heard someone say that he wore a coat that went back to the days of Riel and my reaction is it must have been hung on the way back east.

PHILIP VINEBERG

PART OF THE PICTURE   In the winter, you could see Stephen walking along Sherbrooke Street, sometimes laughing at one of his own jokes, with a hat that looked as if it had been run over by seven taxis, and with a very ancient coon coat, which was similar to the coat that was worn by cab drivers in those days in the winter. And this coat looked as if it had been run over, my goodness, by a herd of mules. And this was part of the picture— the image of himself which he created and which he consistently stuck by.

He carried what we would call in England a walking stick. And he did clomp along with it and I think in winter he perhaps used it to keep steady.

JOHN PEMBERTON

GNARLED LOOK, GNARLED CANE
A gnarled look and a gnarled cane and a steady path, he always walked the same way along the same route right through the campus.

PHILIP VINEBERG

TAP, TAP, TAP   It wasn't a fancy cane, rather a rough-hewn piece of wood. But he never went anywhere without that cane. You could hear it going tap, tap, tap. You could hear him walking up the campus with it and walking up the steps of the Arts Building, where he lectured throughout his McGill career.

He didn't need to use it. I think he liked carrying it. In those days, canes were rather fashionable for people of a certain position in life.

He wasn't always happy. I saw him at times when he looked very grim and serious. You'd catch him at an off-moment and there'd be this set look of sadness on his face.

SENATOR H. CARL GOLDENBERG

PIPE DREAM   He smoked pipes and they were filthy, to my way of thinking. So, one day, I took a knife and I scraped out all the guck out of the pipes, and I used pipe cleaners and I stuffed the end of the pipes and I filled them with brandy. He came home and went to get a pipe and he was horrified. And he said, "Grace, what did you do to my pipes!" And I said, "I cleaned them for you!" And he said, "If you ever get married, a man's pipe is sacred, you don't clean them!"

GRACE REYNOLDS

HE COULD HOLD HIS LIQUOR
I never saw him inebriated at all. I mean, I've seen him drink and he was a social drinker and he enjoyed his liquor and drank slowly, and I suppose he built up a tolerance over a long period of time. It never seemed to affect him; as a matter of fact, it stimulated him to be even more loquacious, although he didn't need much stimulus.

PHILIP VINEBERG

DON'T ASK FOR MY FLASK   He was in great demand for lectures in the United States. He had one suit that had a very, very deep pocket to carry a flask, because they had Prohibition in the United States. Inadvertently, one day, he left his flask in his train compartment and went into the club car. So the customs man came through and said who is occupying bedroom number so-and-so. Dr. Leacock looked at him and said, "I am, sir." The customs officer looked at him and said, "I'm sorry but I have to confiscate your flask." Dr. Leacock said the equivalent of "Like hell you will." And he took the flask and stood between the cars and emptied the flask onto the tracks and kept the flask.

GRACE REYNOLDS

LIQUOR LOOSENS THE TONGUE
There's another version of Leacock's guerilla warfare with the American customs. He was scheduled to address a gathering in Buffalo, but was stopped at the border by a customs officer who told him he could not enter the States with a flask of liquor. Leacock sent a curt wire to the sponsors of the lecture which read, "No hooch, no spooch." Apparently the Buffalo people had enough clout to get Leacock and his flask into the States because the speech was duly delivered.

ALLAN ANDERSON

NEVER FOGGY   He used to say that no student ever smelt liquor on him before four o'clock in the afternoon. I used to see him in the evening at his house when he'd have the Department up there to dinner and the only sign of anything that I could ever see was that his voice, which was naturally rather robust, got perhaps a little louder and the laughter got rather louder.

But there was no sign that, in the slightest degree, was he impaired, except that he did talk and laugh louder than perhaps he would have in the middle of the day.

I never saw him unsteady, I never saw him fogged about anything, his mind remained perfectly clear, his humour flowed as usual.

SENATOR EUGENE FORSEY

DILLY OF A TEMPER   I would always regard Leacock as a gentle man. I never heard him use foul language or never saw him really mad. But he had a dilly of a temper, there's no question about that. But with the students and in a social way, he struck me as a kindly gentleman.

D. LORNE GALES

THE TEN DOLLARS   Never, never, never, he never lost his temper. With some of the young students at McGill it was a time when things were very difficult, and he used to slip some of those students a ten dollar bill to keep them going.

As his secretary in the mid-1920s, I had all the money. One morning, when he went on his walk, he met a cleaning lady who was sort of lost. She didn't know where she was or how to get to where she was going and she was crying, so he gave her ten dollars. Then he came back and he said, "Grace, let me have some more money, please." And I said, "But I just gave you ten dollars." Then he told me the story about this poor old lady who was crying and he gave her the ten dollars.

GRACE REYNOLDS

QUESTIONING THE QUESTIONNAIRE
He had a temper although, on balance, I would say that he lost it very seldom. I have a wonderful recollection of an instance where he lost his temper with justification. It must have been in the year 1935–36. I believe Arthur Eustace Morgan was then the principal of McGill University. He'd come from a small college in England—Liverpool or somewhere—and he had a very different attitude about universities than was customary at McGill, where the administration never interfered with the lecturer.

I happened to be in Leacock's office when he was positively livid with rage. He had received a communication from the principal which, in itself, annoyed him, and he said "Look at this, Vineberg!" It was a questionnaire that he had been asked to fill out. And the first question was "How much time do you spend preparing your lectures?" Leacock was absolutely furious at the impudence of the principal asking him a question like that, and he was ranting at the administration for doing it, when, suddenly, a smile lit up his face, and he stopped being angry. He drew a scratchy pen and scrawled across the questionnaire, "All my life!"

PHILIP VINEBERG

MOSTLY, HE GAVE THEM A BREAK

Leacock was essentially a very emotional person. I have a number of illustrations of that. He was extraordinarily good-hearted. This is one way it came out. I remember a particular student who did a supplemental paper for him in Economics. Leacock gave it to me to mark and it was abysmally awful.

I can give you an idea of it by saying that one of the questions asked was to write a note on Adam Smith's theories of wages. He wrote half a page in beautiful clear handwriting headed "Adam Smith's Theories of Wages" and in the paragraph that followed there was not one word that had the remotest connection with Adam Smith, with wages or with theories of anything. Now this is literally true. It sounds quite incredible. And, of course, I ploughed him; there was nothing else to do.

Leacock said, "Oh, but he's such a nice boy, and he's had such a hard time; he came here with hardly money to buy shoes. You can't fail him."

"But," I said, "Dr. Leacock, this is not an eleemosynary institution—he doesn't know. I know he works hard, I know he's a nice boy, I know he's poor, but he does not know what he is doing. This is a bad paper. It's thoroughly bad."

Leacock's attitude was to be so very kind, you see, he was so sorry for this poor boy; it was a case of George Bernard Shaw's "Kind Hearts and Soft Cruel Ones." Well, Leacock's was a soft cruel heart in these matters. He would let the academic standard go for the sake of being kind with a misplaced kindness for this unfortunate youth who simply did not have the brains. I think he let my mark stand but he was very distressed about it. Well, I was sorry for the boy but I could not be distressed in the same way.

Mind you, there were times when even Leacock's patience was exhausted. I remember another student we had who was thrown out of the honour course because he was no good. And he flustered around in a pass course and, finally, succeeded in getting a pass B.A. How, heaven alone knows, but anyway, he did.

And I'm blessed if he didn't turn up at the beginning of the next year wanting Stephen Leacock to give him a letter of recommendation for a job that required a Ph.D. in Agricultural Economics with a knowledge of both French and German. Incidentally, the boy was a mulatto or a quadroon, which would probably make Leacock all the kinder to him.

And Leacock very kindly said to him, "I'm sorry I can't do this. First of all, have you a Ph.D. in Agricultural Economics?"

"Well, no, sir."

"Well, have you a Ph.D. in anything?"

"Well, no, sir . . . but I thought . . ."

"Well, what have you got?"

"I have a B.A., sir."

"A pass B.A.?"

"Yes, sir . . . but I thought . . ."

"Mr. So-and-So, do you know any German?"

"No, sir, but I thought . . ."

Leacock finally just threw him out after finding out with the greatest care the number of things that he had to have according to the specifications, which weren't within streets of him having.

Even Leacock's patience would give out. But he was extraordinarily kind.

SENATOR EUGENE FORSEY

ONE-UPMANSHIP   I think there was only one person who ever scored off Leacock. Paul Lafleur, the professor of English and Comparative Literature, was from a very distinguished family. His brother, Henri, was the greatest heart surgeon of his time, and another brother was the greatest constitutional lawyer of his time.

Well, Paul was small, precise and very dignified and had a very enormous opinion of his own importance—fully justified, I might add—and he and Leacock had some kind of spat one day, and the next day Leacock, not bearing a grudge—it was all over as far as he was concerned—walked up to Lafleur and slapped him on the back, which, for Lafleur, was like slapping Queen Victoria on the back, and Leacock said "Ho, there, Lafleur, come on and have dinner tonight." Lafleur said, "No thank you." Then Leacock fired out, "All right then, go to hell!" Lafleur instantly replied, "I should much prefer it!"

SENATOR EUGENE FORSEY

CHAPTER TWO

His Family: The Elegant, the Odd and the Tragic

THE OLD JOURNAL I have a journal of John Leacock, Jr., a distant relative of Stephen's and mine, written in 1776. A very neat hand in a small notebook, a little journal. He was a young man when this was written and he was on his way from England to Madeira. He is very graphic in his descriptions. One of the things that I found very touching was how he described what was happening on board ship. Now this was written on the fifth day they were out and it says: *William Peters, the third mate having a quarrel with one of the common men, and he being struck by the sailor, came to the captain and complained to him of the treatment he had met with. The captain, who instead of punishing the sailor's insolence for striking one of his officers, blamed his mate and told him he should no longer be an officer in his ship. The mate replied no more I will and immediately jumped overboard. We were all present and were spectators of the whole affair. He swam in the wake a quarter of an hour at least without having the least thing thrown overboard to him. One of the men was going to cut the lashings of a hen coop but the captain ordered him not to cut the ropes, but to untie them. In the meantime, the poor man was drowned. What a scene was this, to see a young man struggling for his life and even calling out to everyone on board by their names,*

First page of journal kept by John Leacock, Jr., (one of Stephen's ancestors) describing a voyage from London to Madeira in 1776. *Courtesy of Dovie Payne (Leacock).*

begging their assistance to save his life. And for a poor paltry piece of rope the captain let him be drowned. I myself saw him sink.

You can see by this writing that as many years ago as that, over two hundred years ago, the Leacocks had a flair for writing.

DOVIE PAYNE (LEACOCK)

14

Agnes Leacock, in the 1930s. *Courtesy of the Stephen Leacock Memorial Home.*

Agnes, Leacock's mother, at age sixteen. *Courtesy of the Stephen Leacock Memorial Home.*

TINY AND CHIRPY   Agnes Leacock, Stephen's mother, was a wizened-up little soul. Very tiny, chirpy, and very much the lady of the house too. She was the old-type matriarch. She was bright and talky. As long as I saw her, there was nothing wrong mentally with her. She was very alert. She lived in Beaverton with her daughter, Carrie Ulrichsen, Barbara's mother.

Stephen inherited a lot from his mother. I don't think he learned very much from his father. In fact, if he did, he didn't admit it, because he hadn't any use for his father.

JEAN CAIN

THAT "REMARKABLE UNCLE"

My father's father and Stephen Leacock's father were brothers. My grandfather was E.P. Leacock that Stephen writes about in his book *My Remarkable Uncle, Edward Philip Leacock*. He came from England and he married my grandmother in Toronto and then they were out west.

He certainly was a colourful character; he could charm birds off trees if he wanted to. He spoke many, many languages. He had a great sense of humour. I don't remember him that well. I know that when he went back to England, his wife died, and he left his three children here with the grandparents in Toronto.

He would like to have taken my father back to England, but my father's grandparents, whose name was Vickers, wouldn't let him separate the family.

Stephen Leacock thought a great deal of my grandfather and very little of his own father. Stephen Leacock's remarkable uncle had three children—my father and two sisters, Ela and Mary. Ela was one of the first women graduates of the University of Toronto.

Leacock is my second cousin. When I first met Leacock I presume I was a baby because I never knew not knowing him. He was just there. I didn't know him well or intimately at all. I grew up in West-

E.P. Leacock, who was the model for Stephen's story "My Remarkable Uncle."

Walter Peter Leacock (Stephen's father), in Sutton, 1877. *Courtesy of the Stephen Leacock Memorial Home.*

mount. He was a kind man. He was always very good to me, an older person who understood children, although he was pretty hard on his own son, I understand.

It was unfortunate that young Stephen tried to really live up to his father and couldn't. He was put into that environment where all the people were very brilliant; there were professors and everybody there. I think it was too much for him.

Stephen liked to tell stories, and I'm sure my grandfather was a character. I think Stephen said he ended up in a monastery and God knows what all, and he didn't at all. Well, I have a copy of his will and he died in England. He was sending me presents at Christmas, to his granddaughter, and he had a leasehold on property in Cheapside, and it came to the family after he died. So he wasn't as broke as Stephen Leacock wanted him to be. It was a good story, but it wasn't true.

When part of the estate was settled, the silver came over. Stephen would have nothing to do with any of the Leacock possessions—and they were very nice—because he had no use for the Leacock family.

He was devoted to his mother; he disowned his father, as I understand—kind of gave him a one-way ticket down east. He wouldn't accept any of the silver and jewelry and all the things that came over, but his brother George did.

I know that there was a flag that went out west and it had been on a battleship one of their ancestors had been on, as the captain or the admiral or whatever, and it went to his brother out west. I think it was a Peter Leacock.

DOVIE PAYNE (LEACOCK)

TRAGEDY   Charlie Leacock and his brother, Dick, went out west after they finished wiring at Newmarket in the early days of electricity. They went out to Calgary and they done wiring out there. And Charlie came back to Ontario and then on to New York, but he went on to St. Louis and I guess electricity was just coming into its own at the time and he done very well. He established a racing stable and one day they got a wire that his brother Dick had been murdered.

Mrs. Leacock asked Charlie to go over and look into it. And when he got over there they had the groom and the housemaid in jail, and Charlie said, "Let those two innocent people out." He said, "I know my brother and I know what happened. He killed himself." He says, "it's not murder, it's suicide."

So Charlie come back after he had liquidated the estate over there of these race horses and whatever he had. And Mrs. Ulrichsen, Stephen Leacock's sister, looked after Mrs. Leacock, so Stephen gave his share to Mrs. Ulrichsen and George got his share and Dr. Rosamond Leacock, another sister, got a share and Charlie got his share.

And Charlie's mind was on the balance, one way or the other. Charlie went uptown and he give a donation to the Salvation Army and to the Library Board, and he came back to Stephen's and he borrowed twenty-five cents for his fare back to Sutton where he made his home.

JOE GAUDAUR

CHARLIE WAS ODD   Charlie was an electrical engineer, but he was odd, you know. And Stephen Leacock, on his property, had several little wooden buildings and they were all filled with books, see. And Charlie had to close up the cottage, the house. It was a one-storey frame house—it was really a cottage.

And Charlie came in and he told me to get the thing cleaned up. He said get a couple of boys. So I got this Eddie Ball and Bob Russell down there.

And we were supposed to pack these books and he was going to ship them away. And, of course, they were playing around there and Charlie come in and he says, ''Fire those damned kids; they're not doing anything!'' Then another day he'd take it—it'd be all right. And then this day, I think we got the work done, so he decided to take us out in the sailboat. Eddie Ball would be thirteen and Bob Russell would be fourteen, the same as I was. We were all going to school together.

And I don't know what the Sam Hill Charlie did, but he had a pail and it was full of holes, you know. And he set it on the stern of the boat and I don't know what he was going to do, he had cobs of corn or something, but he set a fire in it, you know. And he had the gall-darn thing ablazin' on there and I think the sail caught on fire. We had a panic there for a few minutes, you know. I think he was trying to cook the corn—roast it or something. He was really something.

FRED PERIGO

THE OLD HOMESTEAD　　Sometimes on Sunday afternoon Jack and Tina and myself, with another friend, used to go and visit Stephen's brother at Sutton, on the old Stephen Leacock estate—the original farm. Charlie was living there. So we used to go and visit him.

The land wasn't flat—what I remember of it was driving through the laneway—it was all evergreen trees. The main house was under trees. A plain farmhouse, just a small house. But we didn't go inside too much, we just stayed outside because it was a beautiful day.

And Charlie Leacock would take us to Sutton for dinner at night before we left, to the Tally Ho Inn, it was called in those days.

There was a small barn there, but I don't think there were any animals. Charlie just lived there.

Much later I went back to see if I could buy the place, but there was nothing there—new roads all through there.

I remember the house was very dark, it was all over evergreen trees, very dark, not too much light around the house. And it had small windows. He had the odd bit of furniture. Very plain.

I would say it was a short drive from Sutton. The place was called Egypt, if I'm not mistaken—a little place called Egypt. I would say it was no more than five miles southeast of Sutton.

ALBANIE PELLETIER

A SENSE OF THE RIDICULOUS
All the Leacocks had a sense of the ridiculous. I remember, very early on, when I was quite a small child, one Saturday evening, Uncle Charlie decided to take a group of us children to the early movie at the Opera House and they usually had Wild West and heaven knows what-not. So we all trooped off with Uncle Charlie.

But Saturday night was market night in those days in Orillia and when we came out at nine o'clock there was a tremendous crowd of people milling around.

The family summer cottage during Leacock's boyhood years, on Lake Simcoe at Sutton, Ontario. *Courtesy of the Orillia Public Library.*

The Leacock family at Sutton. Stephen is sitting on the ground (left) holding his knee, while Charlie stands behind him. Mother Agnes is seated (centre), and George sits in the chair with arms folded (far right). *Courtesy of the Stephen Leacock Memorial Home.*

The Leacock farmhouse at Egypt (near Sutton, Ontario). *Courtesy of the Orillia Public Library.*

And someone had left a packing case on the lawn in front of the Opera House and I suppose it just looked like too good an opportunity, because Uncle Charlie hopped up on the box and proceeded to harangue the multitude about something or other and then the police came and broke it up. As far as I can remember, George and Charlie and Stephen were very close. They were certainly very much in evidence up here in Orillia. There was a family resemblance, but not a close one.

ELIZABETH BURROWS LANGDON

THE BROTHERS   When Charlie and George were in Orillia, living here before Stephen, they had an electrical business. My uncle was in with it too. It was a successful business. They wired houses and they sold lighting equipment and bulbs and this sort of thing. I think it lasted around three to four years and then they lost interest and away they went.

George was very tall and straight, a great horseman. Charlie was smaller than Stephen, who was about five feet ten.

JEAN CAIN

CHARLIE AND THE WHEELBARROW
See if you can picture the three of them, Charlie, the professor, and George, coming to meet me this particular morning. George had on a monocle and his housecoat, and Charlie generally always had a rose or some sort of a big bright flower in the lapel of his coat—he was all dressed up.

The professor's got his arm in the air, "Oh Aubrey, oh Aubrey!" He'd keep saying "Oh Aubrey" until you'd say,

"Good morning, sir!" And the three of them talking to me at the same time. I couldn't answer any one of their questions because each one was talking.

I guess you'd call Charlie an oddball. He would come up on the bus from Sutton and get off right in front of our place. Like, for instance, he'd leave his suitcase there. It had old cord wrapped around it and tied in a big knot. Then he'd come over the next day and get my wheelbarrow and take it over to the building.

So, this morning, I heard a noise—you see, we had an apartment over the top of my place of business. This was just at daybreak, and I wondered what the noise was, so I got up and looked out and I couldn't see anything, but I saw my wheelbarrow and my shovel was in the wheelbarrow. So I went back to bed and I told my wife, I said, "My wheelbarrow is down there. It must have been Charlie." And I said I'd left the shovel leaning up against the boiler room door, so I says I suppose he took it and put it in the wheelbarrow so that nobody would steal it. Now I surmised this.

And, sure enough, when Charlie came over he said, "Oh Aubrey, you got your wheelbarrow." And I said, "Yes I did, Charlie." He said, "Did you notice your shovel was in it?" And I said, "Yes I did." "Do you know why?" I said "Why?" "Because I thought if your shovel was in that wheelbarrow, they'd know that they both belong to you and they wouldn't steal it."

They were very clever people, the Leacocks. But I think they were just overbrained and that's the only way I can put it. That's why they were a little queer.

AUBREY GAUDAUR

MEN IN WHITE COATS   Charlie was the nicest fellow I ever met. He used to come down to the boathouse and sit there, oh, all afternoon. But his mind was going at the time. And George, I didn't know him too well. He was an electrician I believe, from New York. George was dressed up pretty well all the time. Charlie, well, he liked his liquor too. I don't remember this, but my son told me that two men came in white coats and took him away one time.

HAROLD ROLAND

STEALING HIS STUFF   When I was young and first working I can recall at home the family talking about Stephen Leacock. My father was a businessman and had very little to do with Stephen himself. He was a good friend of George Leacock's. Dad went to school with George Leacock. And he used to always say that George was the smart one in the family, that George was always cracking the jokes and at parties George was very popular. But Dad said that Stephen was very quick and any time that there was a joke that Stephen would make a note of it on the cuff of his white shirt. I guess in those days they wore stiff cuffs on their shirts. And Dad said that Stephen was very quick and he would write down the jokes and many times they were jokes that his own brother George would make.

SUE MULCAHY

A rhymed placecard composed by Stephen Leacock during the late 1920s or early 1930s. *Courtesy of the Stephen Leacock Memorial Home.*

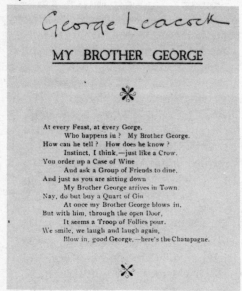

GEORGE LEACOCK, STORYTELLER
One of the guests that we always looked forward to seeing was my Uncle George Leacock. One never knew quite when he would arrive, but he was always a most welcome guest when he did come. The two brothers were very much alike in their sense of humour. They both enjoyed good kindly wit. They were quick to make a story out of some small incident. And very often Uncle George would start telling a story and I could practically see Uncle Stephen writing it. Uncle Stephen made no bones about it; he always said that half his stories had originated from my Uncle George.

BARBARA NIMMO

PASSING THE BUCK   Stephen had a great habit of saying this. He'd be asked a question and he would say, "Well, my brother George is the authority in that field, and I will have to talk to George about this." It was very funny, he'd get out of answering by saying George was the authority.

SENATOR H. CARL GOLDENBERG

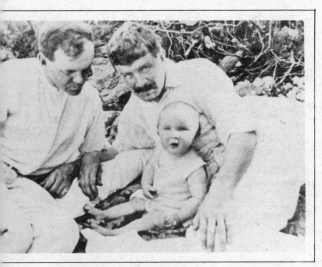

A rare photograph of George Leacock, seen here with Stephen (r.) and Stephen, Jr. *Courtesy of the Orillia Public Library.*

SUMMER OF 1924   I came over from Scotland, from Dundee. And I arrived here at Quebec on August 3, 1923. I worked in Montreal as a maid. One day I had a phone call and it was from Mr. Stephen Leacock and he wanted to know would I like a position as table maid to go up to Orillia, Ontario. I had wanted badly to go to Ontario. I immediately said yes. I thought he looked like a very plain, down-to-earth man, I really did. I liked his appearance. He had a big shock of hair and a big heavy moustache. When he was out around the yard he was just dressed like an old farmer and enjoying it. And his wife never tried to improve on his dress. No. She left him alone. But she dressed very well.

    Mrs. Stephen Leacock was a very nice woman to work for. There were never any cross words. She was a pleasant woman. She was fairly tall and had light brown hair. I would call her a beautiful woman. She was fairly slim and she had good features, more like aristocratic looking. And I think she really was.

    She had a soft voice. She was a very nice woman, not a person to lose her temper. At least I never experienced that. She read and she would go out quite a little bit, walking. The Shaws that were over in the next house were very good friends and they would go back and forth.

    I was there in the summer of 1924. She really wasn't what you'd say a sick woman, but maybe an ailing woman. She didn't have too much energy. She looked all right, she looked very good. In fact, I was surprised when I heard what had happened.

    Her death was quite a shock to him. She wasn't an old woman by any means, a young-looking woman, too. I don't think he ever got over that. I think he loved her.

JENNIE MACKENZIE SMITH

Beatrix and Stevie, Jr., in Atlantic City, 1921. *Courtesy of the Stephen Leacock Memorial Home.*

LIKE A SPANISH DANCER   She was what you would call a handsome woman. She was quite tall, brunette, very composed. There was a picture of her that was taken, I'm sure it was a painting, that painted her in a shawl, as if she was a Spanish dancer. She wore beautiful evening gowns.

GRACE REYNOLDS

TRIXIE WAS HANDSOME   Trixie drew up the plans for the present house. She was always known by the family as Trixie. Now I don't know whether her friends called her Trix or not, but we always called her Trixie.

She was a handsome woman, a very pleasant woman. I would have said she was even-tempered. I didn't know her so terribly well, you see, she was dead in 1926 and we came in 1924.

JEAN CAIN

UNDER A TERRIBLE CLOUD   I have seen Leacock looking sad because one of the years that I was his student he left for England, at the end of the year, at Christmas, taking his wife over for treatment. She was very ill. And that was a very difficult period.

We lost him, for, I don't remember how long, but someone else took over. At that time he was a very sad man, living with a terrible anxiety, naturally, and under a terrible cloud.

MAYSIE MacSPORRAN

THE DEATH OF TRIX   When they found that Mrs. Leacock had cancer they moved the bed from the hospital to the ship to England. The nurses that were looking after her went along. They took one wall out to make a bigger room. They were very cooperative. The nurses and her mother and little Stevie and Dr. Leacock went to Liverpool, where Dr. Blair Bell and Dr. Adami had this new radium treatment or something like that. By the time they got there, the cancer was so far advanced that they couldn't do anything for her. This is when I first started to live in the house.

He gave me power of attorney for six thousand dollars and I lived in the house with the cook and the housemaid.

Mrs. Leacock had beautiful evening gowns and he had me pack all these things and he said she would convalesce on the Riviera. Well, of course, she didn't survive. She died in Liverpool before they got on the boat.

They arrived back in Montreal on the 27th of December, 1926. His brother George came down from Toronto; there were all the nurses and Mrs. Leacock's mother, and we had sort of a brunch.

Then Dr. Leacock called me to the study and said that everybody told him he would have to have someone live in the house to supervise the cook and the housemaid and give little Stevie his medicine, and so on, and he said, "I know how you feel, but I don't want you to talk about it." He telephoned my mother and he said that if she would let me live in the house to supervise that he would look after me as if I was his own daughter. So, of course, my mother gave her permission. This is when I was hired as a secretary. I was his secretary for three years.

GRACE REYNOLDS

HE WAS HEARTBROKEN   I saw Stephen the day he was taking his wife to England. She was suffering from cancer and he was in tears. This was in 1925, I'm sure, and I gave him my best wishes. He was in the Arts Building, he was just getting ready to leave and he was heartbroken. After Trix's death he was downcast for quite a period—for probably a year—then his interest revived.

SENATOR H. CARL GOLDENBERG

THE BLACK BAND SLIPPED   I do recall his referring to the death of his wife. He had this traditional black band around his arm in memory of his wife, when she died in 1926. My picture of him is one of that black band badly sewn on and one end was already coming off.

JUDGE HAROLD B. LANDE

HE KEPT HER ASHES   This is hearsay because I haven't seen this but my father told me—and father and mother had been in his house—that he kept his wife's ashes in a box on the mantelpiece in his study. He wouldn't get them buried; he wanted the remains of his wife, whom he loved dearly, near him.

This was in the house on Côte des Neiges Road. And, to a young fellow, used to people having their forebears buried, and everything else, this came as a bit of a shock, to think that there are the ashes of this man's wife sitting on the mantelpiece when he was in his study. He could sit and think about it.

Now that I'm older I think that it was rather a nice idea, actually. It showed that he was very human and it really meant that he was really a very faithful husband. I think that she was probably the most important woman in his life and he revered her and he loved her and wanted her near him, even if it was her ashes. It meant a lot to him.

FRANK NOBBS

Less than a month after the death of his wife in late 1925, Leacock wrote a letter (January 12, 1926) to his friend, Joe McDougall:

Dear Mr. McDougall. My best thanks to you and Bob for your kind message. I realized how tender and kind was the feeling that inspired your letter. You will be glad to know that I do not intend to take this blow without a kick back. I am starting a campaign against cancer that will knock hell out of it. You'll read all about it in the press in a day or two. Your old friend. Stephen Leacock.

Reprinted courtesy of the Leacock Room, MacLennan Library, McGill University.

Beatrix Leacock after her marriage to Stephen. *Courtesy of the Stephen Leacock Memorial Home.*

A DOMINEERING MOTHER-IN-LAW

Trix's mother, she was a real lady to deal with, and of course Stephen had a lot of dealing with her. She was a very domineering woman, Trix's mother, and she figured she really was quite something. She was a Pellatt, a sister of Sir Henry Pellatt's, and she had lots of money. In Toronto she was very socially prominent and did a tremendous amount of good work with the hospital. She was really a marvellous woman.

But she used to come over and try and run Stephen, and she did that all summer. She lived July and August over there, while young Stevie was growing up. This is all in the 1930s, after Trixie died. She would still come up for the summer.

Cousin Kate, Leacock's mother-in-law, didn't die until 1946. She outlived Stephen. She lived at Stephen's. She had the upstairs bedroom, the big bedroom at the front. It wasn't called Old Brewery Bay

The Old Brewery Bay site about 1913. Seated (l. to r.) are Beatrix, unknown child, Stephen and unknown man. Standing (l. to r.) are Mrs. R.B. Hamilton (Leacock's mother-in-law), Mrs. Anna Biener and her husband. *Courtesy of the Stephen Leacock Memorial Home.*

then; it was Stephen Leacock's home. Even then she was bossy. She came and looked after Stevie and took over. The first time I remember seing very much of young Stevie was when cousin Kate used to bring him over to our place after Trixie died. And they used to come and spend Christmas with us before the house was finished, the present house.

JEAN CAIN

THE BLOWUP They had no well there and I had to go out with two pails of water every day, dip them into the lake and bring them into the house. They drank the water right out of the lake, the people in the house, Leacock and anybody else.

But there was one exception, Leacock's mother-in-law, Mrs. Hamilton. She wouldn't drink the water they were drinking, so she had a small club bag with four large bottles in it and she used to send me with this club bag, and sometimes she'd come with me to visit with Mrs. Stephens over to The Hermitage where there was a pump. And I'd carry this water back from the well.

Well, this one particular day, Stephen was looking for me and he couldn't find me, so he came walking down and here he run into me and Mrs. Hamilton with this club bag I was carrying full of water. And do you know, they had a real set-too. He told her, "If you can't drink the water I'm drinkin', you can hire a boy of your own to bring your water!" It put me on a spot, you know.

Well, I don't know what she said, but she didn't say too much. She didn't argue with him, she just went serenely by and took no notice of him. She was a kind of regal sort of person, you know.

FRED PERIGO

A HELPING HAND   Stephen could be a very generous man and he was very fond of my sister, Barbara, and my father, Frank Stephens. And when her health was very bad—she used to have pneumonia practically every winter—he decided that it was high time she got out of Orillia for the winter, and he took her to Montreal and sent her to Trafalgar, a girls' private school. It was the turning point in her health. She came back and was better from then on. It really was most important. And he paid for everything. This was around 1933 to 1935.

And then you see, he did the same thing for Barbara Ulrichsen, his niece, who is now Barbara Nimmo. He paid for all her education. I don't know what private school she went to, but he put her all through McGill University. And she kept house for him in Montreal.

Barbara kept him straight, financially, and she ran the house. She took over, she came up here to Orillia and was in Montreal until she was married. She was very capable and very efficient.

JEAN CAIN

BARBARA WAS VERY GOOD TO ME
My real contact with Leacock was because I came from Worcester, Massachusetts, and his niece, Barbara Ulrichsen, came from Pittsfield, Massachusetts. She kept house for him then and she was teaching in the English Department at McGill. She was teaching English, but exactly what, I don't know. I think it was first-year students.

When I first went to see him about taking my M.A., he said that he would have his niece look me up, and Barbara was very good to me. Leacock was always very good to me too, but she used to invite me up. I went there often for tea at Leacock's house on Côte des Neiges Road.

The house is still there. It has been changed a little bit; there has been another entrance put on, a sort of a side piece has been added.

Barbara kept track of everything, organized his social activities, looked after his business arrangements, and acted as his secretary. It was a real dedication on her part. I think that when Barbara got married he was really lost. Certainly, I've never heard of anybody who was able to take her place.

I don't know what he did. They moved up to Old Brewery Bay. I didn't keep track.

He had told us about Old Brewery Bay and drew maps showing us where the boathouse was and where the lake was in relation to Lake Simcoe. I've been there, of course, and it's a lovely spot. It wasn't as wild as I had expected it to be.

JEAN VAN VLIET

ONE STORY AFTER ANOTHER
After a lecture was once over, he was at his best and funniest. He'd love to sit over a late supper, enthralling the guests with one story after another. He'd often drive up in a taxi—you'd hear him before the door was open—just off a night train, home from a successful trip. As he had his morning shave, he'd walk back and forth from the bathroom to his study, telling Stevie, his son, and me little bits of the trip. I was always nervous when I heard that taxi

drive up for fear that perhaps I hadn't packed everything, or put that handkerchief in his dinner jacket pocket, or had forgotten that flask. No, I wouldn't have done that, for that headed the list.

BARBARA NIMMO

JUST COUSIN STEPHEN People that are close to you, or that you know everyday, you don't think of them as being famous. And when I saw Stephen Leacock before the war, when I was seeing him all the time, he was just cousin Stephen. He wasn't Stephen Leacock, the author, or Stephen Leacock, Head of Political Science at McGill; he was just cousin Stephen. He was a member of the family.

And you don't think of them as being anything extra. The only time it made me mad was when I came back here to Orillia in 1945-46, when everyone started to tell me what a terrible drunk he was, and how impossible he was and he was this and he was that and he was the other thing.

And I used to just get livid. That's why I joined the Stephen Leacock Associates, because I was darned if I wasn't going to get this business straightened out.

JEAN CAIN

CHOO CHOO CHOO The first thing I did in the morning when I went there, I had to empty the garbage can outside. And we used to take it down to the bush and dump it in the bush. By that time it would be between seven and eight o'clock.

Leacock would be in bed and every morning I could hear him telling stories to this baby in bed. And he'd say, "Choo-choo-choo-choo-choo, Woooo-woooo-woooo, here's the train, here's the train,

it's coming! It's coming!!" And then he'd say, "Look, look, and the engineer, he's waving to that little boy in the red coat. Who's that little boy? Why, it's Stephen Lushington." And he'd tell those stories.

I could hear him every morning. He was in bed, he wasn't a hard man, or drunk or somethin'; he was telling stories to that child.

And then later on, he and his wife, they always went out the front and went to the end of the point. And there was a little bit of a frame structure there and they had their dressing gowns on and they went for a swim every morning. This was in 1917.

FRED PERIGO

Early risers — Leacock and Stevie, Jr., 1918. *Courtesy of the Stephen Leacock Memorial Home.*

A NICE LITTLE BOY   Stevie was a very nice little boy. He was well educated and he was what I would call clever; in fact more so than most children of his age. I would tell my family that he was next to genius.

JENNIE MACKENZIE SMITH

STEVIE JR'S PROGRESS   Stephen was heartbroken about his son. I knew Stevie well. He loved Stevie, but he was very worried. He wanted to make sure that he would have enough to leave for Stevie, because he felt Stevie wouldn't be able to look after himself as he should be. He was proud of him. One day he showed up and he was very happy. Stevie, I believe, was at Lower Canada College at the time, and he had written an article in the student magazine and Leacock proudly pulled it out of his pocket and said, "Goldenberg, look at this, isn't this great!" Well, I don't remember what it was about, but it was by Stephen Leacock, Jr., and he said, "You know, I told Stevie, you don't do that. How would it sound if you saw an historical essay by Lord Macaulay, Jr.?"

SENATOR H. CARL GOLDENBERG

HE SLAVED TO PROVIDE FOR YOUNG STEVIE   I remember on several occasions meeting Leacock with his son and Leacock would be holding him by the hand, and I remember Leacock once telling me with great excitement that his son had passed his French exam as though it was a great accomplishment. As a matter of fact, in the early days, Stephen Leacock, Jr., was regarded by some people as being a child prodigy. It was really a mistake. What happened was that he looked as though he was about eleven years old, when, in fact, he must have been eighteen. And he was able to talk about Social Credit and various other things which he had heard from his father, so that people got the impression that this person who appeared to be so much younger than he was, was infinitely brilliant.

But as time wore on he just disintegrated. I can tell you this, that one of the great motivating factors of Leacock's later years was to make enough money so that his son should be well looked after because he was fully aware that his son would never be able to look after himself. I don't know whether you recall that at one time he was sharply criticized for accepting a position for commercial advertising on the radio. He had accepted some job just to plug some commercial product or another. And he was doing that and some of his pot-boiler writing was being done for the same purpose—to add a little nest egg to look after his son, not appreciating that his son would have an abbreviated lifetime.

PHILIP VINEBERG

THE PEA-SHOOTER   Each of the graduate students was attached to a professor who supervised or was supposed to supervise his thesis. Fortunately, Leacock attached me to himself. I was very lucky. This was his custom, his practice. You were supposed to write a certain amount and then you would come to his house, as he said, "to read with me." And you were supposed to bring what you had written. Well, I did that quite often.

I remember my thesis was on the Canadian budget, 1867 to 1896. Now, this is how Leacock read with you. You would come into his library, and he would pour himself a Scotch and soda. He wouldn't offer anything to the student—nothing. "Now," he'd say, "Goldenberg. Read!" And he would drink his Scotch and shut his eyes, you'd think he was falling asleep, but he wasn't.

I remember this particular occasion. Suddenly, while I was reading to him, young Stevie opened the door, walked in with a pea-shooter, and began shooting peas at me. Well, Leacock said, "Stevie, please don't do that; Mr. Goldenberg is reading with me." And Stevie, whose voice was rather high-pitched, would say, "Yes Daddy," and he'd go off.

Well, I continued reading on this occasion and oh, about fifteen minutes later, Stevie was back with his pea-shooter shooting peas. This would be in 1929. And Leacock would say again, "Stevie, please, I beg you, don't do that. Mr. Goldenberg is reading with me." Always he said "Mr." to his students. It was only later, after I went on the staff that I became Goldenberg.

Now, Stevie went off, I continued reading, Stevie came back a third time. Now the father was getting a little bit fed up and he said, "Stevie, you go downstairs, you will find Mr. Draper waiting for me. Mr. Draper is going to read with me as soon as Mr. Goldenberg leaves. In the meantime you go down and shoot peas at him." And Stevie did! Leith Draper was taking his M.A. at the same time as I was. And young Stevie went down and shot peas at him.

SENATOR H. CARL GOLDENBERG

"LOOK AFTER STEVIE JR." I remember Trix as being quite vivacious. The first time I recall her, Stevie was just a baby, and I was sitting on the verandah at home on a swing that we had, and Trix came to visit and she had Stevie in her arms and she gave him to me to look after. And it was curious because when Leacock was dying, the last time I talked to him, I asked him if there was anything I could do for him. He was in the General Hospital in Toronto, and he said, "Look after little Stevie, look after Stephen if you can." And he chuckled. And that was his last word. Two days later, I guess the next day almost, he was dead.

Well, I tried to look after little Stevie and it was a real problem.

HENRY JANES

A REALLY WILD TEMPER Young Stevie was a dwarf, I'd say about two and a half feet, maybe a little better. But a really wild temper. In my opinion, he was no different as he got older as he was when he was young. Like, when you go to a show where you have to line up, stand in line and wait, and the crowd was shoving around, and you're on the stairs, you know what I mean and somebody moved in the crowd and this woman bumped into him. Young Stephen, he drew up his head and charged her and used abusive language—charged her just like a ram. He would just flare up and have these fancy little tantrums at times.

Possibly, I think, we were maybe making use of him. We used to travel around with the chauffeur and when you rode with him, that eliminated walking. Cars were kind of a scarce commodity.

BOB KILBY

THE BIGGEST CIGAR, THE BIGGEST DRINK   Stevie was a funny kid. Stevie was on drugs and liquor and everything else. I felt sorry for him; he had everything against him. All the young people he went with, like my sister and Dode and Marge Tudhope and all those people, grew up—and he didn't.

He was small. It made him bitter, terribly bitter. He'd smoke the biggest cigar and he'd take the biggest drink because he was Stevie Leacock, and he didn't have to do this and that. And he got so that he was impossible, and then he got in with the wrong people, particularly after Stephen died. Fortunately, his money was tied up, and that is thanks to Barbara Nimmo.

JEAN CAIN

TROUBLE AT THE UNIVERSITY CLUB
There had been sadness in Stephen's life throughout; with his son too, he had great difficulties. It was sad to see him and his son, when they were together, because, although the boy was very bright in certain respects, he was not well developed in other ways, and caused great pain to Leacock at various times.

I am sorry to say that I was on the committee at the University Club when we had a problem with Leacock's son and it was one of the saddest experiences of my life to have him up before the committee because we were all thinking of his father. And I might say that we handled the thing very carefully and I think very justly at that time.

Beatrix and Stephen, Jr., on the dock at Old Brewery Bay, 1917. *Courtesy of the Stephen Leacock Memorial Home.*

It was later that he got into further trouble. But, at that time, we managed to rule on it gently and we were all very sad about it, too. Then, later on, he was banned from the club.

But in this first case he had broken the rules very badly, and the poor boy knew it, and came before the committee very abjectly to apologize for his behaviour.

CHARLIE PETERS

TRYING TO COPE WITH STEVIE, JR.

I was very sad when Leacock had to retire, and I saw him two or three times after that and I felt he was no longer the man he had been. I'd say that the sparkle had gone out of him. His sense of humour wasn't what it had been and he was drinking more. And young Stevie started to drink. Young Stevie finally was expelled by the University Club and started living at the Queen's Hotel. He had to be expelled from the University Club because he'd get drunk there, so he moved over to the old Queen's. He lived there where he could drink and smoke cigars.

I called him one day and asked him to have lunch with me and he did. I took him to the McGill Faculty Club. And I said to him, "Stevie, you've written two pieces on your travels to Mexico for *Saturday Night*, B.K. Sandwell's paper. You write very well, and your father would be very proud of you. Why don't you embark on a writing career?" Well, the little fellow was smoking a big cigar and he said, "Mr. Goldenberg, I don't have to work. My father provided for me very well and I'm enjoying what I'm doing."

And I said, "How could you, living at the Queen's and not doing anything?" "Well," he says, "I go to Old Brewery Bay for the summer." And there he got himself into difficulties. He was one of the few people who was arrested for speeding in a motorboat. And then he would phone John Culliton, who was on staff at McGill, every now and again around four o'clock in the morning. John used to tell me that. It was very sad.

He died in the 1970s. He would have been in his fifties.

SENATOR H. CARL GOLDENBERG

Stevie, Jr., in costume, at the rear of the first house at Old Brewery Bay. *Courtesy of the Stephen Leacock Memorial Home.*

PROMISE UNFULFILLED   Stevie, Jr., I always felt, had a love-hate relationship towards his father. There was no question that he appreciated the genius of his father. On the other hand, in many conversations he told me that his father really had a very poor attitude about Orillia, about its people, that *Sunshine Sketches* was a total putdown, that his father was mocking the town and its petty values, and all that sort of thing. And he said that the people had been fooled all these years into thinking that this was a kindly individual—he was not; he was particularly cruel in his social attitudes.

Stephen Junior resented the lack of his own success. He was a talented individual; he could write very well, and he had a good mind in the years when he had an opportunity to have a career. So resentment was there without a doubt. And I always had the feeling that young Stephen hated himself much more than he hated his father, that he realized what sort of person he'd turned out to be. There had been this enormous promise, and had he had more drive, more discipline, more self-organization, more of those things which I don't think were particularly encouraged when he was growing up, he might have done well. He tended to be ignored. He was first of all over-indulged and then ignored. That was his history. It was a pretty tough row to hoe.

PETE McGARVEY

CHAPTER THREE

Best Friends:
Laughing It Up

A VERY HAPPY MARRIAGE   He had
close women friends, but not to marry. I
don't know how many. I do know that he
certainly enjoyed feminine company, but I
don't think that he probably ever met
anyone who took the place of his wife. I
don't remember her myself but I'm told
that it was a very happy and a very close
marriage.

ELIZABETH BURROWS LANGDON

**THE LIVELY AND TEMPESTUOUS
FITZIE**   I really wouldn't know why he
didn't remarry. I don't think there's
any doubt that he and Trixie were very,
very much in love and I just don't think
he ever thought of marrying again.

And then he had a terrible
problem with young Stevie, I really don't
think it probably ever entered his head
that he might marry again.

You saw very few women around.
But he liked women, he liked Fitzie Shaw.
She's the one that did a lot of his research
on his books in Montreal. He was quite
fond of her. They'd have dinner and be
back and forth to their cottages, and when
Fitzie and her daughter Peggy came up at
Easter and Christmastime they always
stayed with Leacock.

I would say she was the only
person he was close to, not only here but
in Montreal. She was a real companion to
him. Everybody seemed to like to talk
about them, but I never saw any sign. My
sister said that they were just good friends,
which is most likely; but you know how
people like to talk up a bit of a scandal.

Her bedroom at the house was
where the library is now. And that was
originally Trixie's bedroom. And then it
was turned into the library. But there was
talk that they had private doors. Just a lot
of baloney.

Fitzie was a very beautiful
woman—very, very attractive. She had a
terrible jealous streak. She was very, very
jealous of her daughter and her boy
friends and all the young people that used
to come there a lot. She liked the boys.
And, particularly from 1936 to 1939,
when there were a lot of Royal Military
College boys, and boys from Camp
Borden used to come up and they had a
lot of fun, the young people. And she was
always pretty edgy.

She wanted the parties all over
there, she didn't like it when the parties
came to our house. She just had Peggy.

She and her husband hadn't lived together for years; she was separated from Shaw. She was of average height, slim, with reddish hair. She died in a nursing home in Toronto. There was a fondness there. But I'd say that she was the only woman, as far as Stephen was concerned.

JEAN CAIN

THE SHAWS Herbie Shaw was a very successful businessman. He was in the shoe and leather business. The war came in 1940. Peggy, the daughter, got married and went to the United States. I never saw them again. Herbie Shaw and his brother were partners in a firm that was called, I think, Anglo Canadian Leather, or something of that sort, and were very successful.

Mrs. Shaw entertained a great deal for Peggy, and Peggy had a tremendous number of friends who came and went and they had a lovely house up on Redpath Crescent. I was one of the lucky friends who came and went.

BARBARA WHITLEY

THERE'S NOTHING LIKE THEM
Mrs. Shaw bought a cottage from Dr. Edward Ardagh on Old Brewery Bay, to the west of Leacock. She was a high-class Montreal society woman—and, in one way or another, there's nothing like them, they can be very vicious. She used to fly off the handle terribly sometimes.

I was delighted that the doctor had some company because he was terribly lonesome. He'd go over through the swamp. To get to her place, you had to walk through fairly mushy swamp—not too bad, but in the spring it was practically

impossible to get from Old Brewery Bay to the Shaw cottage. You might have to drive around. And she'd walk over with a pair of rubber boots on to Old Brewery Bay.

She was a very pretty woman and I think she lived to be over eighty. She cheered him immensely.

HENRY JANES

WOMAN OF MYSTERY? I met Mrs. Shaw with Leacock two or three times. She was a very nice-looking strawberry blonde and was taller than Leacock. I felt that she was a woman, without knowing the circumstances, who had some tragedy in her life. She gave me that impression every time I met her. She and Leacock were great friends and were together in Montreal and Orillia. Several times I was invited to come and have cocktails or coffee with Leacock, and Mrs. Shaw would be there.

JOE McDOUGALL

Tea outdoors at Old Brewery Bay. Left to right are Leacock, unknown man, Beatrix, Stevie, Jr., and Mrs. H.T. (Fitz) Shaw. *Courtesy of the Stephen Leacock Memorial Home.*

THE REDHEAD FIRED HIM   The recollection I have of Mrs. Shaw is that she was a beautifully built woman. She had lovely long red hair. She was maybe an inch taller than Leacock. And they'd go swimming at the end of the point. She had a good figure. Naturally, at that age, I was watching the figures fairly well. But she was a beautiful woman and, as a matter of fact, she was, up until, I would think, into the late 1940s, still very attractive. She's dead now.

At one time my father and I planted the orchard. That would be around 1927. Leacock had a variety of apple trees. If I recall, he had at least 125 to 130 trees. I know he had Dutch apples; I believe there were Northern Spys, McIntosh, Tallman Sweets, Greenings, and there was no water to water these trees, and it was on a side hill.

Mrs. Shaw fired me once when I was watering the orchard. Her fence was between the orchard and the lake on Leacock's property and I used to have to climb over this doggone fence and carry two five-gallon buckets of water.

I was to water these young apple trees every morning because there was a dry spell when we planted them. They didn't come when they were supposed to have come in the spring—early, you know, before the buds come on. And the outcome was that my job was to carry water and, by midmorning, a young fellow of my age, which was about sixteen or seventeen, my arms would be about four inches longer and I'd be sweating, and she evidently was watching me.

On either side of her dock there was just cat-tails and mud and I had to go right down to the end of the dock in order to get the five-gallon bucket, and I was getting pretty tired around noon. I was sweatin' and a little provoked to think that there wasn't some other method of watering the doggone trees.

But, anyways, I was sitting on the fence in the shade and she come along and she said, "I don't think Mr. Leacock would like it if he knew you were sitting around in the shade when you should be watering the trees." And I said, well, I shouldn't have said it I suppose, but I said, "Well, it's Mr. Leacock who pays me." I was a little provoked because she'd told him different things about me, and I wasn't getting the work that I normally would get if he hadn't have been informed by her, I believe.

Well, she was quite right, I was taking a rest. About these other things, she was not necessarily making up tales, but she was snitching to him. That's how I figured it. Well, right then I went home for dinner. And my Dad said, "Well, you've got yourself into a mess now." And I said, "How is that?" "Well," he says, "Mr. Leacock told me to tell you not to come back this afternoon." And I said, "Did he tell you why?" And he said "No." And I said, "Well, I'll tell you why." So I told my Dad, and I did get a few more days' work, but not near as much as I did before.

When I spoke to her in that tone of voice, and said that Mr. Leacock was the one that paid me, why she was mad at me from then on. I would imagine that she held grudges.

Of course, there was a very close relationship there and she figured that if anything happened to Stephen, she would inherit probably what was left, or part of it. I don't know what the arrangement was, of course, but no doubt she had money in her own right. She was rather touchy in things like that.

She was good for Leacock because his wife died some ten or fifteen years prior to her moving into the old Ardagh place that's on Brewery Bay. That's where the old brewery was. She bought that place from Ardagh, a local doctor. I would think that would be in the early 1920s.

MORLEY YOUNG

A BIG TIME IN MIDLAND One time I drove him to a speaking engagement in Midland. Midland is thirty-five miles from Orillia and at that time he owned a 1927 Pontiac. And its best speed would be forty-five to fifty-five miles an hour on good roads, and he had it mathematically figured out that it would just take us one hour to go to Midland. I think he had to be there at eight o'clock and we left at seven. I knew doggone well it was going to take us longer than that because we didn't get to Coldwater when down come the rain so hard that the windshield wiper couldn't keep up with it. That was getting on in October and it was black dark by that time. I stopped the car and he said, "What are you stopping for?" and I said, "Well, I can't see." "Well," he said, "we'll have a drink." Mrs. Shaw was with him. Of course, they had a drink and Mrs. Shaw said to me, "Would you have one, Morley?" and I said, "No I hadn't better." I very seldom did and I didn't either at

Placecard written by Leacock for Mrs. Shaw.
Courtesy of the Stephen Leacock Memorial Home.

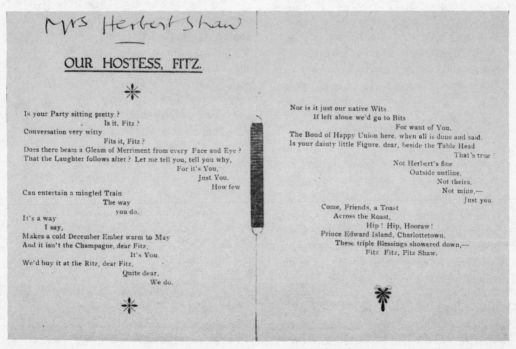

that time. And Leacock said, "We want to get to that meeting in time."

The rain quit and we made the meeting. I believe it was in a church—I'm not sure. He says, "You meet me right here after the meeting," and I said, "O.K." By the time we got there, half an hour late, there was no parking within blocks, so he wouldn't know where to find me and I had to come back to the entrance where I let him out in order to find him.

He said, "We'll be finished, oh, about ten-thirty," so I drove around for a little while and I visited a friend of mine. I went back at ten-thirty and the place was all closed up and darkened—nobody there. So I just pulled up to where I let him out and I went to sleep.

Along about two-thirty or three o'clock, he woke me up—him and her— and they were feeling no pain, and he said, "We're ready to go now."

Somebody had brought them back; evidently they had visited with somebody and I never seen anybody—I was sleeping. He was feeling no pain and she was doing a pretty good chore as far as laughing and talking. They were talking about the different individuals and then they started to sing. I couldn't recall what the song was but they hummed and sang along. Finally, we arrived home.

I think there was some booze left on the way home. He'd never pour while I was driving; he'd say, "Stop the car!" I think that time Mrs. Shaw had to go potty, I'm not sure, but she got out of the car anyways. We, of course, were on a dark country road, No. 12 Highway at that time. This would be about 1930, it would be.

MORLEY YOUNG

THE SHAW HOUSE WAS VERY LIKE LEACOCK'S My husband, James, and I now live in the house that Fitz Shaw had. It's only about 200 yards along a path from the Leacock Memorial Home. It's northwest of Leacock's. Apparently, the house originally was on the corner of Peter and Mississaga in Orillia and was moved around the turn of the century to the spot where Jackson's Brewery had been. The brewery burned down in 1867. It's a big house, like Leacock's and has eleven rooms, including six bedrooms, and is much the same style. Its design is very modern for an 1843 farmhouse, which I understand it was. In one part, it has a huge cathedral ceiling.

Dr. Edward Ardagh, a great friend of Stephen Leacock's, had it at one time. There were two and a half acres around it. Fitz Shaw owned it until she died, and she left it to Barbara Ulrichsen, Leacock's niece, who used to come up every summer for a period of weeks (she still visits Orillia in the summer). We bought it in 1976 from a developer. It had been vandalized and was in bad shape but we've restored it.

KAREN McKEE

CONNOISSEUR I don't think there was any doubt about it that du Roure was Stephen Leacock's closest friend. They were with each other a great deal. I think they were just congenial. I think that's true of a lot of friendships.

I liked du Roure very much. One time we were having a snack in a bar at the golf course at Dixie. We were having some cheese and du Roure said the only way to eat cheese is to have a little red wine with it at the same time, so we proceeded to do this. Funny, you remember little things that he said.

DOUGLAS C. ABBOTT

NEAT AND TIDY   I remember René du Roure. I even stayed at his place in Montreal once. My sister Freda worked for him.

His house was not far from Leacock; you could walk from one place to the other. He had a lot of books in his library. It was a nice big house, fairly well furnished.

He used to come fishing with Dr. Leacock, always neat and well dressed. I would talk French with him. He used to come to Old Brewery Bay and stay two to three weeks at a time. Everybody liked him.

ALBANIE PELLETIER

THE ARISTOCRAT   René du Roure was the head of the French Romance Department at McGill, and I took several of his courses. I always enjoyed his delightful way of speaking French; it was really aristocratic. He was a short, slim man, with a little waxed moustache, very suave and debonair, and slightly stooped.

He used to come into Leacock's lectures before the class was over, and say, "Come on, Leacock, we're going." This was usually just before the bell, five minutes to go in the class.

I got the strong impression that both of them went out to have a few boozes together. It always struck me as odd to see these two people together. They came from such different backgrounds. Here was this debonair Frenchman with all his Continental manners, his

nails polished, and here was Leacock, who looked like a farmer from the country, his hair unkempt and his complexion ruddy, and he towered over little du Roure, and yet those two men seemed to hit it off as great friends.

JUDGE HAROLD B. LANDE

A FRENCH MONARCHIST   I think Leacock gave a graduate class in the afternoon. He stayed long enough to meet René du Roure, whom he always called Captain du Roure, and they'd go to their spot in the University Club for their afternoon drink and play billiards and talk.

I could never figure out this friendship. They admired each other a great deal. Sometimes he would talk about Captain du Roure to me as we were walking and say very proudly, "He is still a French monarchist."

SENATOR H. CARL GOLDENBERG

A rare picture of Leacock's closest friend, Prof. René du Roure (seated on the left) who was honorary president of Le Cercle Francais at McGill. *Courtesy of* **Old McGill**, *1934.*

MILITARY TO THE CORE   René du Roure had been a captain, I don't know if in the regular French force or in the Territorials. Then, in 1914, he went right to war and was away during the whole war and then came back afterwards. He was a captain in the French reservist army.
BRIGADIER GENERAL JIMMY DE LALANNE

FRENCH TO THE TIPS OF HIS FINGERS
I wouldn't say that René du Roure had any exceptional degree of wit; he had a mordant sense of humour sometimes, and he had a very right-wing point of view in politics. He was practically a supporter of L'Action Française which, in those days was a French political party in France which favoured the restoration of the monarchy against the republic. René du Roure's personal associations were with what in France were very right-wing elements.

On the other hand, I think they had the attraction that sometimes comes with a different point of view. For one thing, Leacock was more cosmopolitan than the average country boy that you made him out to be in a sense that he was very much addicted to country life and fishing and the like. But he had a wide interest in the outer world.

René du Roure was a Frenchman to the tips of his fingers, and he was temporarily here, although it might have been for thirty-five years or so. I can only say it was a question of opposites attract.

Besides which, although Leacock had some very distinctive views and was strong about his convictions, he was very easy to get along with. And so it was not hard to be, you know, interested in him

A sketch of Prof. René du Roure. *Courtesy of* **Old McGill**, *1936.*

and friendly with him. He liked different sorts of people.

PHILIP VINEBERG

THE DEBONAIR RENÉ DU ROURE
His soul was French, his blood was blue. The des Royes du Roures, an ancient aristocratic family, represented all that was best in the old régime. A visit to his distinguished father and well-bred sister in the vast, high-ceilinged apartment in the Faubourg St. Germain explained much of René's complex character. His elder brother had been killed in the war and he himself suffered all his life from the effects of an old wound. The second brother had become a Trappist. As the Head of the French Department and Head of the French Summer School (the second oldest on the continent) it was his personality— which seemed to embody so perfectly all the charms and virtues for which his race is most admired—that accounted largely for his success. He was a little man but with a military bearing,

always impeccably turned out and in his later years accompanied by an incongruously large boxer dog known as Tarzan, over which he had hardly any control.

He was the darling of Montreal society, the hostesses' delight. His women friends were numerous but like many bachelors, having failed to win his heart's desire the first time around, he did not love again, although he dallied delightfully.

His boon companions were Stephen Leacock and man-about-town Edward Cholette. How the conversation sparkled when the three were together! On one occasion P.G. Wodehouse of *Very Good, Jeeves* fame was Leacock's guest. René and a pleasant, but not particularly bright, individual made up the four for dinner at the University Club—it was always the University Club. Next morning the faculty room was agog to hear of the sparkling repartee of the celebrated humourists, sure, too, that René would have held up his end. As a matter of fact, he told us, Leacock and Wodehouse were rather shy with each other, never really got going; Mr. ——— did most of the talking—no one else had a chance!

MRS. W.E. BALDWIN (ALICE SHARPLES)

SENSE OF THE RIDICULOUS   All the Leacocks had a great sense of the ridiculous, as the Drinkwaters had, and as my mother's family had. So marvellous! They could make more fun out of the smallest, most insignificant things, and René fitted that role in his French, polished way.

He had a sense of the ridiculous and he loved children. He loved singing and playing games. He was always organizing

games constantly for the whole Christmas period.

MARGE CARTER

AN OLD COUNTRY FRENCHMAN
Du Roure played golf, he played golf at Dixie, the old Royal Montreal Golf Club, and he was an old country Frenchman. He always wore the Legion of Honour in his buttonhole. He was proud that he had served in the first war. My recollection is that he came to McGill after the first war.

He lived until after the second war, but the fall of France just broke that man's heart. He never recovered from it. The world had ended for him.

I would say he was a typical, educated, upper middle-class Frenchman. I got to know French very well because after I finished at McGill and had taken my bar exam, I went back and lived in France for a year to improve my French and to study some bits of lectures at the Université Dijon. So I met a good many people like du Roure in France. I would think he was a man of some personal private means. I don't think he was entirely dependent on his professor's salary and he was a bachelor.

DOUGLAS C. ABBOTT

AFTERMATH   After the fall of France, René just shut himself in his room and drank. He killed himself with drink. It was very disturbing to Dr. Leacock. The whole thing. He was appalled by all that. The war generally. And all it meant. The fact that it happened at all, when it wasn't supposed to.

DODE SPENCER

HE BURST INTO TEARS   My wife recalls wheeling our child down Côtes des Neiges Road below where Leacock lived and he was walking up the hill and looking very, very disconsolate. He was just returning from René du Roure's funeral. He and du Roure were absolutely inseparable buddies and he looked terribly sad, and my wife thought that she should speak to him, and she said, "I'm Allison Walsh's wife. You don't know me, but I want to tell you how sorry I am about the loss of your friend." Somewhat to her embarrassment, he burst into tears. He said, "I've lost a real friend."

THE HON. MR. JUSTICE ALLISON WALSH

ROARS OF LAUGHTER   My father, Sir Arthur Currie, came from a farm outside of Strathroy, Ontario. My father had a very good sense of humour, and presumably he and Leacock must have had something of the same type of sense of humour because they both laughed at the same time and about the same things.

Dorothy McMurray was my father's secretary, and she used to say that whenever Stephen Leacock would drop in and see my father, who was principal of McGill, you could hear the roars of laughter throughout the east wing of the Arts Building. Obviously they enjoyed each others' company. My father didn't have a fund of jokes, but he loved telling stories and reminiscing, and I as a young fellow used to sit down and listen to him tell stories about the First World War and different people in the war, and so on. He had a tremendous memory for people and events—it was a photographic memory—

and that's the kind of memory that Stephen Leacock had.

I'd like to tell you a story about Stephen Leacock that I remember well. When the governor-general, who was then the Earl of Bessborough, when his wife was having her youngest son—who was George St. Lawrence Ponsonby—when she was having him in the hospital, Bessborough came to stay with us in Montreal.

We lived at 3450 McTavish Street, which is now the Faculty Club of McGill University. This one night we were having people for dinner and I noticed my mother getting quite jittery and she signalled another round of drinks. Then I realized that there weren't the exact number of people who were to sit down for dinner. And just then Stephen Leacock arrived. He walked across the room straight up to my mother and said, "Lady Currie, would you tie my tie? My niece, Barbara, is out." So mother tied his bow tie and then introduced him to the governor-general.

The other thing I remember was, when the ladies left and the men moved down to the end of the table to have another port, Leacock was very lively at that time, and there was repartee back and forth and a lot of good fun and jokes between my father, Sir Arthur Currie, and Leacock.

The few times that he would come to dinner at our house and I would be present, there was never any indication that he'd been drinking a lot. But I presume he'd been drinking quite a bit before he got to our house.

GARNER CURRIE

CHAPTER FOUR

The Cosy Home
Life in Montreal

BY OCTOBER, HE HEADED FOR MONTREAL   By the beginning of October, the country life got pretty dull. There's nothing new in the garden, there's nothing new in the farm, fishing isn't very good, things begin to look a little bleak and cold, and he started thinking of Montreal and the University Club and his game of billiards and the theatre, which he enjoyed attending, and his many friends and his love of entertaining and seeing his friends. And therefore he always went back.

BARBARA NIMMO

THE CÔTE DES NEIGES HOUSE
It was semi-detached. When you looked at the building you saw that it was half a house. But you'd think it was a whole house. But it wasn't a very big house. I suppose it was less than twelve hundred square feet of floor.

It was a brick house, red pressed brick. The architectural style was mid-Victorian.

It probably would have been worth $17,000 or $10,000 or something at that time.

FRANK NOBBS

GRACE REYNOLDS   I don't think he was very much interested in household decorations. I don't think the furniture was especially interesting, not valuable antiques, I doubt it.

Grace Reynolds was his secretary for many years. I don't think she was particularly tall, average height, brown hair, large eyes, very animated, very friendly, and very outspoken. Apparently they got on very well, though she wasn't a bit intellectual. I haven't seen her for at least twenty, twenty-five years.

LAURENCE TOMBS

ROUGHING IT ON THE PORCH
I was about eighteen, I guess, when I went to work for Dr. Leacock. In those days Mrs. Leacock was still alive and so I worked in the house from about ten to four o'clock, and then I would have a cup of tea with Mrs. Leacock and then go home. I lived in Cartierville with my mother.

The Leacock house was right next to the Montreal General Hospital, at Pine and Cedar. It was a very big house. You had to go up quite a few steps because it was on the slope on the hill. There was a heavy oak door and an inside entrance hall, and then there was a long hall, and off that was the drawing room on one side and the dining room on the other side. There was a fireplace in the study upstairs.

From the dining room you went through a butler's pantry into the kitchen. He had a cook and a housemaid. Mary was the cook and Betty was the housemaid. Then we had a man who used to clean out the fireplace and do jobs like that. We had a fire in the fireplace every day in the study.

There was a hallway at the back of the kitchen, and there was a great big cold cupboard. This was built of glass and extended outside of the house, and in the wintertime, if you put anything out there it would freeze. And then, if I recall, a stairway went down to the basement from that little hallway. There was also a door into

the back hallway from the entrance hallway. From the dining room there was a door into the butler's pantry and then you went into the kitchen from that. There were some grounds at the back of the house, big enough so that we had a skating rink built.

There were very wide, shallow, very dark oak steps going up to the second floor. When you went up to the second floor, there were two bedrooms and Dr. Leacock's study. In the study there was a fireplace. Because we were up so high, there was a window seat, and you could sit on the window seat and look out over Montreal. It was at the front of the house. There was a third floor where the cook and the housemaid lived. They had their own floor.

The Leacock home in Montreal.

There was a big gallery off Dr. Leacock's study and he used to sleep there in the wintertime. The housemaid used to take the warming pan, and then he wore his raccoon coat to go out to bed. The raccoon coat was like his dressing gown when he went outdoors. Literally, there was snow on top of the bed.

He used to get up around six o'clock in the morning. He didn't work at night. He went to bed around ten or eleven, depending on the circumstances. The cook used to leave a tray in the kitchen, and the very first thing that he did in the morning was light a fire in the fireplace in the study, and then he went down to the kitchen and he brought up the morning tea. Of course, this was when I was actually living in the house.

He knocked on my door and he knocked on little Stevie's door and we went into the study and had tea. This was just morning tea. By that time he had a robe on, a dressing gown.

Then he went into the bathroom and got dressed and went for a walk on the mountain. He went for a walk on the mountain every morning. This was before breakfast, around seven-thirty to eight o'clock. He would come back and have breakfast. Then he walked Stevie to school and walked to McGill to give his lectures.

GRACE REYNOLDS

ICEBOUND   Dr. Leacock's study in his Montreal home had a red carpet and red-papered walls. He believed this colour stimulated his mind and increased his energy. Off this room was a balcony, open except for a railing, and this is where he slept, even in the coldest weather, some-times with snow blowing around his bed. There was a sofa in the room, so it was possible that he did sleep inside when the weather was too forbidding. Every night, hot-water bottles would be placed in his bed on the verandah, but I am sure that if he was very late getting home, the bottles would be frozen solid.

One morning, when he did not appear for breakfast, Mrs. Leacock investigated and found the door would not open, and Dr. Leacock was trapped on his balcony. Luckily, he had placed his coonskin coat on the bed when he retired. Garbed in this, he danced around and clapped his hands to keep warm. As the door seemed to be frozen and would not budge, a ladder was found, and Dr. Leacock climbed down and finally got back into his warm house after a thorough chilling. He did not suffer any ill effects and just laughed about the incident.

M.D.

WE DRESSED FOR DINNER EVERY NIGHT   Dr. Leacock wrote shorthand and I wrote shorthand and so we used to converse with each other in shorthand and it drove the cook and the housemaid crazy because they couldn't read shorthand. He had a man up in Orillia, Bill Jones, and Leacock would write in shorthand, "Did you pay the cook, did you pay Jones?" And of course they couldn't read the shorthand.

When I was his secretary, girls my age who went out on a date wore black evening gowns. When I was going out, I had to stand on a hassock in the study and turn around and Dr. Leacock would give me the once over. He said, "I don't like that dress. You look like a widow." I said, "But Dr. Leacock, all the girls are wearing black evening gowns." And he said, "I still think you look like a widow." So he telephoned a florist in the Mount Royal Hotel and told him to send the largest corsage of pink carnations immediately by taxi. So I had a corsage of pink carnations that started at the shoulder and went down to the waist. At least I didn't look like a widow.

We dressed for dinner every night. He wore a dinner jacket. He wasn't very good at tying a bow, so he used to just take the back ends of the tie and sort of loop it over.

Young Stephen and Dr. Leacock and I sat at the dining room table. He liked to serve the soup from a tureen, then the housemaid passed the soup.

There was a bell under the carpet and he used to put his foot on the bell to call the housemaid back. He always had wine with dinner. We had a wine cellar. On the other hand, he didn't buy expensive wine. He said a lot of the wine that was expensive wasn't any better than some of the wine you could buy in the keg. Every month we had the Political Economy Club and they all came for dinner. Now this included Professor Day, who was a senior member of his staff, and Professor Hemmeon. It was quite a group. In those days we had charge accounts at Gatehouse and that was where you could buy any kind of fish, so that it was very easy to order a dinner, you understand, because you could order this or that and it got delivered.

Dr. Leacock never had a drink till after the day's work was finished. When all his lectures were finished at McGill, he used to go to the University Club and he'd play billiards with René du Roure, who had been a prisoner of war in Germany. That is when he would have a Scotch.

GRACE REYNOLDS

WATER WAS HER DOWNFALL   He liked his Scotch and soda very much. But I never saw him drunk. I have seen him a little happier than he might have been when he came to the Political Economy Club after an early evening at the University Club.

He would have a dinner party at his house for all the staff at the beginning of each year, and when I was there, there was Leacock, Hemmeon, Day, Culliton, Forsey and myself. We were six. And his niece, Barbara, well, she was in charge. He was a widower and the rest of us were unmarried. So he'd have her bring six girls from Royal Victoria College.

And I've often told this story. He had a wonderful bar in his dining room— all kinds of liquor would be served. The maid went around to one of the girls, who I think was in her first year. The girl said something to the maid and Dr. Leacock said "Oh, what did you say?" Well, she felt very bashful and said, "I would like a glass of water." And he said, "Water? Water? Oh yes! I remember, I had some of that forty-five years ago. It's good for you. Bring the young lady a glass of water!"

She could have gone through the floor, the poor little girl.

SENATOR H. CARL GOLDENBERG

BANG WENT THE DRUM   Barbara Ulrichsen was very attractive and blonde, very friendly, and we got along very well together. She was tall, with a good figure and she was dressy. She didn't intimidate me. She was very intelligent, a good conversationalist. I really only knew her one year particularly because she used to invite me up for tea.

It was very cosy, they always had a fire in the fireplace when you came in. Downstairs there was a sort of den, and that was where we usually had tea. I think she introduced me to crumpets.

Often, Leacock would come in and have tea with us and sometimes little Stevie would be there; but usually it was just Barbara and me. The maid would serve the tea and it was a fairly formal tea. I never was in the kitchen myself. It was nice china, very nicely served; actually, I don't remember whether we had silver or china.

Leacock was always very pleasant. He had a lot of bachelors in the Economics Department, Culliton and Dr. King, and when they had staff dinner parties, they needed some women to fill it out, so I went up there to several parties.

But it wasn't always just his staff. Professor du Roure would sit at one end of the table, and Leacock at the other end, and exchange stories back and forth. A very nice, panelled dining room with a lovely warm fireplace. It was very homey, comfortable.

I have the impression of a lot of woodwork. The dining room was panelled but it was certainly dark. Always a fire in the fireplace when you came in.

When there was a party, then we would have drinks upstairs, there was a big sort of a library upstairs. Lots of books on the walls.

I remember one party I went to. An English company was putting on *Green Hat* at her Majesty's Theatre, and Leacock had a theatre party in which I was included. Someone in this company was a friend of his. We all trooped in and sat in the front row. Leacock leaned over to speak to somebody and his foot hit the drum in the orchestra pit, which would entertain me at that age of course. Then we went back to his house afterwards with the cast of the play and had drinks and food.

JEAN VAN VLIET

ASKING BARBARA   I just got the impression that Barbara ran everything for him at home. Anything he wanted he'd say, "Barbara, remember we got a letter from so-and-so," or "Remember I asked you to go to the bank," or "Remember you took such-and-such a cheque." This sort of thing he asked her.

She was a blonde and pleasant-looking. She had a lively personality.

GARNER CURRIE

HIS PARTIES WERE FAMOUS
My uncle wrote in the early morning, often (especially in Montreal) being up and at his desk in the early hours when I arrived home from a very late party. If he couldn't write on a new book or article, there were always letters to answer, plans for the farm to draw up, outlines for McGill work, some treatise or other that he could work on until at another time his mind, rested and refreshed, was ready for something "real."

He loved entertaining and almost always made some visiting celebrity an excuse for a party—an author, actor or explorer. (He was always fascinated with explorers. He nearly went on an expedition to the South Pole with Shackleton or Vilhjalmur Stefansson—I have forgotten which one it was. He knew them both but when he found he could not take along his own supply of whiskey, the long cold nights of the sub-arctic seemed too much.)

So many famous and interesting people have been gathered together in the Côte des Neiges house or have been asked for dinner or supper at the University Club. At home we'd have cocktails first in his study upstairs, an attractive book-lined room, books clear to the ceiling, a large window all across one side of the room, giving a beautiful view down over the city and harbour he loved.

His dinner parties were really known in Montreal as very successful, fun, intellectual evenings. No bridge was played, no games were played, but there was always a rapid-fire of conversation, of witty, clever stories. There would be many good stories. It's amazing how much fun sometimes was crowded into one evening. I have never heard people laugh as they did around his dining-room table and I never expect to hear people laugh like that again.

BARBARA NIMMO

DON'T WATCH THE SPIDER   My association was more with Barbara Ulrichsen, his niece, than it was with Stephen. Barbara and I were of a similar age and Leacock was older than God, as I saw it at that time. She used to have these little dinners to which she would invite my fiancée, later my wife, and myself—about three couples, quite formal little dinners as a matter of fact, because that was the sort of thing that was done in those days and that was a beautiful house to have them in

on the corner of Pine Avenue.

I was there with some frequency. I remember one episode—I had left McGill and joined the editorial staff of the *Montreal Star* and I'd been there for about a year and I was getting pretty cheesed off with no promotions and no light at the end of my humble tunnel. So one evening at Leacock's I said, "Excuse me, sir, could I have a second of your time for some advice?" And he said, "Go ahead, go ahead, Bob." So I said, "Well, I've been on the *Star* for a year and nothing's been happening and I don't know what to do. What should I do?"

And he said, "Well, you remember that old Scottish story about the spider coming down from the ceiling and then trying to climb back up again and Robert the Bruce lying and hiding in the cave and watching it—and he was feeling pretty depressed about his efforts to clean the English out of Scotland and he thought he might just as well give up. But he watched the spider and the spider kept on trying and, after many tries, by pure perseverance, it succeeded in getting to the top and that was all he wanted as an augur for what he should do—that if he kept on trying he would get to the top, and he dashed out into the fray again."

So Leacock then said, "All right, then, you remember that story?" And I said, "Yes, I do." And he said, "Now, referring back to you and the *Montreal Star*, I'm going to change the admonition, or the inference of that spider's story, if I may." And I said, "Certainly, sir." And he said, "Well, in terms of you and the *Star*, Bob, I suggest that if at first you don't succeed, quit, quit at once."

BOB CAMPBELL

TEA IN HIS SALON   I recall being a visitor for tea at his home. I remember a big salon, or living room, in which he seemed to have everything, his desk, sofa, easy-chair, the library with books of all kinds, but they were not in very good order. It was comfortable and it had a fireplace.

He would ask about half a dozen of his students for tea. In the later years he was left with about six or ten pupils, at the most, as we progressed to our senior year.

If I recall correctly, he would bring in the tea tray himself. He had a house-keeper, but she was rather old and was not the type who would be serving guests. At one time the students, Miss Greaves and Miss Best, did the honours at tea in his salon. It was a happy occasion, the fire would be going, Leacock would be pleasant and chatty. We would discuss the events of the day and there were plenty taking place at that time.

JUDGE HAROLD B. LANDE

HE'D LISTEN   When I was doing post-graduate work for an M.A. degree, occasionally I used to go up to Leacock's house with two or three other students for consultations.

He would take you into a fairly large study; I can't remember whether it had a fireplace, but you have never seen such an untidy room in your life. Things were piled everywhere, there wasn't a spot of space to put anything down. How he ever found anything, I really wouldn't know. But this was the way he liked it, and these were very stimulating and interesting sessions which we used to have. Just with a very small group of postgraduate students.

Leacock was particularly good in a very small group. Informal, lively, very stimulating. He'd listen to what was being said, he wasn't a bad listener, particularly in a small group like that. I think he did like to be centre stage, and he was used to that—but not to the degree that he wouldn't listen to graduate students who wanted to express their views.

JOHN PEMBERTON

WRONG WAY SNOW STORM   There was a story about Leacock one time, in the winter, when he was caught shovelling snow into the house instead of out of it.

He, no doubt, had been having a good time and went out to shovel snow off his steps. He was found by some students shovelling the snow into the house, and of course, they looked after the old gentleman and persuaded him to go in himself, and forget about it.

You never could tell what he was going to do next.

CHARLIE PETERS

A SMALL PIECE OF ROMANCE
A cleaning lady who came as a substitute when the regular was ill was a fanatical admirer of Leacock. She was a tall, heavy woman who would have looked more becoming garbed in a man's suit than a woman's dress. She would drop the mop and run to get a glimpse of Dr. Leacock as he was leaving the house in the morning. She confided to Mrs. Leacock that she would love to kiss his hand or the hem of his gown.

Mrs. Leacock, very amused, told her husband about the woman's request. It happened that he had just brought his gown home for repairs. Part of the hem was ripped and dangling. Dr. Leacock tore the piece off, handed it to Mrs. Leacock, saying "Give her this. She can take it home and kiss it every day for the rest of her life."

M.D.

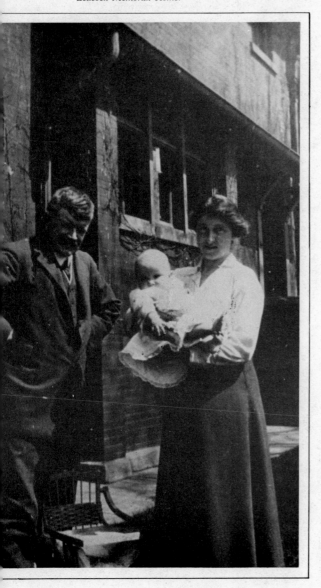

Stephen, Beatrix and Stevie, Jr., in front of their Montreal home, about 1916. *Courtesy of the Stephen Leacock Memorial Home.*

PAPER ROUTED   Back in the early 1930s I used to deliver the *Montreal Gazette* in the morning. My territory started at Sherbrooke, up Côte des Neiges Road as far as Cedar, back along McGregor Street—which is now called Professor Penfield, or Dr. Penfield—and down Simpson. There would be fifty or sixty papers most days.

I used to get up at five-thirty in the morning, pick up the *Gazettes* in the lobby of the Linton apartments, and head up Côtes des Neiges, dropping them off to the customers.

In those days, of course, the *Gazette* boys did not collect for the paper as they do today. The subscribers in that area, which was a rather exclusive area, used to pay for the paper by the year. So my contact with most of them was sketchy.

Professor Leacock was at the top of my route in the last house on the right below Cedar Avenue. I would normally get there six-thirty or a quarter to seven. Well, if I was as much as five minutes late in reaching Leacock's house, sometimes I would see him out looking to see if I was approaching. But, more often, if I happened to be five minutes late or ten minutes late, I discovered that he would immediately phone the circulation department at the *Montreal Gazette* to complain about the service.

Once or twice I saw him outside, in nice weather, looking to see if I was approaching and actually tapping his foot in impatience, waiting for the paper.

BOB TAIT

CHAPTER FIVE

McGill: The Man in the Tattered Gown

A REALLY TRAINED MIND   I think Leacock stimulated all his students enormously. I think he did instill in everybody a desire to learn and I think I would go a little further than that and say that he stimulated a desire to learn in an orderly manner. He was a very good example of a really trained mind in operation.

JOHN PEMBERTON

UNUSUAL QUALITIES, UNIVERSAL APPEAL   At McGill, Leacock had an adoring class. I can't think of any dissonant voice among the students. Many students who were not registered in his class came just for the pleasure of hearing him. He was a great speaker and he had an infectious way of attracting his hearers. You couldn't refuse to listen to the man, he was just magnetic. It made no difference what the subject was, he just made it so interesting.

As a public lecturer, he could have spoken on any subject. He was endowed with some unusual qualities, qualities that had a universal appeal, but he personally preferred to voice his sentiments and express his thoughts in the university atmosphere.

He could have been a success in any intellectual pursuit. He had a great personality, the ability to attract friends, people from high and low, because they all adored him. The oddities of his appearance, his dress, I think, simply added to his charm.

I think the era in which he lived and taught at McGill would be very much impoverished, if you subtracted Leacock from that scene.

JUDGE HAROLD B. LANDE

The Arts Building at McGill University. Year after year, Leacock shuffled up the path to his classes here.

NOBODY FELL ASLEEP   He was a great educator, in the very best sense of the word, in making you think way beyond the subject you were taking and in having you read avidly in all sorts of areas that would tie into a Liberal Arts education. I think perhaps too much stress was laid on him as a humourist—he was far more than a humourist. He was a very brilliant satirist. It was kindly satire and not too acidic.

His lectures were certainly enlivened by his wit. I remember a great many of them seemed to be given at two o'clock in the afternoon, when everybody's a little sleepy after lunch, in the big lecture hall in the back of the Arts Building, overlooking the reservoir. Almost anybody but Leacock would have had us drowsing off during the lecture but he kept us awake by being so challenging and interesting.

I think, though, that stressing him as a humourist, we perhaps overlook the fact that he was a very good educator in the best sense.

THE HON. MR. JUSTICE ALLISON WALSH

STUDENTS ALL SPOKE TO HIM
He lectured at McGill three days a week, which gave him three free days for outside lectures and literary work. He'd started there under the reign of Queen Victoria—1901—giving just one lecture under her reign. He stayed on the staff there as head of the Department of Economics and Political Science from 1908 until his retirement in 1936. McGill was one of the great interests of his life and he was one of the outstanding figures of McGill. You could always tell when he came into the Arts Building from his sure, heavy step and the loud thump of his cane on the marble floor, even if he didn't chance to pass anyone and greet him in his deep, resonant voice. Students all spoke to him, and he always made a good pretence at knowing them even if he didn't.

BARBARA NIMMO

THE DRAMATIC STRUGGLE   His entry to the crowded classroom was a dramatic one. Now as the door would open, the doorway was filled with the figure of a man engaged in a violent struggle to rid himself of his gown while the gown seemed equally determined to cling around its wearer. It was the most awful-looking garment that you could possibly conceive. Tattered and torn, full of ragged holes, it hung from his shoulders and clung around his form like some damp and bedraggled garment without a name. Eventually, however, the man seized the collar of the gown firmly on both sides with both hands and gave it a violent tug, which settled it close to his shoulders, where the gown seemed to cease to defy its wearer. The animated conflict was evidently over for the time being.

S. MORGAN-POWELL

HE SLEPT IN IT?   Stephen Leacock was always very dishevelled-looking and when I knew him, he had grey hair which was usually all over the place. Around the Arts Building, at lectures, he had this frightful old gown that has become famous because it was almost in tatters. But, in addition to that, I'm sure he slept in it because even with its age and being worn, it couldn't possibly get that wrinkled.

G. MEREDITH ROUNTREE

HE LOOKED STRAIGHT AT YOU

Stephen Leacock would come to the class in a torn professor's gown, half off the shoulder, probably dragging on the floor. Whether he was dressed in his latest blue suit or a grey suit, it didn't matter, there certainly might be some food spilled on the front of it. But that didn't matter.

It was from the neck up that you were impressed, his sort of beak face, in essence, and his sparkling eyes. I remember his eyes were very piercing and very intelligent and he looked directly at you. It was the character of the man that shone, and his vibrancy.

SENATOR ALAN A. MACNAUGHTON

THE FINGERNAIL TREATMENT

His gown became more and more bedraggled each time he lectured because he was always digging his fingernails into it and bringing out new tatters.

He had a way of putting his thumbs inside it and having his fingers loose so he could move them up and down. That was his typical position when he was lecturing. He was in constant motion.

HERBERT H. TEES

AND A WATCH-CHAIN

Stephen Leacock had a very heavy watch-chain across his expanded waistline. It was a companion and he played with it. I also remember, in the good old days, that Leacock would take a corner of his gown and he would play with it and twist it. And all these mannerisms would distract the class slightly. He wasn't relaxed, he was busy, busy all the time. But it was a privilege to be in his class.

I think he was such a friendly man; he reached out to everybody. He spoke to students whether they were in his class or whether they weren't, just because they were students.

MARGARET STEPHEN

THE OLD FOB WATCH

It was mostly his watch that he used to handle in my day. I always remember that big watch that he used to bring out. He had it in his vest pocket. He never looked at the watch but he used to twirl it around. It was one of these old fob watches that used to be popular in those days, and he would take it out often and twirl it around in his hand.

CHARLIE PETERS

A LITTLE BIT OF AN ACTOR

As one gets older, one gets perhaps a little careless—especially if you're a so-called absent-minded professor. So therefore your clothing, as long as you're clothed, really doesn't make a great deal of difference. As long as you can get by the police. Then, on the other hand, he was a little bit of an actor. He had a reputation which he had to maintain and probably enjoyed—playing to the audience, the audience being the new student class.

SENATOR ALAN A. MACNAUGHTON

SHAGGY STEVIE, OR LEAKY STEAMCOCK

He gave me a very strong feeling of shagginess. He had a windblown look about him—hastily thrown together. And I'm quite sure that some of this was studied carelessness. As I got to know him better through the course of sittings for his portrait, he gave me a strong impression of ruddiness, of high colour, with the contrast of his sparkly bright blue eyes, twinkling through his shaggy eyebrows.

He was familiarly known to almost everybody as Stevie and frequently as Leaky Steamcock.

FREDERICK TAYLOR

Painting of Leacock in the classroom. *Reproduced courtesy of Imperial Oil.*

NO KIDDING   *The McGill Daily* stops in April when the students are all writing their exams and the Mongrel issue comes out. And the Mongrel issue, which was just a lark, said something about "Leaky Steamcock says," and so on. And you know, he never forgave them. He was terribly hurt by it.

You couldn't play a joke on Leacock. As long as he had the floor, and he made the jokes, then everything was fine. But you couldn't joke with him, you had to be on the receiving end—from my experience. Some of the students would have some repartee with him, but that wouldn't produce, in my memory, any friendly reaction. He'd clam up and he wouldn't enjoy a joke on himself. I really felt that.

He had another thing. I remember this so well. Before he told you a joke, he would start laughing. And I think it was that he thought it was so funny he started to laugh before he told you. He would convulse, he wouldn't just stand there and laugh. His whole body would shake, and his whole upper torso would move with the laughter. And, of course, it was sort of infectious because the students would all be sitting on the edge of their chairs listening to him laugh and wondering what he was going to say. But the laughter would come from him before he told a joke almost on every occasion.

FRANK NOBBS

AN ICY RESPONSE   You could almost see the laughter, the humour in his face. I can recall on one occasion sitting in the back of a classroom. It was at the back of Moyse Hall actually, and it must have been at the end of a lecture because Leacock came down off the stage and walked to the back where some of us were sitting.

On the aisle was Celeste V. Belnap, now Mrs. Gordon Liersch. Leacock was leaning with his leg against the side of a chair. He was rambling on and as I recall, he was talking about exports and imports. It was an economic class and he was giving some examples and said, "Take for instance Iceland." Then he looked aside for a moment and sort of smiled and said, "God knows what they'd export," and Celeste looked at him—she was a very pretty girl—she looked at him with a cute smile and said "Ice, sir."

You could feel the laughter coming from Leacock's feet. You could see his body start to shake the whole way up. And then, finally, he said, "ice" and just laughed.

That was the feeling you got from Leacock when you were talking to him about one thing or another when he wasn't serious. You'd feel that laughter coming, it was near the surface, but it came all through his body.

D. LORNE GALES

ON THE WAVELENGTH   To his face we always addressed him as Dr. Leacock. There was no other way of addressing him, we never thought of him in any other way. Informally, we referred to him as Stevie, or as Leacock, but it was always with a feeling of affection. So often when you refer to teachers, you speak about them with disdain and, if you use a term that may not sound polite or respectful, you mean it. But in his case, even though we'd call him the Old Boy or Stevie—which was really not the most respectful way to

approach a professor—we always did it with a great sense of affection.

He certainly was on the wavelength of the students. You would never consider that there was such a disparity in age between the teacher and the class as you so often assumed to be the case. He was down to our level; he was in a sense one of the boys, although he never used untoward language. He infused us with the importance and the joy of learning and that you could really make it a pleasant chore and he taught us the value of doing this without making it burdensome or boring.

JUDGE HAROLD B. LANDE

HAM ON WRY   Leacock had unpredictable ways of being funny. He was not reluctant on occasion to ham it up.

I remember when Varsity was playing against McGill. Leacock was both a Varsity graduate and a McGill professor. He appeared at the smoker after the game. He had a few thoughts, he said, which he had noted down while on the long ride down in the slow-moving streetcar.

Whereupon he unfurled a roll of toilet paper. He had, he said, composed a long poem in blank verse and pretended that it was all written on the paper. With one hand he held an end of the roll, while, with the other hand, he kept letting the paper out on to the floor as he read.

COL. H. WYATT JOHNSTON

YOU KEPT ALERT   Sometimes he'd just be humourous for the whole class. But you never knew when he was going to turn serious and throw a question at you. So you always sat right on the edge of your seat to be sure that you heard the question and hoped that you'd be able to answer it.

FRED STONE

HE LAUGHED LIKE SANTA CLAUS

My memories of Leacock in the class-room are those of a very vibrant teacher who awakened interest and kept that interest sustained time after time, every time. He had a way of telling some sort of story to illustrate his point and the class would laugh. Then all of a sudden he would hunch himself up and laugh like Santa Claus, "That's good, that's good, ha, ha, ha. I never saw it that way before." Then the class, of course, would continue to laugh, but, this time, at the professor's reaction.

As I think back upon Leacock as the teacher, I think of a most stimulating person whose mind roamed over a vast field of knowledge and had so many comparisons to bring forth that he was not the ordinary kind that kept to an outline, A, B, C, 1, 2, 3 in a pedantic way. He was anything but pedantic.

I feel that a great teacher does more for his students by having that vast encyclopaedic approach and encouraging the student to see the comparisons, whether it's Plato or Thomas Aquinas. He's roaming forth and back in a most enlightened and stimulating way for the young student.

MAYSIE MacSPORRAN

A DICKENSIAN CHARACTER

Stephen Leacock looked flustered, he looked like a typical Dickensian character. He used to usually come into the lecture after we were all waiting for him. He would come in late, and rush up to the front and then start to tell some wonderful big joke, which was a good way to start the lecture and get everybody in a good humour.

FRANK NOBBS

A RESTLESS MAN   He was a restless lecturer and he seldom sat down. I think the times I remember him sitting on the edge of a desk were after he'd written something on the blackboard and then he'd give the students an opportunity to absorb what he'd written by just standing back and relaxing for a minute.

HERBERT H. TEES

REMEMBER THIS   I do remember that he did wander around and around the board with a piece of chalk in his hand. And he seemed to stop and all of a sudden he'd think of something and he'd write it down on the board and he'd say, "Well, now, keep this in mind. This is one of the basic things you must remember."

COL. CHARLES PETCH

BACK AND FORTH, BACK AND FORTH

Leacock never remained still, he was talking all the time, he'd walk up and down in the front. He'd go over to the window and look out and still talk. And he'd come back, and so on. One student might ask a question—something that had appeared in the *Montreal Gazette* that morning or something, ask him a question on that, and away he'd go. He'd give this wonderful answer that had nothing to do with the lecture he was giving.

GARNER CURRIE

HE'D START RIGHT IN   One of his characteristics, of course, was to start lecturing the instant he entered the classroom. So he wouldn't wait until he would get up to the podium or anything like that. He didn't want to waste any time. He entered and instantly started lecturing even as he was striding up to the front of the classroom. On occasions, he would write a great deal on the blackboard or give you a chart or something else like that. On other occasions he might just sprawl across the desk, but most of the time he was walking up and down or standing at the head of the class.

I don't remember his ever being ill and I don't remember his missing lectures. He was a very regular performer even though he was a very busy man and had a lot of important activities.

PHILIP VINEBERG

THIS, THAT AND THE OTHER THING
As soon as Professor Leacock entered the lecture room he started to talk. His lectures were crowded—Adam Smith, John Stuart Mill, Malthus, would come to life again. And he, before Winston Churchill, saved the British Empire every Monday, Wednesday and Friday at three o'clock in Room 20.

JOHN CULLITON

HE WAS A GREAT ATTRACTION
He must have been a voracious reader when he was young. You know, he went to the University of Chicago, that's where he got his doctorate in the early 1900s. He took courses other than theories, but I don't think it ever got beyond that stage. I think that his studies at Chicago ended

there. I don't think he actually learned any more. He was too interested in everything to just concentrate on a particular subject that was assigned to him or for which he was noted at McGill.

In fact, isn't it true that when you speak of Dr. Leacock to people who never knew him personally say, when you tell them he was a Professor of Economics, they express great amazement? They thought he was a literary person whose writings and humour were his specialty. They are surprised to find that he gave courses in economics and political science. I found that several times in my travels.

He had a prodigious memory and he could quote chapter and verse and you could see that he seemed to have a picture memory. I think he was a great historian. He knew more history than economics or political science at that time, probably because, as the handmaidens of history, they were developing into separate sciences. It was really only by 1910 or the

Professor Stephen Leacock — the early years at McGill. *Courtesy of the Stephen Leacock Memorial Home.*

beginning of the First World War that they really were becoming specialty sciences of their own. This has been my impression.

I think that he was really given the job at McGill because of his outstanding personality. McGill was glad to have him because he was such a great personality and they really kept him on, not because he was teaching people a lot about economics, but because he was a great attraction.

JUDGE HAROLD B. LANDE

READ THIS, READ THAT   I came to McGill in 1924 as an undergraduate in the Arts Faculty. I began taking Honours Economics and Political Science the following year in 1925 and I took a course from Leacock: Introductory Political Science. I became rather friendly with him. I may have been a very forward fellow—I probably was. We would talk occasionally when we met in the corridor of the Arts Building, or walking down the street. We'd talk politics. I was very interested in politics.

In his course on Elements of Political Science, there was political theory from Plato to modern times. He taught political economy, particularly the history of political economy. The economists who had written major books—the major contributors to economics—were his main subjects.

He was an excellent lecturer, he was a great teacher. It amazed and impressed me, his memory, the width of his knowledge.

I was greatly indebted to him for many things, but one in particular. I was always a great reader—I never participated in athletics, my hobby was reading—and he would recommend books and would say, "Now you don't have to read that now, but keep that on your list—read it sometime." And I read a great deal more than was required for any of the courses because he interested me so much in what he was teaching and then gave me those references. Now, he did the same for all the class.

SENATOR H. CARL GOLDENBERG

HEMMEON WOULD SORT OF SMILE
Actually, Leacock taught us more political science than economics. We got our economic theory from Dr. Hemmeon, his associate. Whenever you said to Dr. Hemmeon, "Well, Dr. Leacock said thus-and-thus," Hemmeon would sort of smile and say, "Well."

I think Leacock did more for McGill than McGill did for Leacock. He was an outstanding personality, he was a brilliant lecturer and you could just listen to him talk on any subject.

I have never considered him much of an economist, and I only realized that when I began to cram for exams and started looking at my class notes I had taken and compared them with what I had received, say, from Dr. Hemmeon for example, or Dr. J.P. Day, who was another one of the associates in the department. Now, Day was a sound man on money and banking and international finance and international trade.

I enjoyed my course in economics and political science—they went together at the time—because I learned my facts from Day and Hemmeon, but I developed an interest through Leacock's very, very charismatic talks on everything in the world but economics.

JUDGE HAROLD B. LANDE

SOME WHIMSICAL THEORIES It was the Department of Economics and Political Science. In the universities of today, political science and economics are separate departments. But because of the historical evolution at McGill—and that was then true of many other universities—political science and economics were taught by the same people. I think Leacock was essentially a political scientist as far as his intellectual background is concerned. When it came to economics, his general interest was the writings of the economists in the sense of the history of economic literature. But he could hardly be considered a deep student of economics.

He was not terribly concerned with modern economics even as it was evolving at the time. I couldn't imagine Leacock, for example, sitting down and reading Keynes's *Treatise on Money.* When he was interested in Keynes, he was interested in such a book as *The Economic Consequences of the Peace Treaty.* That was one of his favourite subjects, as a matter of fact, and he shared Keynes's view that the Versailles Peace Treaty sowed the seeds of what became the catastrophe of World War II, that it was a great mistake. He was a devotee of Keynes the political scientist and not Keynes the economist. He just wasn't as much interested in economics, although he talked about it and he lectured on the subject. But I cannot say he had the same enthusiasm for it.

In his lectures, too, he had some whimsical theories that he only took half-seriously, but he liked to try them on his students. For example, he had an idea that Napoleon was a great naval man as well as a great military leader. And he would delve into this with some profundity, defending Napoleon the sailor rather than Napoleon the soldier, which was a novel idea at the time.

Incidentally, he had a great interest in sailing and knew a great deal about it. I suppose it was because of some of his activities around Orillia, but that crept into his lectures. He loved the navy and sailing.

PHILIP VINEBERG

BUNGLERS ALL I didn't have much use for Leacock as an economist, but as a political scientist, I thought he was very sound and his courses in political science were very good.

I think it was in the economics classes that we got most of his humour. I always felt that he tried out the material for his books on the class, and some of it sounded that way.

And there's one particular episode I remember, along those lines. I don't remember what the course was, but somehow or other he got on the American Revolution. And he proceeded to tell us, as he put it, what a great general George Washington was. And he said George Washington had his forces nicely collected in the upper reaches of the Hudson, but he moved them down and divided them into three parts, putting two parts on Long Island and one on Manhattan Island, so that the British could defeat each part separately. But, he said, there was one worse general than George Washington and that was General Howe who opposed him; and General Howe very carefully avoided cutting off the various parts of Washington's army and enabled him to bring them together and eventually win the battle. Now this went on for about ten or fifteen minutes you know, and he had the class in fits.

G. MEREDITH ROUNTREE

A DAZZLING MOSAIC OF IDEAS
I have never listened to anyone who was so well oriented as Leacock in the fields of history, literature, political economy and philosophy. With seeming ease and assurance, he drew on his wide-ranging knowledge to illuminate his lectures, which frequently sparkled with wit and humour. If he began talking about the French Revolution, he went right back to the Roman Empire or forward to World War I.

Whatever route he took, he unfolded a dazzling mosaic of human thought and action. He chuckled his way through the humourous parts and joined freely in the hilarity they usually produced. Whether in serious or humourous mood, the inimitable Leacock style was characterized by a certain free-wheeling animal thrust. Few in the audience or in the classroom, wanted to, or could, escape its grip. Generally, it was impossible to retell any part of a Leacock lecture and make it sound funny.

FRED STONE

AN UNBIASED VIEW
I remember him talking about Prince Kropotkin, who was the anarchist, and discussing anarchist theory and showing us why they thought that way, and why it was very good reasoning, without expressing an opinion that they were right or wrong. I remember him telling us that there was one anarchist who had shown that the world could produce enough wheat to give every man, woman, and child a full, nutritional diet and keep them in good health. The world had the capacity to produce enough shoes to give every man, woman, and child two or three pairs of shoes a year, including the heathen Chinese. And the world could produce enough coats and suits and clothing to keep everyone well clothed. In the end he said that, because of our free enterprise and capitalist system, this just does not take effect. So he was presenting the other side, but he didn't present it in a way that you thought he was a Communist.

And then he would quote some of these early authors, Kier Hardie, the first Labour member of the British Parliament —he was elected in 1885—and how everyone in Britain was outraged that a Labour member should be elected to Parliament. With his usual humour and a couple of chuckles he would describe the outraged feelings of the upper gentility in England.

JUDGE HAROLD B. LANDE

SILVER IN INDIA
During the course of an hour you might have him talk on subjects as varied as silver in India, as the basis of their currency, language problems in South Africa, and why big ships are getting smaller because of economic reasons.

He'd talk about the Afrikaans language, which was the imported Dutch language that came with the early settlers

—that it had never been a written language until the time of the South African war, when national pride in language caused it to become an important subject in the universities. And the leading sponsors of the Afrikaans language were given the opportunity of devising a perfect language. In other words a language that didn't have the disadvantages of English spelling and wouldn't have the disadvantages of gender in the sense that the Latin languages have it.

His economic opinions were based on patriotism, on loyalty to the British Empire. He was all in favour of preferential treatment for members of the Empire.

He'd talk on half a dozen unrelated subjects, all in the course of an hour.

I can remember he would give students assignments. Mine may have been on silver in India and I did some research on it. Then you'd come to the lecture and Leacock would say, "Well, I see that Mr. Tees has in his hand some notes. I can tell that he's been doing some vast research. Would you let me see your notes, Mr. Tees?" So you'd hand him the notes. And he'd take them and might even tear them up and say, "Now, you don't need those notes, you've done research. Just tell the class what you've found out."

HERBERT H. TEES

A ONE-MAN SHOW There were many students who weren't taking his courses at all; they used to visit his class and attend it, extra-curricular, just to hear the man talk, because he was a one-man show in himself.

He always had a smile or a smirk on his face, like he was just ready to burst into a guffaw of laughter, which I found so characteristic of the man. In fact, you always knew when one of his jokes was coming up because he'd laugh way ahead of the class.

I never really learned anything directly from his lectures. When it came to examination time and I looked at my notes I found they were just hopeless, and I always considered myself a conscientious note-taker in class. In place of actual facts, which we were there to learn, he always gave us reference books which covered the hiatus. His lectures were so interesting and he had such an encyclopaedic knowledge of everything.

It just took the slightest word to turn him on and he would go off on a tangent and spend the rest of his time, the rest of the hour, telling you about something that was completely irrelevant, but there was some word or some expression that hit him. One day the word "chaos" came up in class, and he stopped and he said, "Do you know where the word 'chaos' comes from?" He told us it comes from the same origin as the word "gas." Then he said, "Now, that is a Dutch word," and the next thing we knew, he was talking about the Boers in South Africa and the rest of the lecture was all about what was happening in South Africa, the way in which the British took South Africa or the early invasion of South Africa, which took it away from the Boers and pushed them up into the Transvaal. The whole lecture was taken up with the history of South Africa, without any reference whatsoever to the purpose of that particular lecture.

JUDGE HAROLD B. LANDE

WE CAN ALL STAND ON BERMUDA

He wrote a book called *Economic Prosperity in the British Empire*, which is a little small book—red—and it was most amusing and he told the students we had to have it. And so we all went down and got it. And it was a real wonderful thing. And he lectured from the book. He said, "Now, if you will turn to page thirty-five, we have a vast country here and I don't think anybody in this country can realize how many eggs we can produce. Now, we can produce enough eggs in Canada not only for the Empire but for the whole world. And the number of eggs, which is in the billions, which we can get per day in Canada, is in the book." And this is the sort of thing he'd tell you.

So then he said, "When it comes to the number of people there are in the world, everybody can stand up on Bermuda." Everybody in the world can stand up on Bermuda he said, and there's sixty-five square miles left still unstood on. It would make such an impression telling you these ridiculous things, which may or may not have made sense in terms of *Economic Prosperity in the British Empire*, that you had to remember these funny, wonderful stories. It was the afternoon amusement park we went to.

FRANK NOBBS

HANG ON TO YOUR PANTS

I studied under Leacock during the middle of the Depression and I remember he used to comment frequently about it. Someone once asked him the difference between the words "recession," "depression," and "panic." "Look," Leacock said, "a recession is a period in which you tighten your belt. In a depression, you have no belt to tighten. In a panic you have no pants left to hold up."

ALLAN ANDERSON

CATASTROPHE

One story I remember Leacock telling in class. He was describing what a philosopher was. He didn't have too much to say in favour of philosophy. He described a philosopher as a blind man in a dark room looking for a black cat that wasn't there.

HERBERT H. TEES

HIS LECTURES WERE MORE ENTERTAINING THAN HIS BOOKS

His lectures were the most fascinating that I ever took at McGill and, in my opinion, his lectures and his talks were vastly more entertaining and humourous than any book he ever wrote.

He would come into the lecture room and the first five minutes everything would be very orderly. He would spell out chapter and verse, then, four or five minutes later, he would start his digressions, which were always fascinating and interesting. And then, with about five minutes left to go with his lecture period time, he would come back to the subject matter and dictate a series of books that he would recommend that you read before the next lecture.

If students read all the books that he suggested, they would never have had time to read a book on any other subject they were taking at the same time at the university.

TRUEMAN SEELY

COMING TO THE RYE   One little thing I still remember, he would come in and it would be a lecture on economics—let's say—on General Principles. So after fifty minutes of rambling around the North American continent, you probably end up with a phrase about turning the waving, golden grain of the West into . . . rye! I always remember the phraseology, the richness, and the imagery of his language.

SENATOR ALAN A. MACNAUGHTON

HE LIKED ATHLETES   They were always jovial classes, he was always getting off the subject. Especially if you were a football player like I was and some of the other fellows, he'd always seem to direct the questions to you to see if you were paying attention or not. And being an economics course that we were taking with him, it just seemed to me that he had a glint in his eye for anybody who was kind of athletic. Whether they were academic or not didn't seem to make any difference. He was always for us. He'd kind of look at us, and say, well, you oughta know this, you know what I mean.

I seem to remember him coming to football practice and Frank Shaughnessy was our coach then. He was a great friend of Frank Shaughnessy and Frank used to be trying to get us all passing our exams, and whatnot. Shaughnessy was the ex-coach at Notre Dame, great, tall, bow-legged, and tough, and chewed tobacco. And Stevie, as we used to call him, used to always be around seeing how all of his favourite students were doing. Well, he was interested in his students I think; I don't know whether he was interested in football. But he'd come around and say hello and see how we were doing.

COL. CHARLES PETCH

NOW, LOOK AND SEE   An essential part of Leacock's vocabulary was a command word at the start of a sentence. It was said pleasantly and, probably, the original purpose was to focus one's attention on what he was saying. Eventually, it became a habit. So Leacock would often begin a sentence with one of a little corps of words he used. He would say, "Look," or "Now," or "See," and other such categoric words. In the classroom, we liked to hear them, because they were so much a part of him.

ALLAN ANDERSON

GENTLE HANDLING   He was enormously kind to all his students and he used to ask different ones to make reports on one subject or another, and some of these reports were very poor indeed, but he would always comment upon them in some such way as this: "Now, Mr. So-and-So, I like very much the way you brought out A, B, C. And I think, Mr. So-and-So, that I quite agree with you when you say that Dickens took that point of view and I commend you for emphasizing something else. I would like to add, however, that if I myself had been giving that report I would have brought in . . ." And then he delivered a little talk the way it might have been done. But Mr. So-and-So never knew that it had been somewhat inadequate.

I never, never heard him make fun of anyone in the classroom, or belittle anyone.

MAYSIE MacSPORRAN

PLAY UP, PLAY UP, AND PLAY THE GAME   Leacock was always very generous-hearted with his students. Once, in the mid-1930s, when I was news editor of *The McGill Daily*, I asked him if he would contribute a piece to the paper. I was in some of his classes and he knew me well. He came through with an important essay on spectatorial sports. He thought students should play games and not just sit on their fannies and watch them. He was very strict about being paid for his writing and he knew very well *The Daily* had no money for contributors, but that didn't stop him for a moment. I was very grateful to him.

He adored his students, especially if they worked hard and showed some indication of intelligence. I remember I was doing a paper for him and I met him in the corridor outside the classroom just before the class was to start. I said "Dr. Leacock, I've done the paper on 'The Ports of the World' but I just couldn't find much on Melbourne, Australia." Leacock said, "Come!" which was one of his peremptory commands, and we toddled over to the Redpath Library. Leacock showed me carefully where I should have found the information I needed. We then headed back for the class, twenty minutes late.

ALLAN ANDERSON

THE UNKNOWN GRETA GARBO
In many ways, he lived in a different world than his students and he had quite a tolerance for their ignorance in some subjects. I remember an incident in the classroom once when he was cross-questioning one of the students about a series of things, and the student couldn't answer a single question. After about ten minutes of that, when all the answers were still negative, because the student just didn't know, Stephen Leacock looked at him and said, "Well, I suppose you could ask me a lot of questions about Greta Garbo and I wouldn't know the answers."

PHILIP VINEBERG

HIS FAIRNESS SOMETIMES REBOUNDED
He was very much interested in teaching for teaching's sake. I remember the course he gave on Advanced Political Theory. Leacock himself was an arch-Conservative. But he handed out a reading list which, in those days of Depression and left-wing politics, brought many of his students to a devotion to a left-wing radical, socialist or communist point of view, because of what they had learned—not from Stephen Leacock who was opposed to all of this— but rather from the vast body of recommended reading to which they became exposed by reason of his teachings.

PHILIP VINEBERG

TOO MUCH LECTURING   Stephen Leacock always contended that at McGill they were required to do too much lecturing. I think he told me once that no professor should be required to give more than nine lectures a week which was one and a half a day. In those days we used to work six days a week.

He felt that if professors really did their preparations, and if they were going to bring credit to the university and to themselves, they had to spend time writing books as well.

BRIGADIER GENERAL JIMMY DE LALANNE

JUMPING THE GUN   In those days the professors had to call the roll. They don't do it anymore. He didn't like it, so he'd come in early, when there was scarcely anybody in the class, he'd take out his glasses; he would clean them and put them on his forehead, where they'd stand for the rest of the lecture; and he'd start calling the roll with nobody there. Everybody, of course, would be present. So that, at five minutes after, when the lecture was supposed to start, he could just go into his subject. I don't think he ever looked at his notes. He'd come in with notes, but he'd never look at his notes.

SENATOR H. CARL GOLDENBERG

NO FRIENDS?   A former student of Leacock's once told me of Leacock's disapproval of a rule that was instituted at McGill whereby the roll had to be called in classes. There was nothing for Leacock to do but conform, and I'm told that his roll call, on at least one occasion, went something like this: "Mr. Abernathy—here. Mr. Bawden—here. Mr. Cawthra—here. Mr. Dennison; Mr. Dennison; Mr. Dennison . . . Hasn't Mr. Dennison any friends in this class?"

JOE McDOUGALL

TIME WAITS FOR NO MAN? WRONG! There is a story from the days before mine, told to me by the late Frank B. Common, Q.C., who had been a student of Leacock's. As in my time, the students were then required to attend seven-eighths of the lecture periods. To check this, attendance was taken in each class by the professor. In one of Leacock's classes there was a notorious backslider in this matter

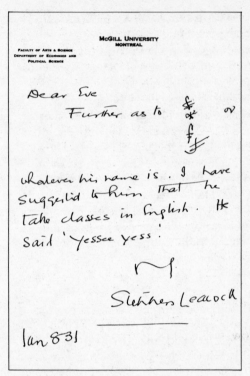

Reprinted courtesy of the Leacock Room, MacLennan Library, McGill University.

of attendance. It was coming to the end of the school year, and it was absolutely imperative that this chap show up at the final lecture in order to get the attendance to qualify as having taken the course.

The lecture began. It was in a lecture room on the top floor of the Arts Building, just opposite what used to be the German department. At the start of the lecture this chap was absent. As Mr. Common told the story, Dr. Leacock looked around the room before taking attendance, and must have noticed that the fellow was not present. Dr. Leacock seemed to forget about the attendance for the moment and started the lecture. When it was nearly over, steps could be heard coming up the corridor stairs, getting slower and slower as they approached the room. Now all the students in the class could think of nothing but the approaching footsteps. The mood in the room became tense. What was going to happen?

Dr. Leacock went right on addressing the class, but as he did so he strolled over to the window and looked out, still talking. He stayed there, continuing to talk while peering outside. Steps came ever closer in the corridor. Nobody in the class dared to breathe. The sound of the steps changed as they moved off the linoleum onto wood; the feet were now in the classroom. The steps stopped, a seat squeaked as a body lowered itself into place. The whole class sighed with relief.

Leacock now turned from the window, walked briskly to the teacher's desk, and said, "Now I think it is time to take the attendance." The class burst into applause.

WILLIAM H. PUGSLEY

ASK AND YE SHALL BE TOLD   The father of one of his students used to go over his son's homework and was dissatisfied with his son's progress. He wrote Leacock about this, complaining that "The boy has been with you six months and yet his knowledge of economics is very limited. What's the trouble?"

Leacock looked at the note for a minute and then scrawled on it; "It must be hereditary."

ALLAN ANDERSON

IT'S A TOSSUP   He seemed to me to be quite casual about exams. The story went—and this is probably apocryphal— that he used to toss all the exam papers up above the stairs, and those that landed on the highest steps got better marks than those that landed further down. And although this is probably not true, nevertheless, it seems to me that he was not particularly interested in what the examination marks showed. He was more interested in the interest that the students took in their work and judged them more on that basis.

CHARLIE PETERS

CHECKING OUT VINER   Jacob Viner was such a good student that Leacock decided—Stevie told me this at the University Club—he decided that he wanted to find out just how good he was. So, he checked with his associate in Chicago— the professor there—and arranged with him to send Viner's examination paper to this chap in Chicago and let him correct it, because a lot of people thought that he played favourites.

And when he got the results back from Chicago, they were much better than he had marked the paper. And Viner got a fellowship right away and went to Chicago and he got degrees and degrees from other places.

BRIGADIER GENERAL JIMMY DE LALANNE

UPPING THE MARKS   One of the brilliant men in my generation at McGill was a fellow called Arthur Bloomfield. He became a great economist. He became attached to the Federal Reserve System in the United States. And I suppose I was an

M.A. student at the time, as was Arthur.

Leacock gave me half of the exam papers to mark and Bloomfield the other half. It was a questionable thing because we didn't have the same standards. I marked exam papers on the basis of a small number of people getting a first class, a small number of people failing, and most everybody getting a second class or a third class or something else like that. Bloomfield, who was a perfectionist and a workaholic, failed everybody. So, Leacock brought him in and said, "Now, look, Bloomfield, give everybody an extra twenty marks, and see what happens." And that's the way he balanced our two markings.

PHILIP VINEBERG

MIND YOUR OWN BUSINESS   While he appeared very brusque, he was really very kindly. There was one year, for some reason or other, I was very anxious to find out what my standing was at the end of the year. I think it was some question of a scholarship I was probably hoping for. So I got hold of John Culliton and asked him what my mark was. John and Stephen shared the same office, so John took me into the office and he was in the process of looking it up and Stephen came in and he wanted to know what we were doing. Very brusque and business-like.

I said, "Well, I wanted to find out what my over-all mark was." He said very firmly, "You get first class, that's all you're entitled to know, isn't it?" And I said, "Yes," very meekly and departed.

Later on, I found that at that time first class was 75, and, afterwards, I found out that my average, arithmetically was

74.6. He had rounded it out to 75, but he didn't want me to know that. He wanted me just to know that I got first class. It was a little act of generosity on his part.

G. MEREDITH ROUNTREE

BREVITY PAID OFF   His top student, in 1915, that people thought he favoured a little bit, was Hilary Robertson. Hilary became a lawyer. Hilary was in the Meredith firm of lawyers for many years. He's dead now.

But Leacock always said that he was one of the best students he ever had. If you remember those books that we used to write our examinations in, I think there were about eight sheets, and he said that Hilary never used more than one book for his complete examination and he never used more than one page in answer to any question.

Leacock said that that was the mark of a good student because he could tell you in one page whether he knew what he was talking about or not. Hilary Robertson had curt answers; either you could look at them and say no good or good. And that's what Leacock said made him a great student. He was very fond of him.

BRIGADIER GENERAL JIMMY DE LALANNE

THE GERMAN STUDENT   He had a phenomenal capacity for languages quite apart from anything else. A Polish Jew came into our class in the third year who had seven languages, I think, but neither English or French. He was brilliant; he went on to a splendid career. But Leacock dealt with this by saying every now and again in a lecture, "Verstehen Sie, Herr

Reich?" "Nein, Herr Professor." And then Leacock would give him a short summary in excellent German of what he had just been saying; "Verstehen Sie jetzt, Herr Reich?" "Jawohl, Herr Professor."

Leacock simply switched to French or German without turning a hair. This of course is not by itself a great intellectual achievement, but it's an indication of the versatility and variety of Leacock's gifts.

SENATOR EUGENE FORSEY

HE GOBBLED UP BOOKS   It was part of the pattern that he didn't limit himself to the lectures as they were given earlier, especially in the fields in which he was interested. He kept abreast of the latest literature. He was an omnivorous reader; not many people appreciated that. He could read a book in a day or two and absorb it very quickly. So he knew what was going on in a way that was beyond most professors. He didn't have a closed mind as far as that was concerned.

He addressed himself to new problems and new issues and the like. I remember quite a few lectures from Leacock on Social Credit. It was a new thing and he hadn't talked about it before, but that didn't prevent him from writing about it, talking about it, and dealing with it.

He would deal with all the new political movements and the new sociological movements and the new ideas. His mind was not ready to embrace new convictions, but it was ready to consider new ideas.

PHILIP VINEBERG

THE HANDOUT   The first time I was on the campus at McGill University, having come from the West, it just so happened that Leacock was the first man I met.

And he said, "How are you getting on?" And I said, "Oh, pretty well, but I'm broke." "Oh," he said, "you're broke are you. Well, we'll have to try and get you some money." And he says, "Here's two dollars anyway to go along with."

So, then, I recall, he took me into the Registrar's and he said, "Here's a Red Indian friend of mine from way out in the woods somewhere, some awful place in British Columbia, you know. And he'll probably be quite a pupil though, a good student; he may do us a bit of good. So let's get him a little more money—give him another eight dollars—he's broke."

So, I was given ten dollars and I'm glad to say I paid it back in due course. But I had a scholarship, so that helped. But from that time on, our friendship became increasingly intimate.

GLADSTONE MURRAY

HALF AND HALF   There was a fellow student of mine who was in charge of a dance that was going to take place in the Arts Faculty. He went to see Stephen Leacock to sell him a ticket. The tickets were ten dollars each. So Leacock took the ticket and said, "Here's five dollars. With the other five dollars, I'll buy myself a bottle of Scotch and I'll have a much better time than I'll ever have at your dance!"

HERBERT H. TEES

68

HOUNDED INTO IT   A number of us were standing at the head of the stairs, outside of the Arts Building one day. It was a sunny morning. Leacock was walking up the campus with his dog, bent as usual, looking down. I was standing there with an Economics student, Gordon Nairn, and a number of others.

Leacock walks up the steps and he says, "Mr. Nairn, when is your next lecture?" and Nairn said, "Well I don't have another one before one o'clock." And Leacock said, "Fine, I hereby appoint you Master of the Hound." He gave up the leash and went and lectured for two hours and Nairn had to stand outside with that dog for two hours.

He brought the dog to the campus a number of times.

SENATOR H. CARL GOLDENBERG

A CERTAIN LITTLE TRUTH TO IT
My first lectures with him were the latter part of March, 1919, when I got back from the war. He was a real character, of course, and I remember the first lecture in second year economics, with all these students—second year students were lads who had not been in the services. They were all too young, you know; they were about seventeen or eighteen. Of course, I had had my twenty-second birthday after the Armistice.

I'll always remember the first course. After about a twenty-minute lecture, Stevie said, "Now look, gentlemen, do you understand that?" And some chap got up and gave him quite an argument and he said, "Well, I'd better explain that all over again." So he went at it again for about another fifteen minutes and when

he finished, he looked at this gentleman and he said, "Now, Mr. X, do you understand that a little better now?" And the chap said, "Well, I suppose there's a certain little truth to it." So Leacock said, "If my four honoured gentlemen in the back row don't mind, we'll call this lecture terminated." That was my first lecture with Leacock.

BRIGADIER GENERAL JIMMY DE LALANNE

MY GREAT MISTAKE   Once, I made a great mistake with Leacock. I told him I was looking for a summer job. This was exactly the kind of challenge Leacock liked. My father was an executive in the CPR and, a week later, he got me a summer job at the Algonquin Hotel at St. Andrews in New Brunswick. I told Leacock this but it meant absolutely nothing to him. He said, "Here," and gave me a letter addressed to one of his important business friends. The letter praised me as an excellent student and went on to say that Leacock would be delighted if his friend would come across with a summer job for me.

This continued, week after week, until Leacock tired of the game. Each week I would say, "But, Dr. Leacock, I have a job!"—Leacock would interrupt me with instructions as to where to take the current letter.

He also gave me letters to aid me in some of my research for the projects he used to hand out. I have one of these letters still, framed, and proudly displayed in my home.

ALLAN ANDERSON

A BARE PASS   About 1924, I had a chance to get a job on a ship that was bound for Africa and would stop at ports on the east and west coasts. It was a wonderful opportunity to see a bit of the world but my father, a very strict man, told me I couldn't go unless I had passed all my exams. The only subject I was worried about was Leacock's course in Economics. I decided to see Leacock and explain my problem. He at once encouraged me to go. He said this experience would be far more beneficial than any course he could give me, and he told me to tell my father that I had passed his course.

I had a marvellous summer—one of the greatest experiences of my life—and, when I returned, I went at once to look up my marks. I had done well in all my courses except Economics. In it I got 51. I went again to see Leacock. His comment to me was, "Well, Miller, I can only say that this was not one of your better efforts!" It was clear to me that Leacock had just seen to it that I got a bare pass, as he had promised, however poorly I had done in the exam.

THE HON. MR. JUSTICE MILLER HYDE

YOU'VE GOT A GIRL, HAVEN'T YOU?
In my third year Arts, I did very well. In my last year, I didn't do quite as well. I was around fourth or fifth in my class. And Leacock asked me to come to his office after the marks were out. He invited me to his office and he said, "Becket, now look, you didn't do quite so well," and I said "No, I didn't, sir—I was very disappointed." And he said, "Well, now look, you've got a girl, haven't you?" And I said, "Yes sir, I have, I'm engaged to be married." He said, "I thought so."

So then he said to me, "Well, now, look, I can arrange, and I'd like to arrange, for a scholarship for you at the London School of Economics." He said, "I'd like you to go."

And I said, "Well, you know, I want to go into law because I've told you this." "But," he said, "you ought to take your M.A. anyway and that's the best place to take it. Go to London. And I'll look after that."

And I said, "Well sir, I want to get into law. I don't have all that much time, and I'm working my way through and I'd like to get right into law."

And he said, "Well, look, I've got a job for you this summer, you know, right here in my office. I want you to take on that Beauharnois Power Study of the consumption of power, I've undertaken it and I'd like you to do that. You'll use my office, I'll get you an adding machine and you can go to it."

And I worked there for four months. It used to be wonderful there, looking over the campus.

When he came back from Orillia, I turned over my reports and oh, he thanked me very much and I was very well paid for it.

Before I ever started that summer job for him, he knew I was not going to London. This was quite clear. But he still gave me that job.

WILSON BECKET

THE IMPACT OF A BOMB   I remember going to get a recommendation from him when I was about to apply for admission to the Harvard Business School. I put before him the usual form, which—

then as now—contained down the left-hand side various characteristics, and across the page space for the recommender to state how much potential he thought the student had, i.e., good, bad, or indifferent. He looked at the form for a few minutes and then said: "They can't expect a person like me to fill in a thing like this." He then drew a line diagonally across the classification table, and at the bottom of the page under "General remarks" wrote: "Mr. Pugsley has taken a good course with us at McGill, and is qualified not only to enter your college but to adorn it." His signature took up practically all the remaining space on the page. When this thing hit the B. School, it had the impact of a bomb, because Leacock had an even greater reputation in American academe than he had here. Then, as now, we had a dismaying disregard for home talent.

WILLIAM H. PUGSLEY

RAH, RAH, RAH, McGILL!   I happened to be the class valedictorian in 1928. I went to Leacock and asked him for a few words that I might put into my speech. Because, when you're writing your own speech and you're only a wee guy, you don't think of too many things.

And he said, "Petch, there are things that every student can do for McGill after he graduates. Every grad should be a missionary for his alma mater, go out into this world muttering 'McGill' at every social gathering. You should keep on saying, 'When I was at McGill.' Every grad should try to create in his mind a mythical recollection when he was on the football team, took a gold medal (since

lost by his wife), was president of the Student Council. . . ."

He also said that of such stuff is the real graduate made. And that if he ever gets rich McGill shall hear from him. He will never get rich but some of his friends may get rich, and it is sweeter and nobler to get one's friends to give than to keep to oneself the whole pleasure of giving.

He said it and I wrote it down. But he spelled out the idea.

"My Old College," he says as he points to the picture on the wall of his library. "That's my old college." As he says it he realized that there are no other three words that can bring such emotion into the graduate's voice as just those three. "My Old College." The man's touched. But is he touched enough to pay three dollars to the Graduate Society? No. "You can see the old joint in a better light from this side," he goes on. He has a dozen affectionate names for the college — the old joint and the old shop and the old shack. Will he pay three dollars for the love of any one of them? He won't. You begin to realize that he's asked you to dinner mainly to talk of the old place. "This picture," he says, "Is really a little later than my time. That small chimney wasn't there. Now if you look close up, you'll see the difference in the bricks. My that's interesting. Let's look close up that chimney. Perhaps he's got three dollars up that."

COL. CHARLES PETCH

McGILL COLLEGE – OLD BUILDING
MOLSON HALL IN LEFT FOREGROUND

McGILL COLLEGE – OLD BUILDING
NOTE THE COW IN THE FOREGROUND

Early views of McGill University, probably taken in the mid-1890s. Note the cow in the foreground of the picture on the right. *Courtesy of* **Old McGill**, *1934.*

TEACHER AND FRIEND McGill was his home. He was preoccupied with many other activities, such as his writing, but his first love was his teaching and his students.

As as matter of fact, when he retired in 1936 I had the honour of being designated by the student body to propose a toast to Stephen Leacock. And I remember to this day the concluding words of my toast in which I said "To Stephen Leacock, teacher and friend."

Not many people know how much Stephen Leacock befriended those students to whom he took a liking—usually because they were good students. He got a lot of jobs for a lot of students. Graham Towers got his first position at the Royal Bank because he was recommended by Stephen Leacock. He went out of his way to correspond with his students.

As you can see, I have a lot of correspondence with Stephen Leacock. He tried to suggest various things to them to encourage them. He couldn't do that with all of his students, but certainly for those whom he felt had a show of promise he did a great deal in the way of personal help and friendship. That was relatively rare for a professor, especially a busy professor like Stephen Leacock.

One of his great letters, I think it is the first one I got from him, reads as follows: "Dear Vineberg: Your handwriting is worse than mine. I can't say more than that. Yours truly, Stephen Leacock."

He wrote with what was almost a quill pen, he never used a fountain pen. He used one of those old-fashioned pens with old-fashioned nibs.

PHILIP VINEBERG

HE TAUGHT HER GREEK   There was an English family in the States, and all the girls were sent to Canada to school, and Lois, the eldest, went to McGill. This would be in the teens—about the time of the First World War. She elected Greek as one of her subjects and apparently she was about the only one who did because there was no classroom set up. She went to Stephen Leacock's office and sat across the desk from him when she needed instruction in Greek. Oh, he was a very erudite guy. Of course, his big subjects were Economics and Political Science.

So Lois used to go to his office and sit across the desk from him and she said, "He spat all over me and I loved him." Apparently he was just a charming guy.

GRACE ANNESLEY

CLASS MEMORIES, 1917   I went into Professor Leacock's classes in Arts in 1917. He was teaching Political Science. He was the most intriguing person. He had a great many mannerisms, you know. For instance, he used to come into the classroom, and he was always dragging his gown on his right shoulder, it was always

dragging along behind him. Then he would always have a big load of books in his arms, and this was why the gown was dragging behind; he couldn't hold onto it. Then he'd plop these books onto the desk, just drop them all like that. Then he would begin to perambulate around the room. He was always walking back and forth and up and down the aisles.

There were only two or three girls in our class and he wasn't very keen on having girls in his class. He would come up the aisle behind us and he would stop right behind a girl and he would shoot a question at her quickly, you see. Frighten the life out of her.

All my impressions of him were action, action. He would start at one blackboard and go along and cover the whole room, writing, writing, writing. He was always moving, doing things, smiling, talking. That's the thing that struck me. Well, he kept you alive, there were no dull moments. He kept you thinking all the time. You couldn't go to sleep.

We all wore gowns in those 1917 days. We attended Victoria College—we were part of McGill—and we had to put our gown on before going into class. There weren't a great many women around, but still it was a big class.

In my original class we had, I would say, twenty or thirty women. In Leacock's class there were only two or three. We were treated very well at McGill, although they didn't all like having the women around. As far as I know I did all right.

We used to have a skating rink on the campus. In the winter they had skating and the bands, the military bands, used to play out on the campus. We used to take our skates to class, and, the minute the lecture was over, out we tore to the skating rinks.

EILEEN FLANAGAN

NOT PREJUDICED AGAINST WOMEN STUDENTS   From my experience I don't believe he was prejudiced against women in class. We had a very small class; we had about ten in the class who were taking Honours in Economics and Political Science. We had two women who were very bright, a Miss Greaves and Miss Best. Miss Greaves had an English accent.

These were typical women, who were almost mannish in their ways, and they were very good economists. They were probably the best in the class. Greaves and Best were there during the early 1930s.

Leacock frequently addressed his questions to them, I think because he felt he would get a sensible response. I'm convinced that the more intelligent and the more competent the student was, the more interested he was. I don't think that he was prejudiced against them because of their sex, their background, or personality.

JUDGE HAROLD B. LANDE

THE JAZZY STOCKINGS   When I attended McGill (1925-26) I did not have the feeling that Leacock objected to having women in his classroom. But after I left McGill, I heard that he really was not in favour of co-education. I had read it somewhere. I didn't have that impression.

However, when Jane Belnap was at McGill, she sat up in the second or third row. It was in the era when ladies' hosiery came out with a rosebud at the knee. None of my contemporaries can remember the rosebud at the knee. They all remember a couple of years later we had black embroidered clocks coming up the side of the ankle.

Jane Belnap went to Simpson's on the way to McGill and bought a pair of these and displayed them in the classroom. And I thought, when I heard this report, no wonder Stephen Leacock didn't want women in the classroom if they were a disturbance, a distraction, like that. I don't know why she did it, but she did it.

MARGARET STEPHEN

I GOT YOUR LETTER FROM SOME GOD-FORSAKEN PLACE   My studies with Leacock were political science rather than economics and he would assign topics, for example, on the influence of Charles Dickens on social reform. He seemed to me to have treated women on a parity with men, except that, when he assigned speeches and reports, he frequently left them out. I never remember that he called upon women to deliver the little reports.

I happened to be involved in the Delta Sigma Society, the Debating Society at the Royal Victoria College, and, one summer, I was in Europe and I wrote to him asking if he would address our society during the coming session. I didn't hear from him, but when I saw him the first time he said, "Oh hello, I got your letter from some Godforsaken place or other and I just want you to know that I would be delighted to come." He remembered.

He did come and he spoke on modern literature, moving backwards, forwards, or sideways. I recall that he was very entertaining on the subject; he said he had just put his hand into a barrel and pulled out the subject. He brought with him, and put on the table beside him, wads of papers, they were old proof sheets, and he had decided what to speak about when he looked at these papers.

The one thing I do remember was his comparing the days of, let's say, Colonial times in the States when Priscilla in church was able to exchange a little bit of an eye flicker with John and that was very pleasant, they were near one another; whereas today the same two just had to sort of clutch antennae. They were just each at their own machines, not near enough to catch those electric flashes. He assumed they were both sitting listening to their radios. That's what he meant.

MAYSIE MacSPORRAN

THE WANDERING TIE   Leacock never missed a meeting of the Political Economy Club, which, I believe, he founded way back in his early days at McGill. The Political Economy Club met once a month in the evening. For its undergraduate members, it was a prestigious affair. One student each month would read a paper on which he had slaved for weeks and weeks. I remember I did Social Credit, which was then in its infancy in Alberta, and I think I put more effort into preparing that essay than anything else I worked on.

The members of the department would be there: Leacock, Hemmeon and Day. One faced the awesome scrutiny of professors and peers alike.

I was secretary of the Political Economy Club in 1935–36—1936, of course, was the year that Leacock was

forced to retire. He felt very bitter about it and I think he began drinking more than he had in the past.

He would always turn up at the Political Economy Club before the meeting began. There was a handy barometer to the degree of drinking that Leacock had done that evening. If his tie was slightly awry, then Leacock had only downed a few. If his tie had been moved almost halfway around his neck, then Leacock had been putting them away. If his tie had been jerked almost around out of sight, then Leacock had been tossing back a good many Scotch and sodas. I suppose the more he drank, the hotter his neck got.

Anyway, Leacock would sit there, prepared for the worst. We always

The executive of the Political Economy Club, 1935-36. Professors J.P. Day and J.C. Hemmeon are seated on the left while the author stands behind Professor Leacock on the right. *Courtesy of* **Old McGill**, *1936.*

regarded Leacock's economic point of view as pre-Adam Smith, and he looked on many of our economic points of view with foreboding and despair. Whoever was giving the paper that night would get off to a brave start. Leacock's face would get red and then still redder. At a certain time that was almost predictable, Leacock would jump to his feet, as much as it was possible for him to do so. He would shout, "Stop!" He would amble up to the podium, while the poor fellow who was giving the paper stood hapless on one foot, as it were, and Leacock would tell all of us off properly. We were ignoramuses, we had learned nothing, he had been wasting his time on us, where did we ever get these ridiculous notions! He would give us a sound, brief lecture, and then shuffle back to his seat and listen quietly, though undoubtedly despondently, to the rest of the paper, as the undergraduate at the lectern warily read it.

It didn't happen all the time, but, when it did, it was quite a performance. I always looked forward to it.

ALLAN ANDERSON

ONE DAY ISN'T AS GOOD AS THE NEXT He certainly hated stupidity. One time, at a meeting of the Political Economy Club, I saw him in a rage at Professor Day. They were taking opposite sides on some subject. And when it was Leacock's turn to speak, he compared Day's arguments on one side of an economic question and his own side of the same question to two engineers who might be arguing in the boiler-room of a ship. One was saying, "Oh look, the pressure's going up and up and up, what can we do? What kind of

valves can we adjust here so the pressure won't go too high?" And the other one just reached up—this was Professor Day— and took the indicator down. That was his attitude about Day's thinking. And Professor Day didn't like it. Leacock said some rather rude things to Day.

When we were getting ready to have our picture taken for the executive of the Political Economy Club Leacock said, "I'll have to get Professor Day to have his hair cut so we can all get in the same picture."

HERBERT H. TEES

SENATOR LEACOCK? We were six on the staff of the department in the early 1930s—Leacock, J.C. Hemmeon, J.P. Day, John Culliton, Eugene Forsey, and myself. Forsey and I are now the sole survivors and by a turn of fate found ourselves colleagues again, this time in the Canadian Senate. If Leacock were aware of this, he would be chuckling. Perhaps he would remember that in one of his books he wrote: "I do not desire office but would take a seat in the Canadian Senate at five minutes' notice."

SENATOR H. CARL GOLDENBERG

DOING THE DONKEY WORK Hemmeon was devoted to Leacock and for years did a great deal of the donkey work of the department for Leacock. They were at opposite poles ideologically and temperamentally, but Hemmeon was devoted to him, he would do anything for him and did an enormous amount of the whole administrative work.

SENATOR EUGENE FORSEY

SABLE FOR A WIFE Those were the days of bachelor professors in Economics, such as John Culliton and J.C. Hemmeon. It was rumoured that Hemmeon actually was married, but kept his wife on Sable Island. There was a story that someone asked him if this was true, and he replied, slowly, "No, it is not true that I have a wife, but if I did have one I *would* keep her on Sable Island."

F. MUNROE BOURNE

MY YOU'RE IGNORANT GOLDENBERG! He appointed me to the staff as a sessional lecturer in 1932, the year I was called to the bar. John Culliton, who was a lecturer in Economics, had won a fellowship which required him to travel around what was then the Empire.

Leacock called me one day—I had just been admitted to the bar—and he said, "Would you like to lecture two or three times a week? I'll give you a hundred dollars a month." Well, my God, in those days a hundred dollars a month for a law-yer . . . I had just started, I had no practice, and it was the depth of the Depression. So I said, "I'm coming right up." I came up and he said, "You can share my office." Well, that was a treat! I sat at his desk facing him.

Occasionally he'd say to me, "Now, I'll be away next Monday, or Wednesday or Friday, would you take my lecture?" And I remember one particular occasion when he said to me, "I'll be away Friday. Would you take my eleven o'clock course in Political Science?" I said, "Well, I'll be glad to do that Dr. Leacock. Now, what are you lecturing on, or where are you in your lectures?" He said, "Well, that doesn't matter. What book are you reading now?" And, I remember, I said I was reading Bertrand Russell's recent book, *Freedom and Civilization*. He said, "Good. You lecture on Bertrand Russell. Where are you in the book?" And I told him. He said, "You just lecture there."

I said, "Where are you going?" He said, "Oh, I'm going to get an honourary degree." I said, "Congratulations. What university is honouring you?" He said, "Heidelberg." I said, "Heidelberg! When will you be back?" He said, "Monday."

Well, of course, this was before the days of airplanes. I said, "How will you get back from Heidelberg on Monday?" He said, "My, you're ignorant, Goldenberg. Have you never heard of Heidelberg University, Tiffin, Ohio?"

I checked and there was a Heidelberg University, Tiffin, Ohio, and he probably got a fee of a few hundred dollars to come down to deliver the convocation address at Heidelberg.

SENATOR H. CARL GOLDENBERG

THE MESSY OFFICE What was noteworthy about Leacock's office was the piles of papers, books, disorderly state of affairs, everything in disarray. He wasn't a tidy man, and he didn't believe in the clean-desk executive method of treatment. His desk was cluttered with all kinds of correspondence, and this and that and the other thing. It was a reflection of the busy kind of life he led and the indiscriminate way in which he dealt with a dozen things at a time. His office was lined on both sides with books all the way and both sides completely filled, there wasn't a space left where there wasn't a book.

PHILIP VINEBERG

ONE GOOD TURN DESERVES ANOTHER

Harry Barker was known as the Poet Laureate of the Arts Building. Harry Barker was what we would call today a cleaner and he was a very loquacious and cheery little soul with his mop and his bucket of water, and always, if he'd buttonhole you, he'd unload his latest poetry on you. And, some time when I was there, the students got together and published some of Harry Barker's poetry. I guess it was that publication that Harry initialled and gave to Leacock and Leacock shortly afterwards, gave him an autographed copy of one of his books. He said, "One good turn deserves another." That would be typical of Leacock.

D. LORNE GALES

ROLLING IN THE AISLES   I recall seeing Leacock with little Stevie beside him in the front row at one of the Red and White Revues when John Pratt was in it. It was the closing night and he did one of the songs he later introduced into the Navy Show, "You'll Get Used to It."

And Pratt was a natural comedian, too, with a serious side to him and he kept coming on and on for encores giving a new irreverent verse each time which he made up on the spur of the moment, you see. Everybody had had a few drinks—and Leacock was practically rolling in the aisles. I mean, it was his type of humour you know—satire on the college characters.

THE HON. MR. JUSTICE ALLISON WALSH

THE OTHER PROFESSORS GOT TURNED OFF

I don't think my father, Professor Nobbs, liked him or disliked him. I think he enjoyed his presence but I think Leacock wore a little thin after the years with him. In his early years, Leacock was quite something at McGill. The professors all said this, you know. But this kept on and on and on for thirty years, and they got a little tired of the act.

FRANK NOBBS

A LICE WAY OF DOING THINGS

The story is that Leacock was having his late afternoon drink with his cronies in the University Club and Willie Birks was there. And Leacock was really against the Board of Governors and the appointment of Morgan, an Englishman, as head of McGill, and so on and so forth. And Willie said, "Now, listen Stephen, enough is enough. You've got to realize that finding a principal for McGill is no easy job and we combed Canada and we combed the United States of America, we combed Europe, we combed England with a fine-toothed comb." And Leacock stopped him and said, "And that's just what you get with a fine-toothed comb!"

D. LORNE GALES

MAD AT EVERYBODY   Leacock was absolutely furious with the way he was treated by McGill when he was retired. You have to remember that there was a reverence for professors. Everybody greatly respected Leacock the teacher even though they didn't think he was the greatest lecturer in the world.

They showed him a great deal of respect and the longer he was there, the more respect he had. And Leacock had always been treated as the outstanding star at McGill and with good reason.

To be suddenly crushed and eliminated at one fell swoop was a terrible thing. It's one thing to know ten years in advance there's a compulsory retirement age of sixty-five and to prepare for it mentally and accept it. But it was quite another thing to have the mandatory retirement age introduced retroactively, without respect and without a transitional period.

I think he was generally mad at everybody, including the Board of Governors.
PHILIP VINEBERG

MORGAN WAS A BAD CHOICE   In the case of Leacock, he should have been handled on a personal basis as to whether this was the right time and the right way to do it. And to have his career at McGill end with this bitterness at a university that he loved so much, was very sad for all of us who knew him and who realized what he had contributed to McGill.

I think Morgan was a poor choice for McGill and, of course, he was not there for a very long period. And even if one says that the Board was responsible for Leacock's retirement, I think there could have been more effort on the part of the principal to handle this case in a different manner.

You must remember that Morgan had no McGill tradition behind him at all—no Canadian tradition behind him. He was brought over from England and put in a tough spot, and it didn't work out.
CHARLIE PETERS

A STUPID THING TO DO   My own reaction was that it was a stupid thing to do and very unkind. If Leacock was fired, it was perfectly stupid and very unkind. I think—again I'm guessing—but he wasn't the greatest statistician in the economic world and you know, courses change and times change and systems change. For example, I don't remember being tossed statistics at all in his courses. And of course, it's essential. So it may be that the powers that be thought that he was getting a little bit out of date.
SENATOR ALAN A. MACNAUGHTON

MORGAN ENFORCED THE RULE   I think it was just Morgan who stood in the way of Leacock's term being extended. Now, I don't know for how long it could be extended. Today, I am a Governor of McGill—I have been for thirteen years. And we grant an extension of up to three years after sixty-five. I'm not sure what the provision was at that time in the University statutes. But the general feeling among the faculty, and I remember it very well, was that Leacock would not have to retire.

They decided to enforce the sixty-five year rule. Morgan was not picking on Leacock as an individual. Morgan decided that he was going to enforce the rule. Anyone attaining the age of sixty-five would have to stop teaching. That was it. Of course, there was a great deal of sympathy for Leacock. I don't think anyone worried about anyone else. Leacock was an institution. He was McGill. If you told anyone you came from McGill, they would immediately say, "Oh, that's Leacock's university. Do you know Dr. Leacock?"
SENATOR H. CARL GOLDENBERG

ALL ETERNITY   When he received that letter about his retirement, the *Montreal Star* asked him if he had any comments to make and he replied, "Yes. And I shall spend eternity shouting them down to the Governors."

SENATOR EUGENE FORSEY

THE McGUILLOTINE   There's a marvellous cartoon in his place in Orillia. It's a picture of himself, Susan Vaughan, and René du Roure with their necks in a guillotine. He drew it.

Susan Vaughan was the warden of the Royal Victoria College. They were all retired at the age of sixty-five. They were all tremendously powerful and long-time influential McGill teaching staff. And their necks are in a triple guillotine and the heading on the sketch is "The McGuillotine."

D. LORNE GALES

HAW, HAW!   Hemmeon told me, about 1937, I guess, when I came back down to Montreal that when the word came through that Principal Morgan had been let out, Hemmeon got a wire from Leacock from Orillia and all it said was, *Haw, Haw! (signed) Leacock.*

FRED STONE

TELLING THEM APART   When Stephen Leacock went out West, after he retired from McGill, he was invited to be the speaker at dinners where graduates of McGill, Queen's, and the University of Toronto would be present. And when he got back to Montreal somebody said to him, "And how could you tell them apart?" And he said, "It was very easy. At the time the dinner began, the Queens students would be saying grace, the Varsity students would look at each other and say, "What are they doing?", and the McGill students would be halfway through their soup.

HERBERT H. TEES

McGILL WAS A REAL FRATERNITY   I was at McGill from 1928 to 1932. I loved McGill. I think after I graduated from McGill and travelled around the world and had been to a lot of places, I began to realize that McGill was a real fraternity and you could meet a McGill man anywhere in the world and there was a bond right away. I have many happy memories of McGill and, of course, of Stephen Leacock. Mind you, we were about twenty years old, most of us, at that time when we got into Stevie's classes. We knew he was a great man, perhaps some of us realized it more than others. We knew if not great, that he was well known, even internationally, and so we seemed to regard him I think with at least some awe. But you know, as Bernard Shaw said, it's such a tragedy that youth is wasted on young people. I just wish I could do that all over again and take his lectures all over again and how much more I would appreciate them.

BOB BOWMAN

SOMEBODY HAS GOT TO START AND RE-UNITE CANADA   I was news editor of the McGill *Daily* during the 1936-37 season and Leacock, by this time, had been unceremoniously booted out of McGill simply because he had the bad judgement to reach the age of sixty-five. He had gone off to take a look at Western Canada and his observations thereon were later set down in *My Discovery of the West*.

Someone, whose byline was "W.W. Goforth," sent the *Daily* a detailed account of Leacock's tour and the joyful Western reaction to it, and this lengthy column appeared in the January 29th, 1937, issue of the *Daily*. The column ends with a direct quote from Leacock, which is wry, witty, and prescient:

Somebody has got to start and re-unite Canada. Nova Scotia weeps her salt tears into the Bay of Fundy regretting her irrevocable union. French Canada mutters its curses around the hay-stacks and swears in its barnyards about the needs of petite nation, and the West, half silly with drought and distress, prints paper money, and sits chuckling over it, like an idiot with dead leaves. British Columbia sits with her back turned, like a sulky girl at a dance, looking for new Pacific admirers.

. . . this is the home of Social Credit, with the world's new bad man at its head, at whom the eastern capitalist puts his head under the bedclothes — just as he did a hundred years ago at the mention of a liberal.

Take next your Alberta paper money, your "Prosperity Scrip" that so frightened all the economists of America. Here it is — a prosperity certificate — one dollar — with a little insert picture of what I take to be God creating Alberta . . . Guard these certificates well. They have been a pleasant interlude in a dull world. They have been a wonderful object lesson as to how and why real money circulates. And now their life work being over, they can be "retired" as I have been; they will always maintain, as I do, a value as a curiosity.

I have vagrantly changed my politics, except of course in Quebec, where we have to change our politics every now and then and send them to the laundry.

We must not think that all races are different. The Frenchman and the Italian is not unlike us — the Canadian may be a bit superior to the rest.

We used to think of the Frenchman as wearing a bell hat and gloves and going after other people's wives. He was supposed to have excellent taste and low morals.

The Irishman was thought to have no respect for law and order or anything else. He made a fine policeman.

The Scotsman is hard and dour, and believes strongly in hell and means to go there.

ALLAN ANDERSON

CHAPTER SIX

The University Club: Good Food, Good Friends, Good Talk—And Bad Billiards

The University Club in Montreal, Leacock's "home away from home." *Photo by Brian Merrett, courtesy of the University Club of Montreal.*

HOME AWAY FROM HOME The University Club was really Leacock's home away from home, and of course, it was very close to the university. He was a founding member. I would think he probably used the club more than any other member and he was, you might say, an institution at the University Club. The University Club was founded in 1907. It wasn't on the present site until 1913.

JOHN PEMBERTON

THE UNIVERSITY CLUB I knew Stephen Leacock at the University Club of Montreal in the years immediately before the war and during the early years of the war, in other words, in the late 1930s and early 1940s. The University Club was then, and still is, within a block of McGill University. The club was formed in the days when to have a university degree was an exceptional thing and, hence, it was supposed to be very exclusive.

The magnificent stairway to the first floor of the University Club, from the main hall. *Photo by Brian Merrett, courtesy of the University Club of Montreal.*

People who knew Leacock better than I mentioned that he regarded the University Club as his second home. He pre ferred, along with many other staff members at McGill, not to use the McGill Faculty Club because that was too much of a trade union meeting ground. A lot of them didn't care for their fellow faculty members and preferred to mix outside the university circle to prevent the horrible inbreeding that you see in most academic institutions.

The University Club was quite a small building—three storeys—but, to my mind, was the finest and most suitable club building I have ever been in. It was very beautifully constructed.

In the entrance hall, the floor was tiled and the walls were panelled in wood, the porter's desk was there. Guests waited on the ground floor until the member who had invited them appeared to get them. On the first floor there was a very nice fireplace, a table with magazines and papers and so forth. The rest of the first floor was probably devoted to kitchens and other offices.

To get upstairs, there was a winding staircase. Nothing was grandiose, but everything was fine. The second floor had a lounge and cloakroom and what they called the billiard room. Most of the billiard room was devoted to tables and was also used as a bar.

The dining room was on the next floor and there were card rooms either on the dining room floor or the next floor above it. The food was first class and could not have been better. The dining room was run on English lines with no smoking allowed. If someone went in with a guest who inadvertently lit a cigarette, the waiter would be over instantly to stop it.

It was a club of the finest type for men who wanted a good quiet lunch and to meet their friends for a drink. A lot of businessmen went there for lunch, as I did, and left after lunch, but a lot of the university staff who didn't have duties that afternoon stayed on.

There was a small library. There were, of course, all the usual magazines—particularly the English magazines and newspapers—and there was always good conversation. There was a big fireplace in each of the rooms and so it was very comfortable in winter. It was not in any way plush, as the new St. James's Club is. It was more in the style of the older St. James's Club—which of course, has now disappeared—but was smaller in scale. It was beautifully suited to its function.

The club was used a great deal, but they kept the membership down to the point where it was never crowded. There was no criterion in joining the club, except being recommended by a number of members and having a university degree and being passed by the committee. I would judge from remembering the membership that there were other characteristics as to suitability that were required. I think that if just any dentist wanted to be admitted he would have to impress the committee as being a man of a certain quality, and a certain intellectual level, and not merely the possessor of a degree.

At that time there were many more applicants for club memberships than there were openings, and so the committee could afford to be very selective. It was exclusively male. There was that horror of all horrors, a woman's annex with a separate entrance, and members were allowed to take their wives to it and eat in the separate dining room, so that they would not contaminate the men's quarters. And even when there was a general mixed party going on, the ladies were not allowed to go up the elevator the men normally used. They were taken up separately by back stairs or another elevator, I don't know, but they were not allowed to use the members' elevator.

The club was not to any appreciable extent an "old boys club." Why that should be, I don't know, but it was true. Partly because there was a very definite attempt made on the part of the members and the committees to keep down any of the type of pomposity that we saw at the St. James's Club or the Mount Royal Club. To keep down this pomposity meant that, when they admitted new members, they had to admit relatively young men to membership.

There were a few old-timers there who were somewhat colourful characters and who made it their second home. I well remember one. He was a very prominent lawyer in Montreal, my lawyer at the time, and he'd been made an officer, my God, in the Boer war in the cavalry, and he'd never forgotten it—and he was about five feet three inches high. He arrived at the club in the early afternoon and started drinking and would continue drinking till he left the club at eleven or twelve o'clock.

The club porter would carefully take the old gentleman by the elbow and edge him out onto Sherbrooke Street to the bus stop and stand with him until the bus came and then he would very carefully put him in the bus and the bus driver knew where the Colonel's stop was and when the Colonel got to that stop the bus driver would carefully take him by the elbow and help him out onto the sidewalk and then he still had to cross the street.

It was an everlasting sorrow to him that one day when getting out of the bus his foot slipped and he went down and got a very bad scratch on his nose and the other club members failed to take a sympathetic point of view and continually asked the Colonel for months afterwards how the scratch on his nose was coming along.

CHARLES FISHER

HE WAS THE UNIVERSITY CLUB

Leacock, of course, really was the University Club for many years. He spent many happy times there. There's a lounge on the second floor, and just inside the door, on the left, there is a chair where Leacock always sat and which has been known for many years as "the Leacock chair." It's a padded chair; it seems to me there's a McGill crest on the back of it. Here he held court with his many friends in the University Club for years.

Over the chair, there is a portrait of Leacock which is very much honoured by the members of the club. When you pass by the chair you come to another little room which is a library where, no doubt, Leacock spent considerable time as well. It was a very fine place to relax and read.

On the east side there is a large room where one assembles for drinks— let's say, before lunch or dinner—and beyond that, where there used to be a billiard room, there's now a snack bar. But in Leacock's day this was a billiard room and he enjoyed billiards and played very often on those tables.

On the third floor, there is the main dining room, which you reach by another semi-circular stairway, and there are two private dining rooms. And then there is the fourth floor, where there are a series of dining rooms and sitting rooms which are now used a great deal by the members of The Canadian Women's University Club and their guests.

Women, now, of course, have full access to all the rooms in the University Club, which was certainly not so in Leacock's day.

CHARLIE PETERS

NOBODY BUT LEACOCK SAT THERE
My father, Percy Nobbs, was one of the original members of the University Club and it was on lower Mansfield Street. And then, in 1908 or 1909, they bought this site on Mansfield Street, just south of Sherbrooke, on the east side, and my father was the architect of the club. And not only was he the architect of the club, he designed the furniture, he designed the cutlery, he designed the curtains, he was the interior decorator of the club, and the whole thing is a memorial to my father in his expertise as an architect.

Leacock always sat in a chair in the same place in the club in the lounge, and as far as I remember Leacock was always in the chair on the right-hand side on the inside wall when you came in. That was his chair.

But I got the impression that if he was in the club, nobody would sit in that chair, that was his when he came up to sit in it you know, that was it.

FRANK NOBBS

THE LADIES' DEPARTMENT   It was busier at lunchtime than at any other time. The Ladies' Department would be busy in the evenings, especially Thursday evenings, which was maid's night out—when people still had maids. They owned the property next door and they called it the Ladies' Department. It was a very nice lounge. It was a separate building.

DOUGLAS C. ABBOTT

THE BIG ARMCHAIR AT THE UNIVER-SITY CLUB   The thing I remember best about Stephen Leacock is that he would come to the University Club, have a few drinks before, during and after dinner, and he'd come in a very talkative mood and talk continuously and extremely well. He would not brook any interruptions whatever.

He had a particular corner of the lounge and he'd sit in a big leather armchair in the corner and his listeners would sit around him in a semicircle. He would talk continuously for several hours on any subject he happened to be interested in—maybe the latest scandal in the city administration, maybe the latest stupidity that had been committed in academic circles—any one of a thousand things that appealed to him, and maybe on the French-English problem.

There would be a group close to him and a group further back. Everyone in the room would have his chair pulled over and would be listening to him, maybe twenty men. There would be at least one or two of the people, who, as soon as they saw he was in a talkative mood, would go to the telephone and telephone their friends and their friends would come over.

Other members would come in as soon as they knew Leacock was about to hold forth. They made sure he was supplied with a drink beside him at all times.

I think that at the University Club, in his life there, Leacock showed his true nature. He was mixing with men who were more or less his intellectual equals, educated about as well as he was, men of substance and men that he could feel considerable sympathy with. Therefore he neither strove to impress them nor did he strive to make jokes that they would laugh at. He simply was himself in a perfectly natural manner and his enormous gift for continued narration showed through. Someone has said—I think it was Norman Douglas—that history should be written as one gentleman addressing another gentleman, and that is exactly the way that Leacock was at these club sessions.

At the University Club on the evenings when Leacock was holding forth, he would start immediately after dinner, seven-thirty or eight o'clock, and might go on till eleven or eleven-thirty.

CHARLES FISHER

A GREAT RACONTEUR   He had a twinkle in his eye, he had a loud, carrying voice, he loved to laugh at his own jokes, he told jokes very well. He was a great raconteur and he got on well with people, because he was universally popular in the milieu where I saw him at close range and that was at the University Club.

DOUGLAS C. ABBOTT

The lounge at the University Club where Leacock spent many evenings regaling the members. *Photo by Brian Merrett, courtesy of the University Club of Montreal.*

The Leacock corner at the University Club. The chair (right corner) is reputed to be the one Leacock used. The portrait is by Richard Jack. *Photograph by Louis Jaques, courtesy of the University Club of Montreal.*

THEY WERE BOTH POOR BILLIARD PLAYERS   Leacock used to go to the University Club a great deal with his friend, René du Roure. I think that Leacock and du Roure had rather an unusual relationship, which you could study if you wanted to by just observing them together at the University Club. Leacock, of course, must have been very fond of du Roure. He was a very close friend, he called him "mon capitaine"

or René. And he used to tease him unmercifully the whole time and they played a lot of billiards together. In those days there was much more billiards played than now.

Leacock was a very poor billiard player and so was du Roure. I won the championship at the University Club twice, so I know a little bit about billiards. But Leacock assumed that he was vastly superior to du Roure and would annoy du Roure almost to a point of distraction by constantly coaching him and telling him what shots he should play, and you could sort of see du Roure's blood pressure rising while this was going on.

"Now, René, it's very simple, this is what you do, you see, you play just on the right hand of that ball there and you go into that pocket there and the ball goes over there." René would just look at him, daggers, absolute daggers.

And it was tremendous, it was just an entertainment to watch them play together. I never saw Leacock play with anybody else but du Roure. I would say they played two or three times a week at the University Club. I think they might play for about an hour.

I think, as a rule, they played in the late afternoon. They may have often stayed to dinner, but it was very funny, because it was an absolute pattern!

JOHN PEMBERTON

SLOW LEARNER   Leacock enjoyed billiards. He fooled around at it with du Roure, always playing the part of the expert and nagging du Roure with pointers about the game. Yet he must have known his limitations, for he once remarked, "I have worked at billiards for a half-century. I'll need another."

ALLAN ANDERSON

A LEACOCK   I never saw either Leacock or du Roure playing billiards with anybody else and they played billiards at the end table, there were three billiard tables there. They were on the left as you went into the lounge, the table at the end, at the left, next to the rack of cues.

The billiard room was just below the level of the lounge. It was two or three steps down and the rest of us would be sitting in the lounge—we had been playing billiards at some of the other tables. We'd be sitting in a group and having our afternoon aperitif and, as a rule, Dr. Leacock and du Roure would come up and sit down with some friends of theirs and he'd tell some of his stories.

They weren't any better billiard players than I am, but they had a special practice—if they had a chance, they would always sink the opponent's ball which gave them two. I know that, in good billiards, that's not considered the best thing to do. But they'd do that every time and they'd have a dollar bet on it. And one would pay the other. If Leacock sank du Roure's ball, du Roure would pay him a dollar for having done it, you see, and vice versa.

I think we got to call this sinking the white ball "a Leacock."

DOUGLAS C. ABBOTT

AN UNFORGIVABLE AFFRONT   He was to be the guest of honour at a dinner in the University Club and he'd forgotten about it. He'd been for a walk on the mountain and he had forgotten that that was the night. When he went into the club—as soon as he saw this lady—he realized that that was the night that he was the guest of honour at the dinner. He said he was sorry, that he was detained and that he would take a taxi and change and be back in so many minutes. She insisted that he should stay just as he was and he never forgave her. He didn't like the idea of being the guest of honour at a dinner in which he wasn't in a dinner jacket. He wore a dinner jacket when he ate alone at home.

GRACE REYNOLDS

NOT DELINQUENT   In the summer, when he'd come down for a day or two from Orillia, he'd come and have lunch at the University Club.

As you go out of the dining room to the stairway, to the left there is this little corner where they used to post people who were delinquent. They just put up the list of their names.

The rules were that you'd be listed on the 20th of the month. The secretary-treasurer of the club had the list, or the honourary treasurer, or whoever it was, had the list of anybody who had not paid his account for the previous month.

And the last time I remember seeing Stephen there, we were sitting together, and there was a list with about four names on it, and he took a look at it and he said, "I must have been in the country longer than I thought this year; my name's not on the list."

This is how he used to pay his bills. Apparently, he never opened his bills from the club, but when he'd come to the club, he'd always look there and see whether he was listed. If he was, he went upstairs and gave them a cheque.

BRIGADIER GENERAL JIMMY DE LALANNE

THE UNIVERSITY CLUB'S BEST-LIKED CHARACTER   He did down a lot of booze and, in later years, he got very unsteady. If he got up to go to the washroom, someone would take him by the elbow and there would always be a porter in the washroom who would undoubtedly smooth down his hair, straighten his tie and refurbish him a little before he came back. They had an absolutely first-class staff and the staff took a paternal interest in the members. And, as I say, a man like Leacock, if he went to the washroom, there was one of the porters attended him and made sure he got straightened out and got his buttons done up right and so forth.

When he got up to leave, there would be a porter come and take him by the arm and guide him downstairs carefully and see that he got a car or a taxi to wherever he was going.

It was a club that played a great deal of bridge in the evening and, if Leacock was holding forth down below, the card rooms would be abandoned and the card players would hustle down to listen to Leacock. He was urbane to the nth degree and obviously happy and comfortable and pleased. Everybody liked him very much and he liked being there very much. He enjoyed his evenings.

He was the University Club's best-known and best-liked character.

CHARLES FISHER

THE ONLY HONORARY MEMBER
I don't think that the club has had any new furniture since the days of Leacock. I think that room is as it was and I believe that the chair under the Leacock painting, which hangs just inside what used to be known as the reading room, and is now known as the Leacock room, is Leacock's chair. I would be reasonably certain of that.

Leacock used that room so much and sat there so often, that, as a memorial to Leacock, after he died, the room which had been known as the reading room was called the Leacock room.

The University Club has no honorary members, maybe the governor-general, but actually, it has no honorary members. But shortly before Leacock died, the question came up at a council meeting as to whether it wouldn't be appropriate to make Leacock an honorary member of the club. I was on the council at the time and there was a lot of discussion. You can imagine what happened. People said you'd be creating a precedent, we've never done it, and so forth, we'd be open to having to create other honorary members and so forth.

So, I remember saying at this meeting that I didn't feel we would be creating a precedent because, I said, if you consider you are creating a precedent, you are assuming that there might, at some stage in the future, be another Stephen Leacock. And I said in my opinion that is quite impossible!

Nobody said anything for a moment and somebody said, "I vote we make him an honorary member," and we did. Unfortunately, he died three weeks later.

But, for three weeks, he was an honorary member, and the only honorary member of the University Club.

JOHN PEMBERTON

CHAPTER SEVEN

The Great
Radio Caper

During my freshman year, in 1921, at the University of Toronto, several of us started a magazine, humourous in intent, which was called *Goblin*. We started our magazine along rather unconventional lines. At the beginning, we had thirty-five editors and no business staff. This arrangement was criticized by some stuffy people who felt that this was irregular, and we reformed as fast as we could and cut it down to five editors and no business staff.

Goblin was first published in February of 1921 and ran through until approximately six months after the 1929 market crash, when advertising revenues suddenly vanished and we went into voluntary liquidation.

For our first issue, one of us thought it would be a good idea to ask Stephen Leacock, whom we all admired and enjoyed so much, to contribute an article. We wrote to Leacock and explained what we were doing and, with his usual sympathies for undergraduate efforts of this type, he agreed and sent us perhaps two hundred and fifty words under the title of "Sermon on Humour," which we published.

Here are some examples of the wit that was typical of Leacock, which appeared exclusively in this fledgling college magazine, and I do not believe that it has ever been reprinted anywhere since then, although quotations may have occurred here and there.

The best of humour is always kindly. The worst and the cheapest is malicious. The one is arduous and the other facile. But, like the facile descent of Avernus, it leads only to destruction.

And then he goes on to say that it is easy for a college paper to take off on a professor. In the environment of a college paper, the professor stands ready as its victim:

The professor is a queer creature, of a type inviting the laughter of the unwise, his eyes turned in. He sees little of externals and values them hardly at all. Hence in point of costume and appearance he becomes an easy mark. He wears a muffler in April, not having noticed that the winter has gone by! He will put on a white felt

hat without observing that it is the only one in town; and he may be seen with muffetees up on his wrists fifty years after the fashion of wearing them has passed away.

I can myself recall a learned man at the University of Chicago who appeared daily during the summer quarter in an English morningcoat with white flannel trousers and a little round straw hat with a blue and white ribbon on it, fit for a child to wear at the seaside. That man's own impression of his costume was that it was a somewhat sportive and debonair combination, such as any man of taste might assume under the more torrid signs of the Zodiac.

As with dress so is manner. The professor easily falls into the little ways and mannerisms of his own. In the deference of the costume they pass unchallenged and uncorrected. With the passage of the years they wear into his mind like ruts. One I have known who blew imaginary chalk dust off his sleeve at little intervals; one who turned incessantly a pencil up and down. One hitches continuously at a tie; one smooths with meaningless care the ribbons of his college gown.

Needless to say, we were delighted to have received a contribution from so distinguished an author, and we sent him the largest cheque that we felt was possible in the light of our budget. We sent him, as I recall, twenty-five dollars. He acknowledged receipt of this magnificent sum with this sentence—"You are much too kind, but I accept."

Many years later, in fact, in 1933, I was working for an advertising agency, McConnell & Ferguson. At that time we were planning a variety radio show in Toronto. Someone suggested that it would be a brilliant idea, to give a little quality to this program, if someone could obtain the services of Stephen Leacock to read a short humourous sketch or commentary at a certain part of the program. Somebody remembered that I had been editing the magazine which ran the "Sermon on Humour" of Leacock's and, therefore, I must be an authority and I was immediately conscripted to get Leacock to accept a suitable contract.

Accepting the challenge with some trepidation, I wrote to Leacock, outlined what we had in mind and asked for his co-operation. I got no reply. I let a week or so go by and wrote him again—still no reply. A third letter got no reply and, finally, becoming somewhat panicky, because, by now, I had attained a certain status with my colleagues as one who knew Leacock, I sent a telegram to Leacock saying that I would be in his office at nine o'clock in the morning on the following Thursday.

I arrived in Montreal at Leacock's office at approximately nine o'clock to find no one in the office except his assistant, Professor John Culliton. Culliton, who later became a very dear friend of mine, looked at me askance and said, "Mr. McDougall, if you are well-advised, you will put on your hat and coat right away and go back to Toronto because I can tell you Leacock hates radio."

Before I had the chance to respond, the door opened and there was Leacock with his great coon coat half on, his hat over one eye, with wisps of hair showing underneath, and his magnificent heavy walking stick. And before anyone had a chance to say anything, John Culliton said, "Professor Leacock, this is Mr. McDougall from Toronto. He's come about the radio thing. I've told him that you were not interested."

Leacock went around the other side of his desk and hung up his hat and coat, stashed his cane in the corner, and sat down and faced me across the desk. Fixing me with a steady gaze he said to me in severe tones, "Mr. McDougall, I will tell you what you must do. You must go to your hotel room, I presume you have a hotel room, and write me a letter. And in this letter you must set forth the exact terms and payment that your principals are prepared to pay for these services of mine; and I must warn you that I am a very expensive piece of property."

I pointed out that I had already written three letters in which I had included all the details. He said, "I know, Mr. McDougall, but that is the thing for you to do and I must go now." He rose and I helped him on with his coat and we left the office together, down the stairs and out into the snowy path across the campus.

Leacock turned to me and said, "Mr. McDougall, you will bring your letter to me at the University Club at precisely one o'clock. Do you know where the University Club is, Mr. McDougall? You probably do not, you are from Toronto. I will show you. It is over there. You will never find your way. I will take you. I am going to the University Club."

We entered the University Club and in the foyer the great fire was burning very comfortably, and Leacock turned to me and he said, "Mr. McDougall, I am going to have a Scotch and soda. Will you

have a Scotch and soda, Mr. McDougall?" I said that I would. So we sat down and we had a Scotch and soda. And we talked a little bit and I reminded him of his contribution to the magazine, which he recalled very happily and, so much so, that, a little time passed and he said, "Mr. McDougall, I am going to have another Scotch and soda, will you have a Scotch and soda, Mr. McDougall?" I had no alternative of course but to say yes, so I had a Scotch and soda, and, about this time, Leacock recalled a bit of doggerel entitled *Nunc Dimitis* that I had written and published in the magazine about an old professor, and quoted it to me. If there was one characteristic of Leacock's that was outstanding, it was the soft spot in his heart for professors, particularly old ones.

I found it staggering that he had remembered. The verses that I had written turned out to be a tremendously important and happy introduction to a friendship which endured until the time of Leacock's death in 1944.

This is what I had written:

"Gentlemen," thus a Professor,
"That will be all for to-day."
Business of shuffling and scuffling,
Putting of notebooks away;
Business of leaving the classroom,
Business of reaching the air,
Business of laughing and shouting,
Finding the out-of-doors fair.

Years have gone by; the Professor
Dottering doting and grey,
Still tells irreverent classes,
"That will be all for today";
Folds his worn notes in his pocket,
Wearily stumbles his way

Over the dusk-dreaming campus
Counting his miserable pay.

Weary of minds that are vacant,
Wishing for peace and for rest,
Dreaming of shackles discarded,
Wishing the wish that is best,
That someday an angel will tap him
Soft on the shoulder and say,
"Mr. Scolasticus Thompson,
That will be all for to-day!"

I was naturally more flattered than I can describe that this man whom I revered so highly should have actually memorized these verses, which I had written without any such hope for this kind of immortality.

He had seen them in a volume of my poetry which appeared under the title of *If You Know What I Mean*, by Joseph Easton McDougall.

The climate became considerably warmer at this point and Professor Leacock turned to me and he said, "Mr. McDougall, I am going to have a Scotch and soda; will you have a Scotch and soda Mr. McDougall?" I demurred for a moment but, under the circumstances, I agreed.

At this point, the door of the club opened and in came the head of the French department at McGill, Captain René du Roure, an old buddy of Leacock's who was greeted by the professor enthusiastically. "Mon Capitaine, you must come here and meet a very dear friend of mine, Joe McDougall. Sit down mon Capitaine. Joe McDougall and I are going to have a Scotch and soda; will you have a Scotch and soda, mon Capitaine?" Mon Capitaine would.

"Have you ever read *Goblin* magazine mon Capitaine?" said Leacock. "Of course not. You read nothing but those depraved Parisienne journals. I want to tell you that Joe McDougall here is one of the most brilliant young writers in Canada today. Shame on you for not being acquainted with his work."

Mon Capitaine, Dr. Leacock, and I had a Scotch and soda. At this point I felt it wise to look at my watch and, as it was approximately half past eleven in the morning, and I was due to present my letter to Leacock at one o'clock, after going to the hotel and writing it, I suggested that perhaps I should leave. Leacock said, "Yes Joe, you are absolutely right. You must go to your hotel. What hotel are you staying at?" I said that I was at the Mount Royal. "The Mount Royal Hotel," said Leacock, "is a crass, commercial affair. Not fit residence for a talented young man such as you. I will put you up here at the University Club, where you will write the letter; but don't worry about the charges, I'm going to do it anyway."

I regret that I cannot recall the exact form or details of the contract that was drawn up, but it was probably unique in the history of broadcasting in that it contained a clause which required that, on every weekly occasion, when Leacock's contribution from radio station CFCF was cut into the program which emanated from Toronto on a network, I was contracted to come to Montreal to attend a small dinner party at Leacock's home with his friends, following which the whole dinner party would repair to CFCF and sit before Leacock, who could ignore the microphone, which he would refer to as "that damn thing on a stick." We were to be there every week.

It was, originally, I believe, a twenty-six-week contract series of broadcasts. The same contractual provisions were obtained when the university year was over and Leacock went to Brewery Bay to his home there, and I had to go to Brewery Bay and there attend a similar dinner party.

The contribution to the broadcasts by Leacock were about four minutes in length and were partly material that he had already written and published and partly original and partly abridgements of earlier writings of Leacock.

They were little sketches and observations more or less in the vein of the famous "My Banking Career," and little comments on life. The result was that, in the studio, the dinner party guests were invariably convulsed with enjoyment. Probably their pleasure at these broadcasts was heightened by the mood that was engendered by the dinner parties. These were quite unique.

Fortunately, the laughter of this small audience did not go out over the air, and the radio audience had no idea of the circumstances under which Leacock was delivering these little lectures.

The dinner parties themselves were memorable. As a rule, there would be perhaps six people at each dinner party. There would be Leacock, his friend Captain du Roure, and myself, and the other half of the table consisted of his niece Barbara Ulrichsen, who was his housekeeper, and two of her friends. As I recall it, Barbara Ulrichsen's friends were of a quite different stripe from Captain du Roure and other friends of Leacock's.

Captain René du Roure, who was an extraordinarily jolly fellow, would invariably attempt to retell anecdotes (some of his own making I'm quite sure), which never failed to shock the more proper old-Montreal family audience at the other end of the table, much to Leacock's distress, who somewhat impaired René du Roure's delivery by shushing him halfway through.

While the broadcasts were being done from Brewery Bay, I happened to be laid up with a cold at home and for the first time I heard Leacock over the air. To my dismay, I realized that he was not a success on radio. He had a habit, when telling a story or giving his amusing commentary on something, of chuckling in advance, which, if you were present, usually produced a state of expectation and hilarity to such a point, that, when the point of the story came, you were exhausted.

On the air it sounded strangely and incredibly as though he was a very conceited person which, indeed, he was not. Comments from various people began to come in to the effect that Leacock was not anything like as amusing on the air as he was in print. And I suppose the word got to him before it reached us, because he approached us and at the end of perhaps eighteen or twenty of the projected twenty-six weeks of broadcasting, the contract was cut off by agreement. This was in 1934.

This development seemed to have no affect whatsoever on Leacock. If it had any effect, it only served to confirm and add weight to his natural and earlier hatred of radio and everything connected with it.

I do not recall what was paid to

Leacock for his contributions. As far as I know, he never appeared on radio and never took part in a radio broadcast again.

This did not mean that my friendship with Leacock was broken off. In 1934 the advertising agency which employed me moved me to the Montreal office. I had many occasions to meet with Leacock and benefit from his company, and also benefit from a custom of his which applied not only to myself but to many other of his friends. This stemmed from the fact that it was his conviction that anyone whom he liked was capable of accomplishing almost anything.

For example, one morning I received a call from a woman who said she was the secretary of a man I had never heard of and that this man wanted to see me. Out of curiosity, I went to the office of this man and was asked if I would be willing to write an economic history of Canada from the point of view of private enterprise. Not surprisingly, I was so astonished at such a suggestion that I was struck with complete silence and finally got up enough courage to ask how it came that he was asking me to take on such an enterprise, since I did not know him and I was surprised that he had ever heard of me.

He looked somewhat embarrassed, and he said, "Well, Mr. McDougall, I have to confess to you that you are not the first person we approached. We did appeal to Dr. Leacock but, unfortunately, he's at work at present on a somewhat similar enterprise and could not take it on, but he said, "If you can get hold of J. E. McDougall, you couldn't get a better man to do it.""

I said that I'd have to think about it. Back at the office, I phoned to Leacock and I said, "Stephen, did you recommend me to write an economic history of Canada from the point of view of private enterprise? Because if you know me, and you do, when it comes to economics I know exactly nothing."

He agreed. "Yes, Joe," he said, "when it comes to economics you know just nothing! But, I have written a sort of a précis which I am about to go out and mail to you now. If you follow this carefully you will have no trouble whatsoever. They do not want a book, they want an elaborate pamphlet and you'll have no trouble with this at all."

I said, "Now, how much do you think I should charge for this?" "Well," he said, "Joe, I would find out how much money they have and don't ask a cent more!"

The next morning I received in the mail one of Leacock's famous pen-scratch letters, which was guidance for anyone who is not a moron, with such references as, "Section 7—read Thompson's *Influence of the Family Compact on the Economy of Eastern Ontario*, pages 176 to 179. Note—do not read any more of this book as it is balderdash and it will only serve to corrupt your thinking!" As it turned out, the budget that my would-be principal had available was not sufficient to pay for even the pamphlet that they apparently had in mind, so nothing came of it. But it was typical of Leacock.

I've heard of many other people who had no particular qualifications for assignments but who were recommended by Leacock and whose deficiencies were amply made up for by Leacock's own contribution to boost a friend. By the same token, he was from time to time phoning me to recommend for some assignment in my area some young person he thought highly of, much to my dismay, more often than not.

I moved into an apartment house on Cedar Avenue, which was actually only around the corner from Leacock's home, and would frequently run into him. I can see him now, on a blustery, wintry day, plodding up Cedar Avenue dressed in his raggedy coon coat and muffler askew and hat jammed on his head and his great walking stick braving the snowy winds, striding along as if it were the middle of summer.

My last contact with Leacock was that telephone conversation in which he said that he was sending me this digest for the pamphlet. And I am told that the time he went out to mail that to me, that afternoon, was the last time that he went anywhere alone. He was dying at that time and it was nasty weather. I don't think it contributed to his illness in any way but, that was, to the best of my knowledge, the last thing that he did before he became incapacitated and died. This would be in 1944. He looked fairly well and did not appear to be frail at any time.

I didn't know he had cancer of the throat, but I knew he was very ill. I had no idea at all until he died that he was in such bad health at the time he wrote me the memorandum.

I felt that Leacock was essentially a tragic figure. Not only had he lost his wife, but his son, who was a dwarf, was a constant source of agony to him. He would say to me, again and again, occasion after occasion, "Joe, isn't it wonderful,

Stevie was at the doctor's last Thursday and he was measured and he's grown three-quarters of an inch in the last year." If all these reports of Stevie's growth were correct, he would have been one of the tallest men in Montreal. But, to the best of my knowledge, he didn't grow at all.

One of the great regrets of Leacock's life was when he was forced to retire from McGill at age sixty-five. This was a crisis in his life but, with his unfailing sense of humour, he explained the situation to me this way. He said, "Joe, I am now Professor Emeritus. That's from the Latin, Joe; 'E, out, meritus, he ought to be.' " He hated retirement; he loved college life. It really broke his heart when he was forced to retire.

To me, Stephen Leacock was, without a doubt, the most impressive person that I have ever met. In order to encapsulate it, I would have to use that worn-out phrase, "my most unforgettable character." He was unique and he never seemed to portray the tragic side of his life when he was in the company of others. He enjoyed people and the company of others. He appreciated humour and humourous attempts on the part of other people.

I remember, on more than one evening in his home with his usual guests, after dinner we repaired to the sitting room on the other side of the hall, where Leacock urged me to sing to the company an old New York Irish song my father had taught me when I was a child, which has as a refrain:

Will it be one lump or two lumps?
Permit me to pass you the cream.
Oh, Mrs. McSorley, that dress of yours is a
  dream!
Sure, the whole entertainment was governed by
  et-i-quet-té,
Such a high-toned social event was Dooley's first
  five o'clock tea!

Leacock would sit in the corner in a chair with his walking stick, pounding the stick, not attempting to follow the words, but simply repeating over and over again, "One lump, two lumps, one lump, two lumps," enjoying it as he enjoyed all life—in a word, he had gusto!

JOE McDOUGALL

Stephen Leacock, around 1942. *Courtesy of the Stephen Leacock Memorial Home.*

CHAPTER 8

Wonderful Times at Old Brewery Bay

I WANT A PLACE OF MY OWN   (On May 30, 1907, Leacock wrote this letter to his mother, before sailing to Australia from Marseille)

Tell Charlie I am awfully anxious to get a place: if the little point is not too wet I'd like it. If it is not obtainable then the Hughes Point on either shore — make an offer — do something this summer so I can take up the place next spring. The more I see of foreign parts the less I think of them compared with Canada and I want a place of my own.

When Stephen bought the property, Old Brewery Bay, he didn't build on it for two or three years. I think it was 1907 or 1908, but they didn't build on it right away. The first house was almost identical to this one, only it was one floor. It was the same architectural style. There was a verandah at the front and a verandah at the back and the doors went right through. They started from scratch. They lived in that in the summer while the big one was being built. They eventually tore it down.

I'm really not sure when the first house was built, but Leacock lived in it until about 1927. Trixie wasn't alive then.

JEAN CAIN

THE CHORES WERE ENDLESS   At age thirteen, I went to the Orillia cottage as a babysitter but soon took on many other duties. The cottage had no indoor plumbing; water was carried from the lake and heated on the stove for dishwashing.

The first Leacock cottage at Old Brewery Bay, 1916.
Courtesy of the Stephen Leacock Memorial Home.

Needless to say the chores were endless in such a place. But I stayed for several summers and spent the winter of 1918 with them in Montreal. I left Orillia and had little contact with the Leacocks after 1921. Their lifestyle was changing, and after Mrs. Leacock died the old cottage was destroyed and the big house built. I visited Brewery Bay in the fifties and found nothing familiar but the lake and the trees.

M.D.

THE RUSH TO BUILD THE NEW HOUSE

I first met him in 1917. He was a smart-lookin' man and the cheerfulest man you'd want to talk to. He could laugh good, that's what I liked. I went to see what I could see. He had a horse and a cart there.

He had the first house then. It was a small house, it wasn't very big. He called it the Lakeshore House. He had a garden there and a gardener workin' for him. He was just like me. He just dressed ordinary. And he didn't believe in a collar and tie, if he could help it.

Teddy Webb hired me; he had the contract to build the new house. That was 1928. There was a big gang of men. It was a rush job. There were twenty men anyways. There was a bunch of labourers out there and then there were carpenters. It was supposed to be done by the first day of July in that same year of 1928.

I went to work there, I forget what day. I moved to town—back into Orillia on the Thursday and Teddy heard I was here and he came down to see me Friday and wanted me to start Monday morning. This was in May. We had two months to build that house. They had carpenters even from Cookstown. It was pretty well built. Only every room ain't square—I can guarantee you that.

Teddy was to get an extra thousand dollars if he finished in time, by the first of July. According to Stevie he did. I had heard this before and Stevie and me used to talk about it. Teddy was rushin' it because he wanted to get that extra thousand. Leacock was in there every day, or so. He used to come in and use the phone on the wall in the dining room when I was finishing that off. He never opened his yap about anything we were doing. He never said beans to me.

There was a big sitting room in the front facing the south. I went back the day after everybody left and finished it off—half a day left—it wasn't quite done; everything else was done. There was a verandah in front of it and there was a winery in the cellar, on the west side. I guess it's still there, a winery in the basement. I finished it off.

I often talked to Leacock when I was puttin' the winery together—puttin' the shelves in. He'd say, "By God, Oscar, when you get this done and I get my wine all in, I want you to come and have a drink with me." And I never went. I never drank.

I don't remember any porch being on the back. There was the dining room and the next was a room what he wanted for his writing room.

Three Gothic windows come out on the roof on the south side. It was a frame house, pretty well all pine. It was a beautiful place, it was, as far as I'm concerned. I don't know who designed it. Some architect I guess. I would say it was

150 yards back from the water. The main part was white, if I remember right. I don't remember what the other colour was, but I think it was trimmed black. I'm not sure. The roof was all cedar shingles. There were darned few homes along the shoreline then. Very few homes all around there, just an odd one.

When we were finished, Teddy Webb just handed me my cheque and that's it. I got forty-five cents an hour.

OSCAR OLIMER

LITTLE FURNITURE, LOTS OF BOOKS
I was in and out of Stephen Leacock's house in the early 1930s at Old Brewery Bay. Usually, it would be at a party, a gathering. I would not be over there too often.

I remember mostly the house. The furniture seemed sparse. The living room didn't appeal to me. I didn't feel it was a comfortable room. But when there was a party on and a whole group of people, quite often you do push furniture back, so I wouldn't get the idea of what it would be like ordinarily. But it didn't appeal to me particularly as a comfortable room.

His study always looked loaded. His desk would be loaded with stuff and bookshelves and everything. That was a very used place. It looked like an all-year round home, in a way, and yet you didn't have a feeling that they lived there all the time, which they didn't. I believe we went in the main entrance, which was through French doors—there were about three or four sets of them along the front off the verandah. There was a wide verandah and a balcony on top of it, just across the front, I believe.

Going in on the right hand side was the living room, which, as I say, was a nice room; it was airy. I suppose there were high ceilings. There was a fireplace going in the centre of the room. On the left of the living room was the library, or study or den of Stephen's, and when we were there for parties, he would usually be in his den working and, periodically, come in and talk to somebody in the party. He would go and talk to one person. I don't think he would come in and talk to everybody. He would talk to one person, or somebody else would say what he had to say and Leacock would listen and then he would probably go back to his study.

The part of the house I remember most is the place out at the back right through the other side of the house, all glassed in. It's still there. He may have written there, but he did write upstairs in the boathouse.

It was a rambling summer cottage type of house. The exterior looked like a house that was for year-round use; it could have been in a town, it could have been anywhere.

I don't know how many bedrooms they had upstairs, but it was very sparsely furnished. A bedroom would just have an iron cot type of thing and one dresser.

CATHERINE DRINKWATER

THE SCENT OF PHLOX   The dining room in the Leacock house had an ordinary, plain table, nothing ornate about it. Very plain. Well battered too.

There were pictures on the wall, but they were mainly posters and pictures that had been painted by Peggy Shaw perhaps, or her governess, Mademoiselle —pictures of the house, of trees or garden or the arch, if I remember correctly. Things like that.

I think there was also a picture of the *Selwyn*, which was the sailboat. Stevie went to school at Selwyn House in Montreal. But there weren't any Renoirs or Van Goghs around.

Though it was very plainly furnished, it was very comfortable and very homey in the summer, and there were always lots of flowers.

Every summer, I always have great bouquets of phlox in my house, because of the perfume. It reminds me of the Leacock house. When you went inside in the summertime, it always smelled of phlox.

ELIZABETH BURROWS LANGDON

LOTS OF SCREENS   There was no air-conditioning, I think there was sometimes a small fan. It was never very hot, there was lots of screens on the doors, and we used to keep them open. It was close to the lake.

ALBANIE PELLETIER

A LOVELY BILLIARD TABLE   There was a lovely big billiard table downstairs in the basement, just as you went down the stairs, to the right-hand side. It was a nice, very well-lighted table, with beautiful dark-shaded lamps over it, and it's still there.

ELIZABETH BURROWS LANGDON

PEEKABOO   When you come into the Leacock house, there's a little closet on the left where there used to be a phone. The children thought it was a secret phone and delighted in it. In the wall opposite the entrance to the closet there are a number of peepholes. On the other side of that wall, are two small sliding panels and, when they are open, it's possible to see through the peepholes into what was Leacock's study. The study is lined with books on shelves along the walls. I have heard it said that the peepholes were there so that Stephen could see if anyone was stealing his books. Whether that's so or not, I don't know, but, anyway, that's what I heard.

HILDA OUTRIDGE

LIKE MUSSOLINI AFTER HITLER
I was married in June, 1943, and my father, John Drinkwater, asked Stephen Leacock to be master of ceremonies. It was a very informal wedding and the reception was on the lawn at the farm, Northbrook. I do recall that we were all outside just milling around on the lawn and enjoying things. And he did not play the part of a real master of ceremonies as they do at weddings today.

Stephen Leacock showed up dressed in his white ducks and his tweed jacket, exactly the same as I had seen him on any other occasion. And he didn't exactly look too happy about it. We were enjoying being out on the lawn and visiting; this was an absolutely perfect, beautiful day and he came to me and he said we should get on with the cutting of the cake. Obviously he wanted to get going. So we went in to the living room and I did cut the cake for him and he did propose the toast to the bride. But being the bride I do not remember very much of that toast. Our best man had to follow him and he said it was rather like Mussolini after Churchill.

NORAH BASTEDO

HIGH STYLE   One time, when Dr. Bruce was the lieutenant-governor of Ontario, he and Mrs. Bruce were visitin' Mrs. Kilgour over on the point here—the Kilgours from Toronto. The big house used to be right inside the fence; it burnt down.

This morning Mrs. Kilgour—we called her Madam—she called me in and said, "Get a hold of the chauffeur, Ken Ash, and go over tell Dr. Leacock that Dr. Bruce and his wife and myself would like to call around at eleven o'clock." So I said, "Fine, Madam," and so I went and rounded up Ken and we took the car and went over.

Stephen was in the raspberry patch with a white shirt on, he always wore a white shirt, all stained down the front. He'd been eating berries. An old pair of white pants wih a tie on as a belt. Always a tie for a belt. He was just grimy, he was always like that. That's the way he lived—he enjoyed that.

Anyway, we came back and Ken went and told the Madam that this would be fine. They went over at eleven o'clock; lo-and-behold, Stephen came to the door all dressed up. All he had done was put on a long-tailed frockcoat. This was over what he had on before—just the white duck pants and the stained white shirt. Ken said that he was afraid to look around to see the looks on their faces but they were made welcome and made the best of it. Knowing him, they took it for granted, you see.

GEORGE MOASE

A CON JOB   I had a call from Stephen Leacock to come over and have a cup of tea with him. I wasn't sure whether this was another business proposition or not, but he said he'd like me to come over and have a cup of tea. So I went over and I was the first to arrive and I was talking to both Stephen and his brother Charlie in the kitchen. Charlie seemed to be doing the catering and that was cutting the bread and making toast and they had a little pot of crabapple jelly which he finally spread on the toast. It was all piled up on the plate on the middle of the table.

And I asked him—I said—"Who else is coming?" He told me there was a chap coming in with a load of coal, and there was another chap coming with some ice, and he said there was another chap coming in with some refreshments from Barrie. I said oh, well, when do you expect him? He said he should be here by now.

So, we had the afternoon tea and the toast was very delicious and we sat and talked for a little while and I mentioned that I should be going. "Well," he said, "just a minute, I want you to give these men a hand off with the coal and unload the ice and bring the refreshments into the house."

JOHN DRINKWATER

A BASKET CASE?   Mrs. Leacock and the ladies, including the cook, had gone to Orillia to shop. It was a very hot day. I was giving young Stephen his lunch in the kitchen and Dr. Leacock was at a table in front of the cottage, lunching on a roast beef sandwich and gooseberry pie. The dogs started barking, and Leacock, ever curious, looked out and saw an Indian woman coming down the path carrying a load of baskets. He told me to go out and send her away and tell her we did not need any baskets, then or in the future.

I went and spoke to the woman. She looked tired, but was smiling in spite of the heat and her heavy load. She had walked from the reserve at Rama, which was some distance. There was a bench under the trees, and she said she would rest there, if I did not mind. I went back to the house and told Dr. Leacock she was there, afraid that he might be annoyed. I was relieved when he said "Give her a sandwich and some ginger ale and tell her to rest there as long as she wishes."

Dr. Leacock finished his lunch, then went out to talk to the woman. To my surprise, he had changed his mind about the baskets. He bought them all. Looking a little sheepish, he carried them into the living room and piled them on the table, with the remark "Here is a surprise for the ladies. I can shop right here. I don't have to go to town."

M.D.

THE MAID MET A MAN   Supper was finished about seven-thirty. I would sit outside a lot and I'd go up to the park a lot. The park is where the pavillion is down at the waterfront. It would take about half an hour or twenty minutes to walk to the park. That's going in to town to the east. So I'd go to the park and it was pleasant there.

Of course, at that time, there was a band every Friday night in the park, Couchiching Park. A band played every Friday night. Oh, I loved music and I used to go down and listen to it. I met a young man, Roy Smith, at the park and he became my husband.

I don't think the Leacocks were interested in music. They didn't have a Victrola or anything in the house. He had books and he liked fishing, and he liked sailing and swimming, and he had his garden. I don't remember any music being in the house.

I think, if I remember right it was either thirty or thirty-five dollars a month I was paid. It was a good wage, because I was living in and getting my food. I ate after with the cook. I got along with the cook. I got along with everybody there. No trouble. Never had a quarrel. I had every evening off. This was the summer of 1924.

JENNIE MACKENZIE SMITH

AT LEAST SHE COULD BAKE BREAD
He had a maid come and work for him and we'd had her before and we'd broken her in a little bit—it seemed to me that we broke in all of Stephen Leacock's maids that came locally. But he liked the bread she made. Well, that's all she could do, was make bread. She was the sloppiest and the worst—poor old Tina had an awful time with her.

But she could bake bread and Stephen liked it, so there she stayed to make bread for him. She made all kinds of loaves. That's all she did was make bread.

JEAN CAIN

CHEQUE IT OUT   My dad used to drive Stephen Leacock down to Toronto quite frequently. If he had to go, he'd phone dad any old hour of the day. Can you drive me down? And as payment he would write on the back of anything, an IOU for whatever he figured dad's expenses were. Whether he collected or not I don't know, but cheques were often written on the back of a piece of paper.

I don't know what father did with these. Some were cashable, because I remember dad saying he got this cheque on a piece of paper and it was quite legitimate with the bank. He took a great many trips that way with him.

NORAH BASTEDO

SEVENTY-FIVE DOLLARS IN HIS CAP
Stephen Leacock never wrote a cheque, in my estimation. He was building the boathouse and he was buying the stuff from Macnab's Hardware and he run a bill up there and they sent him the bill. Now, he didn't write them a cheque or anything else. He gave me seventy-five dollars.

I was only a kid of fourteen and, in those days, we walked down the CPR track; see, that was closer. We never came up the Atherley Road; the CPR track followed the lakeshore. And where the station is down at the bottom—that's the old CPR station—that was the hangout for tramps you know, and I didn't know what to do. I had this seventy-five dollars and I had to walk down there.

So I tell you what I did. I didn't have anything in my pockets, you know, so I put it in my cap on top of my head and I walked down the railroad track till I got to town and paid the seventy-five dollars. And then I got a ride back because

Macnab's had something to deliver. He always paid in cash when I was there, he never wrote a cheque, he paid cash.

FRED PERIGO

A PROBLEM COLLECTING   We had a hard job getting money out of him. I don't know whether he had it or not. We finally did get it, but we had to go over two or three times to get it. He wouldn't have any on him, or something like that. And we had to row over, there was no such thing as a motorboat then. Well, it was not the distance, it was buttin' the wind, you see, about maybe a mile. My mother was great for collecting the small debts. We were renting boats at that time for three dollars a week or twenty-five cents an hour.

HAROLD ROLAND

BILL JONES   Leacock was good to his help. He had my father and Bill Jones and over the years he had different men. Bill Jones was Sergeant Jones and he eventually became senile. He and his wife lived across the Bay. He used to row to work and any party that Leacock would have, he wore, I think, a special suit. I suppose it would be a dress suit. Bill would dress up in his uniform—at least I called it a uniform. Oh, it would be one of them black tie and stiff collar things, I would think a sort of tuxedo affair, and he'd pour the drinks and serve them. That was his job.

Jones was very dark and he was a military-type man. He had a moustache, fairly well trimmed. If you'd say Leacock was a crazy old bugger for doing this or that, he'd agree, one way or another. But he'd never give us anything to talk about. He didn't want to get into any trouble—he

Leacock and his gardener, Sgt. Jones, at Old Brewery Bay. *Courtesy of the Stephen Leacock Memorial Home.*

just watched himself. Because at that time, a lot of people was looking for his job, or any job they could get. But Jones had a family, two girls, I believe, and I think that they're both dead.

MORLEY YOUNG

ON THE END OF A HOE   Sergeant Jones was really Private Bill Jones and he'd been Les Frost's batman during the First World War and he was with Les when he was injured, I think at Passchendaele.

Bill had been in the Imperial Army as a young man and he was, typically, an Imperial Army soldier. He was a little fellow, but always immaculate. It didn't matter whether he was gardening, or

things like that, he was always neat and tidy, with his shoes shined, and "Yes, sir," and "No, sir," with the professor, and very conscientious. He was quiet and meditative more than anything else.

When we were kids around Old Brewery Bay, if we wanted a boat or anything, we always had to ask Sergeant Jones. He was the guy that ran the place. Years later, I asked Sergeant Jones about Les Frost and Stephen Leacock and the Sergeant said, "Les Frost was a wonderful officer—he looked after his men." And I said, "What about the professor?" and old Bill Jones thought, smoked his pipe for a couple of minutes, and then he said to me, "He was a strange, strange man but very kind, very kind. He was always doing something for somebody."

But, anyway, I was up there going fishing with the professor sometime in the 1940s and I think that somebody was interviewing him, I forget who it was, but anyway, I asked him about Sergeant Jones, and the professor said, "He came to me after the First World War, about 1920, looking for a job. I put a hoe in his hand, and he's been on the end of it ever since." And this was at least twenty years later.

HENRY JANES

LIKE A VALET   Sergeant Jones worked around the house; he did everything for Stephen. He was like a valet really, for Stephen. And Leacock kept him on long after John Kelly came. He became senile and had a home on the Atherley Road and Stephen used to take care of him.

Sergeant Jones hung around and he was a pain in everybody's neck because he wouldn't let them do this or that. And he used to make Stephen kind of mad, too, particularly if he was going on a fishing trip. He had a soft spot for Jones. Jones was different.

But Kelly was a real Irishman. You could never take him for anything else. He was as Irish as Paddy's Pig and as stubborn. The main reason they got along was that he only saw Stephen for the length of two months in the summer and the Christmas and Easter holiday. He ran Brewery Bay. He ran the farm and he did everything he wanted there, and Stephen would say, "I want this done" and he'd do it. He and Tina, his wife, ran Brewery Bay.

JEAN CAIN

TINA, KELLY AND SERGEANT JONES

Kelly's wife, Tina, did much of the cooking. They lived in a little coachhouse. But before that was built, they lived in the servant's quarters in the house.

They didn't have children, but they had brothers and sisters who all came up. Tina's family was very large. There were always numerous maids and outdoor helpers, and people like that. If they ever needed any extra help, the family helped out. Tina was French-Canadian and Kelly was Irish. They were a constant support to Leacock.

Sergeant Jones was also there; he was an old man. I can remember him sort of puttering around.

ELIZABETH BURROWS LANGDON

THE PELLETIERS   Val is my brother that came, in 1941, I believe, to work for Stephen Leacock at Old Brewery Bay. We grew up in New Brunswick. The first to leave to come to work for Mr. Leacock

was my sister, Tina Pelletier. Tina went to Montreal looking for work, which all the girls from our small town did. And she got a job there with—I forget the first person, but then, after, she got a job with Stephen Leacock.

We are seven brothers and three sisters in our family. My father was a labourer, a woodsman—worked in the bush for the International Paper Company.

We did not speak a word of English at home. We all learned our English after we left home. Mr. Leacock spoke French, so they had not too many problems. When I first went to Old Brewery Bay, I was twelve years old. I did not speak a word of English. I started to work in the garden and Mr. Leacock spoke French with me, so did his son Stevie Leacock. To me, he talked French I must say better than average, a sort of Parisienne French mixed with English. He had a very good accent; he could speak it very well. You know, when you are English, and you start to learn French, I wouldn't say you have an accent, but it's different than pure French. His was very good French.

Tina was the second-oldest girl; there was one more older than her and one younger than her. She was in the middle. I would say Tina would be fairly young—seventeen or eighteen—when she first came to Montreal. It was about 1934 or 1935. She was about twenty years old when she first started working for Leacock. She was a housemaid and a cook, at the Côte des Neiges Road house. Then, from Montreal, she used to go to Old Brewery Bay to help open the house there.

Tina was a very pleasant lady. She was a very fine lady and very nice-looking with fair hair and blue eyes. She was about medium height, five feet four or maybe five feet six. She certainly was very full of life and always laughing and always friends with everyone.

Her husband, John Kelly, or Jack as he was called, too, and my sister Tina were like father and mother to me. I was twelve years old when I went there, that was in 1938.

Tina got married in New Brunswick in Val Moral in 1936 or 1937, I'm not sure. John Kelly was from Londonderry, Ireland, and a very fine man. He came to New Brunswick as a young boy and started to work in New Brunswick building a dam for the International Paper Company—he started working on that as a construction foreman, I believe. She met him in Dalhousie, New Brunswick.

Kelly was one of the nicest Irishman I ever met in my life. He was a very fine-looking man. Tall, handsome, brownish hair, and very cheerful. He was killed in a truck accident hauling wood from the Coldwater district up around Orillia to Old Brewery Bay. He was killed in an accident—a train, one of the fast freights hit the truck and that's how he was killed. He was killed in 1939, two weeks after the war was declared.

I was the only one there with Tina, and I was very young and I certainly didn't know exactly what to do, but we done the best we could. She was strong but she had to leave her work for a few months. She went to stay with her sister in Three Rivers to get over the shock and that. And I had to go back to New Brunswick to my parents, so I stayed there the winter, and in the spring I got a letter from my sister, Tina, asking me to go back to stay with her at Old Brewery Bay, Orillia.

Tina and John Kelly had no children. Tina remarried many years after; I don't know the year. She never went back to New Brunswick. After Leacock died, she worked in Toronto and Montreal for Simpson's.

At Old Brewery Bay, Tina was the head maid, the housekeeper, and she had two, sometimes three, maids working under her. After she and Kelly were married, they had their own lodge that Leacock built for them. They called it The

Tina Pelletier at her wedding to John Kelly at St. Maure, New Brunswick, 1935. *Courtesy of Albanie Pelletier.*

Lodge and that's where I stayed with them. It was to the south of the main house. Tina supervised the cooking and, certainly, she cooked, but she wasn't there all the time as cook. Tina would hire local girls or would go and interview them. We ate in the kitchen. There was a kitchen off the main kitchen.

Leacock had to have his soup, that's one thing—he never had his dinner without soup first. Tina used to make all kinds of soup from the garden with vegetables. He liked a clear soup, you never had too much with vegetables in it. It was like a consommé, with croutons. One of my brothers came there, a year before I did, Lou Pelletier, which was Lucienne. He worked there one summer, around 1937. But after Jack Kelly got killed, he came back. He was working in a mine in northern Ontario, and Mr. Leacock needed someone to do some work on the property. I was still fairly young myself, so he asked Tina if my brother Lou would come back. So he came back. Then, my brother Valmont came in.

He must have been kind to do all he did for the Pelletier family. I think we were five of us brothers that were there. I'll name them all, we'll start with myself— Albanie—then Lou, Valmont, Bob, and Yvon. Yvon was the youngest. When we went in the army, my sister brought Yvon up to stay and to work. My sister Freda worked there too for a short time.

I was getting twenty-five dollars a month when I first went there. I was puttin' money away. The Pelletiers will never forget Leacock.

ALBANIE PELLETIER

TINA   Tina was a good friend of mine. We come from the same town in New Brunswick. That was St. Maure, it was just a little town, a farm town near Dalhousie. Tina was a very attractive girl, very pretty. She was about five feet three, a heavy girl with pretty eyes. She had fair eyes. She was pleasant, outgoing and cheerful.

She worked for Leacock for many years. She used to take a lot from him. He was grumpy and would tell her off. For instance, one day he ordered some tomato soup. There were tomatoes growing in his garden and he just said he wanted some tomato soup. He had some guests for dinner. So Tina opened some canned soup and served the tomato soup. When he found out it was tomato soup from a can he came back in the kitchen, made the guests wait, and she had to make the tomato soup from scratch.

Kelly used to look after the farm, the hens and the eggs. They had about thirty hens and Kelly would pick the eggs up and bring them to the lodge. Then Tina, she would be cooking the eggs for his dinner.

He said he wanted boiled eggs for dinner one night. So Tina boiled the eggs and I served them. They had picked the wrong eggs and they had been in the nest for a while so they weren't very good. So Stephen got very angry and come through the kitchen and he was yelling and carrying on about Kelly that had brung those eggs in. And he took some eggs and threw them through the window, the windows were opened and there was a screen, and I remember the eggs were all splattered on the screen and running down.

HILDA ELSLIGER

VERY PLAIN COOKING He liked very plain cooking. He did like his porridge, with brown sugar and cream or milk.

Luncheon would just be what we would have ourselves, just a light snack. But then, the dinner at night, they'd have meat, vegetables and dessert—I think there was mostly puddings. They served wine with dinner, especially if they had company, red or white. They often had fish; they'd be freshly caught because he just loved fishing. He liked lamb, too, and I like lamb also; that's why I remember. They had roast beef on occasion. I think the cook did most of the ordering.

They had just a little hand bell, I guess it was silver. But, there was a little bell that she had to ring for me, when it was time to go in and clear off the table. I would just sit in the kitchen and wait or do something in my own line of work, such as keeping all glassware shining and keeping all silverware clean. I would polish and polish and wash and wash. They had to be spotless. That goes with being a table maid.

I wouldn't say there was a lot of conversation went on. I think it was just a case of get the meal over and get on with it. I don't think they were particularly religious. I don't think they would say grace. I got the impression of a happy couple. I think he was very very kind to her.

JENNIE MACKENZIE SMITH

ONLY FOR THE DOGS There was no filtered tap water at Brewery Bay and as a newcomer I was shown where the bottled drinks were kept. It was a shed with sawdust and ice, and piled along the wall were cases of ginger ale and soda. Another section had a large padlock on it. I was amused at Dr. Leacock's advice: "Don't, under any circumstances, drink any water. Only the dogs drink water here."

M.D.

EATING HIM OUT OF HOUSE AND HOME At the first of each month, the grocery bill from Hatley's store would arrive at Brewery Bay and when Dr. Leacock saw it he could not control his rage. He would storm into the kitchen where Chris, an Irish girl who was cook-general, had carefully saved every bill. Dr. Leacock took possession of these bills and spent some time adding them, hoping to find an error. The cost of supplying the larder was rising steadily. Dr. Leacock's brothers and Mrs. Leacock's mother were visitors for the summer. Young relatives of the family had pitched a tent on the grounds, and lined up at the kitchen door at mealtimes. Add to the family group their friends from Orillia, who would arrive and wait around for refreshments. I have no doubt that the bills were shockers. Mrs. Leacock and Chris took the brunt of these outbursts of temper as Dr. Leacock seemed to believe that all this expense was the result of their extravagance. The Leacocks had acquired their first car, and Mrs. Leacock tried to avoid these encounters by driving off to town to shop or play golf.

The year 1918 brought a friend of Mrs. Leacock's from Montreal to spend the summer at Brewery Bay. Her name was Mrs. Herbert Shaw. She was a slim, attractive redhead and she had thoughtfully brought an elegant wardrobe, which enhanced her natural chic. Dr. Leacock, always polite and controlled when in the presence of a charming lady, did not lose his temper over domestic problems when Mrs. Shaw was within hearing distance. Hatley's bills came as usual, were paid but never mentioned.

M.D.

THE CRASH OF 1929 Until 1929, he was only hiring people; then it was a little rough. He laid my father off, he laid Bill Jones off part-time.

But prior to that time he was evidently drawing a fairly good salary and he was spending a lot of money. I know when they built the new home, why I think it cost him $10,000 at that time. But that was a rumour, we don't know how much it was.

In 1929 he lost a lot of money on the stock market, according to him. He was doing more writing, I know that, and he was not coming up during the winter, which would save quite a bit of money.

MORLEY YOUNG

CHAOS AT CHRISTMAS After getting acquainted with Kelly, it got around to Christmas. He told me that the old man, who was the professor, was coming for Christmas. And he wanted me to give him a hand because he didn't know how he was going to get all this work done. So, my chore was cutting wood and hauling it with the horse and stone boat to the main building.

I threw it in the window to the cellar and then we'd deliver it to the different fireplaces. There was seven of them, including a furnace. Seven fireplaces and two furnaces.

The day that the professor arrived, I was still at this job delivering wood to the cellar and keeping the fires going. Kelly managed them at night. Before the professor arrived, Kelly came to my house one morning about seven o'clock and he was all excited that the pipes had frozen up in the big building.

Well, he had the fireplaces going, but not enough; he let the fires die down. It took all the fires going to even keep the chill off in that big place. It was an enormous big house, you couldn't live in it.

I don't know how he stayed in it for two weeks. He didn't have any electric heaters, just these two furnaces and seven fireplaces. It kept me going steady just bringing wood.

Now, going back to when Kelly came over this morning, excited, as I was having breakfast. He told me that all the pipes had froze up in the building and to get my coat and boots on and let's get going. So I quieted him down and told him to sit down and have some breakfast with me, which he did.

And we got over there. I was surprised to see that he had chopped big holes in the nice hardwood floor with a carpenter's chisel. It was quite a mess. He was looking for the pipes where they might be frozen. I couldn't believe that anybody could be so stupid to chop up a lovely floor like that. I wondered how we would ever get it matched again.

Well, as it turned out, he had a couple of blow torches which I suggested we start heatin' the pipes that we could see in the cellar and therefore we did get them thawed out.

After we got the water thawed out and the fires picked up, why I struck off for the lumber mill to see if I was able to get hardwood flooring, which I did, and I matched it. I was surprised to know I could get it matched.

I worked bringing in wood and keeping the fires going, I worked at the floors and got them repaired, so I made an excellent job on them. So Leacock arrived and I was still at my chores delivering wood and keeping the fires going and I heard him coming down the stairs calling, "Oh Aubrey." When he'd meet someone, it was, "Oh Aubrey, Oh Kelly, Oh Michael" or, whoever he wanted, he'd say, "Oh."

So I had never met the professor before—never. I just thought he was funny, a real professor. And he came to me with his arms stretched out to shake hands, he was glad to meet me. "Kelly's told me all about you. And it was nice of you to come over and give Kelly a hand to get things organized."

"How much wood do we have here?" I said, "I don't know." By guess, he was measuring it up with his hands, this way and that, and to the best of my knowledge I think he said, "I must have a cord." He wanted to know what kind of work I did. So I told him I wasn't working at present and he said, "Well, I would like you to come and work for me next summer and I'll pay you thirty cents an hour." As a matter of fact, he paid me thirty-five cents an hour. I don't know if he thought I was worth more or

what—he'd give me thirty-five cents an hour. Those were top wages in those days.
AUBREY GAUDAUR

A HARD TASKMASTER   He was often a hard taskmaster; he worked hard and energetically himself and expected it of others. I've known him to fire all the maids with a houseful of guests and hire them back the next day at increased pay.
BARBARA NIMMO

AMBLING AROUND   I never saw Stephen sitting sunning himself in a deck chair, ever. He was always ambling about doing something. Or he'd be in his library.
DODE SPENCER

WRITE FICTION   My family came out from England in 1930, my mother and father and myself. We lived in Toronto for a few years. My aunt had a cottage on Lake Couchiching. The cottage was on the eastern shore of Lake Couchiching, not far from Orillia. I was ten years old. She had a boat, a Peterborough canoe, and we lived in that on the lake, my two cousins and I. Stephen Leacock's house was on a sort of ramp dividing Lake Simcoe and Lake Couchiching, outside Orillia, and we used to paddle down there.

We didn't go out too far—it's not a very wide lake—but we went around the shoreline. At one point we were on the Leacock estate. I didn't know he was Professor Leacock, but it was a nice big house and more than a cottage. And I guess it was about 1933 when I first came to his attention. And gradually we got talking; he was puttering around, as I remember.

Young children don't pay that much attention to adults—they are alien beings whom you keep out of the way of, because adults are associated with saying "Don't do this" and "Don't do that." But never Leacock. He didn't seem to mind and he didn't say, "And, well, little man, and what's your name?" and that kind of approach, which puts kids off so much, and I gradually got to know him.

He was a simple man; he was a pleasant man. The first conversation that I remember of any consequence was in the summer, I think, of 1934. My father was a career soldier, Royal Canadian Engineers, and he was being moved to the Royal Military College in Kingston to go on the staff there. I told Mr. Leacock that I wouldn't be there next summer, I'd be going to Kingston. And then he started what other adults do years too early, "Well, what do you think you'll be when you grow up, Harold?" And at age fourteen I said to him, "I think I'd like to write." I had always made 99 in composition at school—in grade school or whatever I was in.

And he said, "Well, let me give you some simple advice, Harold." He said, "You know I write a bit." I didn't read *Nonsense Novels* until much later. "I write a bit," he said. "A lot of people who write will give you all sorts of advice, but just remember this; write fiction!" He said, "Am I the first one that's ever given you advice on how to write?" And I said, "Well, yes, I think so, Mr. Leacock." And he said, "Well, write fiction. If you write anything else but fiction, you're stuck in the libraries and in newspaper files looking things up!" He said, "If you write fiction, all you need is a pencil and paper." And I guess he was talking about his *Nonsense Novels*; he certainly wasn't talking about his economics textbooks.

We were sitting on steps somewhere outside his house, in the garden, when he told me that and he said, "In case I don't see you again, Harold, come into the house." And he took me into his library or study and he looked around the shelf and he pulled out a book which he gave me that summer. I don't know if I still have it or if I loaned it to somebody who built up his library the same way I built up mine. I don't think I got it back.

But anyway, the book was called *The Unsolved Riddle of Social Justice*, and he autographed it for me. He said, "You mightn't understand this for a few years, but I'd like you to have this." And I didn't understand it for a few years.

Class distinction is almost unknown among the young but, my father being a career soldier, I was always aware of certain levels in the hierarchy. And I suppose, if I thought of it at all, I didn't realize until he brought me into the house, that he was the owner and not the gardener. I hadn't thought about it much, but I remember being mildly surprised, because since he was always puttering outside in the garden, I suppose I half thought that he worked there. I guess he was in flannel bags, grass stains. His hands were dirty, I know.

HAL LAWRENCE

THE GYPSIES AND THE MUSHROOMS

Stephen Leacock was robust, as I knew him first. That would be about seventy years ago. I was about seven years old and I used to sell him dew-worms. He was a great friend of my mother's and father's, and I used to collect dew-worms on our lawn and take them down to him.

He'd always greet me with a smile and, perhaps, a pat on the shoulder. This is about 1912. I'd ride down on my bicycle with two baskets of dew-worms on the handlebars.

And the first time I remember him, he was working in the garden with Sergeant Jones. He looked at the dew-worms and said they were just fine. He was going to have a fishing party that afternoon.

And there was a troop of gypsies parked on part of the Old Brewery Bay and he and Sergeant Jones had been picking mushrooms and he said to me, "Take these over to the gypsies and if they're alive tomorrow, we'll eat some of them." And I looked a little puzzled, so he said, "I mean the mushrooms, not the gypsies."

For every fishing trip, usually, he'd pay me a cent a worm, which was a very high price in those days. I'd take him two baskets and he was going fishing with Jake Gaudaur, the father, who was the world's champion oarsman, I think, in 1903 and 1904, and he was a favourite fishing companion of Leacock's.

I got a couple of dollars. And he was meticulous about money. The professor looked after accounts and things like that very well.

HENRY JANES

HE GOT ALONG WITH KIDS

Stephen Leacock, to my way, got along with children and students far better than he did with adults. He had a much easier manner with children. He was in his element when he was writing for them and doing plays for them—children and young people, students.

When it came to the average person that came to his house from Orillia, like Dode, and Jack, and their fathers and mothers, he wasn't particularly interested. And he entertained them because he wanted to have them in the house, but he never entertained them personally. He would have a dinner party and sometimes he ate dinner with you; sometimes he didn't at all.

He would greet you and say, "Welcome to my home, and dinner will be so-and-so, and the drinks are there, good night." And he'd walk down to the boathouse and you wouldn't see him again and maybe he wouldn't be seen for ten days, depending on what he was writing and what he was doing. And his meals were all taken down, he had a room in the boathouse. That's where he did all his writing in Orillia, with the exception of Christmastime. Then he wrote in the end of the sun gallery because that was inside, but the rest of the time he wrote in the boathouse.

I don't think he was very socially inclined.

JEAN CAIN

DISTRACTED

He was looking at us as children and he always seemed to have something else on his mind. He perhaps said five words to me. He wasn't interested in conversing with children. He might come in to a birthday party and start talking to some of the other children about something they were going to do the next day—it never gave one the feeling that he was interested in the party itself.

CATHERINE DRINKWATER

SHRIEKING AROUND   We felt that we could let ourselves go at the Leacock home, more than we could at our own homes. One thing, it was very summer-cottagey. It was sparsely furnished. Stephen didn't really care about possessions and material things. It was of no interest; if he broke glasses, he went out and bought some more. And he didn't have the best crystal or anything; that didn't worry him. Or maybe he might have, but even if he did, and it was broken—so what.

So we would have these marvellous parties; we'd get going on Spin-the-Bottle, or some ridiculous thing. But one of the things we really remember was Crack-the-Whip. Jim Harvey, who was very lively, a very tall chap, much bigger than the rest of us, would usually lead the line and he had very long legs. I was one of the younger ones so I was always on the end.

And so we would go like mad down the hall and up the stairs—really fast up the stairs, and then when you get to the top there was a sharp turn and I'd be sort of swung out around the end and crashed against the wall. And this sort of thing went on all through the house. We thought it was hilarious.

Nobody paid very much attention and René would be there egging us on at the bottom of the stairs, shrieking. And

The living room at Old Brewery Bay in the early 1930s. *Courtesy of the Stephen Leacock Memorial Home.*

Leacock would be there enjoying it too.

We didn't play in the library. Never in the inner sanctum. Nobody ever told us—we just never did. We respected it, I think. It was just a spot we didn't go.

DODE SPENCER

THE PLAYS   I guess I was about six or seven years of age when I first saw Stephen Leacock. We used to go over to the Leacock home, particularly at Christmastime, they came from Montreal, and Stephen would write plays. Now this would be in the late 1920s, probably around 1927, I would think.

The house had wicker furniture in it. It was a cottage. This is the Old Brewery Bay home. This is where we would go at Christmastime. We went there in the summer too. He'd write plays for the kids, the reason being that he had Stevie and he had a friend, Mrs. Shaw, who came with her daughter, Peggy. Peggy was our age, Stevie was a little older.

So, because he knew our parents, we would be invited over to play with Stevie and Peggy, because they didn't know anybody else. And that's sort of where it all started. Leacock started writing plays for us. There were eight kids, all more or less seven or eight years of age, and going up a little bit. We all lived within a radius of about ten miles of the Leacock home. Kelly, latterly, and whoever was the chauffeur before then, came and picked us up every morning. Kelly was the chauffeur for a long time—a jack-of-all trades, he did everything. He was always called Kelly.

Leacock wrote the little plays to keep us occupied and amused and himself amused. And he enjoyed every second of it. As well as that, you see, he would have a party for our parents, every year after the play was performed. The parents were the audience. Then they had a party. And he did love a party.

On looking back, I think the plays were really very witty but the wit was all over our heads. We didn't understand it. It was written for the parents. Dr. Leacock would stand at the back of the room and kill himself laughing and rubbing his hands.

And we'd perform like little puppets, but we didn't know what we were doing. Heaven knows what we were saying! We memorized our lines and our parents thought it was marvellous. Everybody would be laughing, you know.

All I can remember is one line, and probably it was one of the early ones, so I was maybe seven at the time, and it was about Champlain or somebody or other,

who appeared in Butte, Montana, but he had blazed a trail clear through to Milwaukee, and of course, all the parents roared with laughter. I didn't know what it was about.

That was the sort of thing he wrote but we didn't know what we were saying. We didn't know that it was funny.

Leacock was a child at heart. He was delightful. He had a genuine love for children. We all felt very much at home there and had a lovely time. And there was always lemonade and cookies.

He always had programs printed for each play each year. Here's one for 1940—"Third Annual Mid-summer Entertainment of the Old Brewery Players." We graduated from Christmas to doing them outside in the summer. We would do them out on the lawn. We'd do them outside—rain or shine, or thunder or lightning, you name it, we were in it. One-shot occasions.

This is a later program—"A Discovery of the Play by the Babes in the Woods" by Stephen Leacock. And "Leap Year Lapses"—a one-act play by Peggy Shaw was done. Peggy was a great friend of young Stephen Leacock's. The next one was "Courage, A Dramatic Interlude of the South Coast" by Stephen Leacock. The scene was a village pub on the south coast of England.

They were small one-act plays, a little longer than five or ten minutes. Dreadful things occurred like pails of water landing on people's heads, a gun wouldn't go off and someone shouted, "Bang—he's dead!" Dr. Leacock said, "This is terrible," and left. He said that one wasn't so damned good! At the beginning of the play he was sitting in the audience saying, "Damned good stuff, my God, this is damned good stuff!" and then the gun proceeded not to function and Peggy Shaw ran on and said, "Bang!" and Stephen got up in a huff and left the audience.

This is one I really remember, one of the early plays, New Year's Eve, 1929. The Old Brewery Players present "Beauty

Below: Old Brewery Players' playbill for "Beauty and the Boss."

Right: The Old Brewery Players in costume for Leacock's Red Riding Hood play, Aug. 14, 1929. *Courtesy of the Stephen Leacock Memorial Home.*

Below, right: Play program for Red Riding Hood, with illustrations by Peggy Shaw. *Courtesy of the Stephen Leacock Memorial Home.*

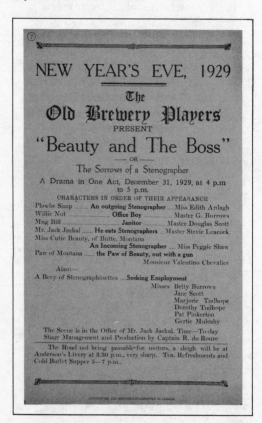

and the Boss, or The Sorrows of a Stenographer." It was in the living room of the Leacock's home and there was a bay window. The place where the wire for the curtain went is still there. This is where we put on the actual play itself—within the confines of this bay window. The piano came out beyond that a little way. It was the west end of the living room and there was a fireplace and all the chairs sort of extended out from the west end of the fireplace. It was a big, well-lit room. There would be twenty or thirty people there.

We regarded Leacock as a kindly uncle. He'd chat and joke with us and tell us stories. I was Lady Godiva one year and had to ride side-saddle through the woods to the stage on Silver, Leacock's horse, and Silver would run away with us so often. I

Marge Tudhope, as Lady Godiva, and John Kelly as a groom, Aug. 3, 1938. *Courtesy of the Stephen Leacock Memorial Home.*

was just terrified. And mother had made hemp hair that trailed on the ground yards behind the horse and it finally became wound all around his hooves. And on this wig I had a flashing light that went on and off on my hair as I emerged through the bushes, and if Kelly hadn't been hanging on to that darned horse—which he was, for dear life, because he was leading us holding the lantern—I don't know what might have happened. Kelly was made up as a Beefeater.

DODE SPENCER, MARGE CARTER AND ELIZABETH BURROWS LANGDON

TOO LATE!   I can remember after one of the rehearsals for *Lady Godiva* I said to Dr. Leacock, "Do you need me any more, Dr. Leacock?" and he said, "Margery, I'm too old for that sort of thing!" I was about twelve years old, but that's the sort of rapport we had.

MARGE CARTER

LADY GODIVA   Our parents, I imagine, were the large percentage of the crowd. The lights were probably several extension cords with a couple of 100-watt bulbs in them. The stage was sort of makeshift.

I remember the year I was there, Marge Tudhope was Lady Godiva, with the curls from the Canada Woods Specialty—the woodshavings—and wearing a white bathing suit and on Stephen's great big horse.

I think he had a 100 or 200-watt bulb hanging over the audience area and one in front of the stage. The stage was a curtain rod with something or other hanging on it. His electrical system defied anything. They called them octopuses: about ten outlets on one little extension cord.

As Lady Godiva was riding her white horse across the front of the stage—I think this would be a fill-in for a change of costumes, sort of a little intermission—the horse stepped on this octopus-light thing and all the lights went out in the whole area. So we had a temporary time-out for fixing the light bulbs.

This was in the year of the Dionne quintuplets. And I was Dr. Dafoe, and five minutes before we were going on the stage, Stephen decided he'd change all my opening lines and I got on and of course got stage-fright and couldn't think of anything to say, so I went back to the original lines. I don't know if that went over very well with him or not.

CATHERINE DRINKWATER

CHANGING HIS MIND   Leacock was around for rehearsals. He would give one direction and then come back half an hour later and give an opposite direction.

ELIZABETH BURROWS LANGDON

SET DESTROYER   I can still see young Jimmy Armstrong. His father was the head of the Theology Department at Princeton University. And he was, oh, he was so excited about it. And they were in changing their clothes, getting ready to go on stage, and Mrs. Shaw had cedar panelling, the same kind of panelling there is in the home, and the wind was blowing like a fool and he put his hand right through the wall.

JEAN CAIN

FREE MOVIES   At night, we used to go out to the movies. Twice a week Leacock used to pay for anybody who wanted to go to the show in Orillia. It was only fifteen cents. Kelly would take us in the car. Young Stevie, of course, was very fond of the movies. About four of us would go. There were three movie houses, the Opera House, the Princess and the Geneva.

ALBANIE PELLETIER

THE FUNNY OLD CAR AND BRESSO'S HACK   He had the funniest old car. The very first time I saw the car, Mam'selle was the governess of Peggy Shaw, and she was from France, and she came up with them for the summer. She was a gay lady, oh she loved fun, a good time. And he had an old Star I think it was.

He had that old Star, and it was the worst-looking old car you ever saw. It was a sedan. And this is what we used to travel around in. The windows were broken, the curtains were torn, but we had a ball in that old Star the first two years that Mam'selle was here. That would be in early 1929-30. We used to have a lot of fun. Just jolly around. Go in to town. Just have a good time. There wasn't anything much to do in Orillia. It was very quiet.

We'd spend time down at the lake, fiddling around, but that car was a great source of fun. That was the first car he had—the worst-looking thing you ever saw. This was before Kelly and Tina. He never rode in it. Oh Lord no! He went in Bresso's hack. Bresso had a livery stable and eventually had taxis.

When he called Bresso's hack, it used to be a horse-drawn affair, they'd come and pick him up and trot him into town. When I first came here, that was our mode into town. This was in 1924 or 1925. Horse and cart. He didn't have his own. It was covered—you couldn't see, there were little windows in it. And in the winter, of course, that was for protection, to keep you from being frozen to death.

He never drove a car. And he wouldn't stay in a car while it crossed a railway track, either. No sir! He made the car stop and he got out and walked across, and then the car came across, and he got back in again. He was afraid of being hit and he didn't trust cars.

He had a private road put in going into Brewery Bay. That was on a lease, a ninety-nine year lease from the CNR. We thought that when he got his own private road that he wouldn't do it, but no way. When he came out of the house and got to the tracks, the taxi would stop and let him out and he walked across the track and then got back in again. And you know, going to Montreal, that's quite often he did that—because there were lots of railway crossings between here and Montreal in those days.

JEAN CAIN

THE DeSOTO   He had a car, like he bought a car after Jack died. I think the first car was a De Soto. That's the one he had when I came about 1937. That wasn't his first car. I heard that he had an older car before. Kelly was his chauffeur. Kelly had a suit—when he used to take Leacock out, he had to be dressed in a chauffeur's suit. My brother, Lou, drove him sometimes.

ALBANIE PELLETIER

HOW'S THE GAS SUPPLY?   He never learned to drive a car and knew nothing about a car except, as he often said, that it needed gasoline. "How's the gas supply?" he'd always ask a parting guest. As long as a person had a licence, that was all Uncle Stephen asked about their driving. However, the rule of the road when you drove for Uncle Stephen was to "get her up to thirty-five and hold her there." I've had many a trip between Montreal and Orillia at that speed—the difficulty was to keep the chauffeur awake.

BARBARA NIMMO

THE FABULOUS TRIP TO THE FOOT- BALL GAME   I drove him to Toronto for a football game once and, of course, we were late getting started. On the way down I said to him, "I don't know Toronto, I don't know where Varsity Stadium is, I don't know nothing. I'm a country boy." He said, "No problem—I'll direct you." He would sit in the back seat and Mrs. Shaw was with him.

We stopped twice, I think, once around Bradford and then again just before we got to Yonge Street. The first time we stopped was to have a drink, I believe, because I could hear the glasses rattling around—I didn't turn around— and once he'd get poured and maybe have a sip or two, why he'd say "O.K., you can drive on now." And he knew we were late and he didn't take too long to pour.

We stopped just before we come to this overhead railroad bridge. "Now," he said, "when we get to that overhead bridge, you take the first turn to your left and I'll direct you from there."

So I makes the first turn to the left after the overhead bridge and we ended up in a cattle yard. And he said, "Where in the hell are we going?" And he was giving me a bawling out and Mrs. Shaw said, "Now, the boy has done what you told him. Don't go after him, you made the mistake. It's the second turn past the overhead bridge." He was quite provoked.

Anyways, I had to go right on down, right into this holding place, I don't know whether it was an abbatoir or whether it was a railroad cattle corral-type thing, you know. But I had to go right down—I couldn't turn around there—which would be a quarter of a mile anyway from the highway, and then found a space where we could get turned around. We came back and he was so mad and provoked that she gave me directions from then on. He'd swear; he did on that occasion. He wasn't a cusser, I wouldn't call him a cusser, but he'd swear when necessary.

I let them out at an entrance and he said, "Just park over there." And, of course, there was the whole street and nobody parked. So I go over and parked and along came a Mounted Policeman and he said, "What are you doing here?" I says, "I'm parked, I'm waiting for Mr. Leacock." "Well," he says, "can't you read?" I was in a No Parking zone.

And I had to drive around, I was afraid of losing the Varsity Stadium, and I drove for about a good three hours. He had said, "Meet me here when the game is over." I drove and drove and drove, around and around the square block around the stadium. And I'd be trying to get out onto an intersection and the taxi drivers would be behind me honking the horn and I was just about out of gas.

But, anyways, fortunately, I was at the entrance where I let them out first and they got in the car. They were about the last ones out of the stadium. Well, I didn't know whether I'd missed him but out he come, Mrs. Shaw and him, and there was another couple with them.

One man got in the front and the two women and Leacock got in the back. I dropped the other couple off on the way back to Orillia some place along on Yonge Street. He didn't introduce me to anybody, you know, I was just the driver.

On the way home, I said to him, "Mr. Leacock, we're just about out of gas." And he said, "That can't be, we had a full tank when we started." And I said, "I've been driving ever since I dropped you off. I couldn't find a parking space within six blocks of here in any direction." Well, he was a little provoked, but he said, "O.K., pull into the first service station."

MORLEY YOUNG

BURN THAT SHED!   This is only hearsay, but I can remember being told that Kelly was driving Dr. Leacock back to Montreal one very cold night in early January, at the beginning of the semester, and something happened to the car. They had a flat tire or something and they had to get out and wait for help to come.

So they were standing, freezing, and there was an old rather broken-down shed at the side of the road and Dr. Leacock said "Kelly, set fire to that." And so he did. They warmed themselves at the fire until they were rescued.

ELIZABETH BURROWS LANGDON

CHAPTER NINE

Boozing and Boating on Old Brewery Bay

JACKSON'S BREWERY   On old maps, it shows that there was Jackson's Brewery on the shore there in that bay where, later, Stephen Leacock's home was built. So that's why it was called Old Brewery Bay. In a map of 1867 it does show that the brewery was there at that time. And there is a picture on the outside of the map showing a sketch of the brewery. And when you look at the picture, it certainly was a substantial brewery.

SUE MULCAHY

Looking up the garden path to the house at Old Brewery Bay, 1957. *Courtesy of the Stephen Leacock Memorial Home.*

THIRSTY IN NEVADA   The summers were spent in Orillia at his country house there, Old Brewery Bay. He'd judge his visitors by that name. He used to say, "If they like the name Old Brewery Bay, they're all right. They can have everything on the place. I have known that name, Old Brewery Bay, to make people feel thirsty by correspondence as far away as Nevada."

BARBARA NIMMO

THE LEACOCK PLACE   I used to say "Sir" to him at all times. That's the way I was brought up, anyway. I said "Mr. Leacock" but I would say "Sir," things like that.

He had writing paper with the heading on it "Old Brewery Bay" and all the mail, the envelopes, they all had "Old Brewery Bay." We just used to call it "the Leacock place."

ALBANIE PELLETIER

BOOZE IN THE BASEMENT   There was no liquor store in Orillia. We had to go to Barrie for the liquor and the beer. But that was done once a year, for the beer.

Jack used to go with a truck and take all the empties, and just about fill up the truck and that was for the summer. It was put in a room down in what we called a cellar. It was kept cool, and it was locked and the beer was put in there. Tina had the key and when they had parties, she would say, "Well, we need so much beer." There was one room like that and another room for the hard liquor.

As far as I know, the beer was IPA—India Pale Ale, we used to call it. It was made, I believe, by Labatt's and that was Mr. Jones's beer. And Mr. Jones used to get one bottle of beer. I don't know if he got one in the morning but I know every afternoon he used to get one bottle of beer.

I used to go in the kitchen and Tina, or the maid, would prepare a nice basket with a big pot of tea, that was for the men in the field, and I had to pick that up and take it to the men, and they all come, and we had our tea. I think we had our tea around three o'clock in the afternoon.

There was more beer drank for the friends, there wasn't that much liquor drank, just at the dinner parties. Scotch was the drink that he liked.

ALBANIE PELLETIER

SUN OVER THE YARD-ARM   His rule was "Never drink till the day's work is done." That was a complete rule with him. He never took a drink in the early part of the day, and I guess there's nobody living that saw him over so many years as I did because from the time I was seven, you see, until he died, 1912 to 1944, I never

saw him drunk. He drank rye, but his preference was for Scotch. I'll tell you a story about that.

When Prohibition was coming—and you know his fight against Prohibition—we had a big house with two cellars in it in Orillia, and he and my father got together and they filled—between the two of them—one cellar completely with booze.

And the Johnny Walker Company, I think they gave him half a carload full of whisky and there was a mistake in the order and they sent gin and he didn't like Holland gin. There were five gallon kegs, very thick and syrupy. I used to pour some off for myself because they wouldn't drink it. He once was given a quantity of Red Label Scotch, which he liked.

There were cases of Bass's Ale and cases of Labatt's. I think Labatt's gave him quite a present. He liked beer and one of the little sunshine benefits of old Sergeant Jones, and the men that were working around Brewery Bay, was a bottle of beer at lunchtime, or in the afternoon when they were through work, they always had a bottle of beer. He liked beer, the Bass's Ale particularly, and Labatt's Special, it was a heavy ale.

HENRY JANES

DOES THIS GUY BATHE IN BOOZE?
I remember delivering his booze on a regular basis. It came by train on the CN express every week from Barrie—a case of rye whisky, I think it was. I would deliver it to the caretaker. Finally, one week I said to him, "Does the guy bathe in this?" And he said to me "Don't talk like that or you

can get the hell off this property!'' This was about 1941.

BILL McGILL

DON'T DRINK HER STRAIGHT   I never did see him drink very much. One day I took a drink of straight whisky. And he says, ''Joe, don't drink whisky that way. Take a long drink you'll last longer.'' I don't know if he meant I would stay sober longer or what.

That's the way he drank, Scotch with either soda water or water. Soda water if he was home, but water on the lake.

JOE GAUDAUR

RED AS A BEET   After seeing him drink all afternoon, you wouldn't see too much difference in him as far as his character goes. He was always calm, pleasant, but his face was as red as a beet. I never saw Mr. Leacock drunk. I didn't even know that he drank. He drank quietly. Well, if he did drink a lot, he wouldn't be doing his writing, or while he was writing.

HILDA ELSLIGER

SNEAKING A FEW   Some of us younger bucks that used to float around there used to sneak in and the custodian of this place always managed to sneak a bottle of whisky or two when he went and got some for a party and once in a while some of us would end up over there. Drinking with the custodian at his place—Kelly. We'd have a few drinks at Kelly's. Not too much.

BOB KILBY

A DRINK WHEN THE DOOR WAS SLAMMED   One New Year's Eve they were having a party. The guests would have to stop at Forest Avenue, which is at the Atherley Road, because the roads were not ploughed. My job was to get the guests as they arrived by automobile or by taxi and then to bring them down to the main house on the sleighs with hay. I had hay. You couldn't get down by car.

This party lasted well on, I got home at three o'clock in the morning from delivering the last batch out to the road. I knew the two girls who were helping to cater along with Jones—Jones was mixing the drinks, the girls were scattered amongst the guests and there'd be some that didn't drink and, in between trips, I'd be in the basement between the two furnaces. During the course of the evening, the girls would slam the door and that was the signal that there was a drink there for me. And I would come up and get the drink and come back and sit between the furnaces. They had two furnaces in the house at the time.

Anyway, when the last guest had left, I was pretty well fixed myself. I just hung the reins over the post in the sleigh and the horse went right home and I put her in the barn. I don't remember parts of going home.

The next day, Leacock was going back, I believe, and he asked me to come over and bring his grips and stuff over before he could catch a taxi. I went over and he said to me, ''Would you have a drink?'' I said, ''No thank you, I never touch the stuff.'' ''Well,'' he said, ''I tell you, if you ever do, never take a drink straight, always cut it with water, the best man to be alone fishing, and that. A great man to be alone.

GEORGE MOASE

SAILING WAS HIS GREATEST HOBBY

Sailing was his greatest hobby. He liked to row, but sailing was his main hobby. He would take a lunch and lots of times he'd go alone. It'd be calm and, I know that one man picked him up twice, when he was becalmed.

Of course there was no wind, and he couldn't go no place, and he'd let a sail down and run up some flag, either his shirt or some part of his apparel, and this fellow, evidently, he lived on Cedar Island, a man by the name of Van Vlack—I've forgotten his first name, but he was an elderly

retired man—he had an old motor boat and he could look out and if there was anybody in distress or needed help, why, he'd get the old boat going and he'd tow them or pick them up and take them wherever.

Van Vlack is dead and gone these thirty or forty years, I guess, but I know of two occasions where he picked him up and towed him in to Leacock's Bay. I don't think Van Vlack drank but Leacock, I think, maybe gave him a dollar or something for gas.

MORLEY YOUNG

Stephen Leacock, aged 6, was already a budding sailor in England in 1875. *Courtesy of the Stephen Leacock Memorial Home.*

Leacock (standing) in his element, out in one of his sailboats on Lake Couchiching. *Courtesy of the Leacock Room, MacLennan Library, McGill University.*

FIND STEPHEN   Mrs. Stephen Leacock—Trix, Beatrix, that was her name—she'd call me up about two o'clock in the morning to go out and look for Stephen. I'd go out and tow the old boat back with him in it. He had fallen asleep or got tight, or something, I don't know. I had a sneaking idea where he was all the time, by the way the wind would be blowing. So I could find him.

HAROLD ROLAND

RED BOW IN THE SUNSET   He loved his sailboat, the *Selwyn*, and it was an old beat-up thing and, so help me, you'd hardly want to go out in it. But he went out and you'd see him sitting out there at the entrance to the Bay with his boat and his fishing line over the side.

Leacock used to go out fishing a lot and he'd get in the sun and he'd be thinking and, the first thing you know, he'd nod off. No one could find him. They wouldn't know where he was and they'd be hunting. So Kelly got kind of fed up with this hunting business and he painted the bow of the boat bright red. He had no trouble after that. All he had to do was to look to see where the red bow was and he'd go and haul him in.

JEAN CAIN

THE ABSENT-MINDED PROFESSOR
There was never any new boats. I never recalled a new boat. Then he bought this twenty-six-foot motorboat from the Kilgour's for $500. We ended up with that. I don't recall the name, there was no name on it when we got it. Well, Leacock—now this is only hearsay, I wasn't there—but there was a drain plug in that boat, like a plug that you use to drain a boat when there's water in it, the momentum would carry the water out.

If you open that and stop the boat, naturally the water is going to come back the other way. So that's what occurred one time. I believe Harold Roland was fishing at the Limestone, a location on Lake Couchiching about six or seven miles down on the lake, and it's quite shallow in spots, but there's lots of water off the Limestone, you can get twenty-eight or thirty feet of water.

Anyways, evidently on the way down, Leacock opened the valve to drain the boat, and then when he anchored, why he forgot it was opened and he could hear water running but he didn't know where it was coming from. He started to shout, I don't know whether there was anybody with him—must have been somebody else with him.

But, evidently, Harold Roland went over and picked him off and whoever was with him and got into the boat before it sank, or before it filled, and shut the valve off. And that was the last for Leacock—no more damned boats. You just can't trust them.

He didn't sell it. He put it in the boathouse, which was down at the waterfront and he left it there for about three years. He had no use for motorboats from then on and, as long as I can recall, he'd go out in a sailboat, or a rowboat.

MORLEY YOUNG

THEY WERE FOR THINKING, NOT DRINKING   Some young fellows in Orillia saw Sergeant Jones and one or two other workers at Old Brewery Bay digging a great big pit and putting boxes and boxes of stuff in this pit and then covering it up with earth and they thought that the professor, who would be going back to McGill soon, was making a hideout for his booze.

Actually, there was a collection of books and things that he didn't want, and he was having them buried. Well, anyway, these fellows went out, when they were short of liquor in the wintertime, and they dug up the cache and found these old school books, and stuff like that, instead of the liquor.

HENRY JANES

POP IT DOWN   They had this ice house out from the house. I used to go up to it in the morning and get two blocks of ice, or whatever it was, and bring them in and put them in the refrigerator. Well, there was no such a thing as Coca Cola or Pepsi Cola or small bottles of pop in those days. And Stephen bought his hard liquor in bottles.

But there was a pop factory down here right on Front Street. It was F.P. Hinds and they made soft drinks. And they made ginger ale and ginger beer and it was in big bottles. And he would get a couple of cases—a case of ginger ale and a case of ginger beer.

And I would keep them in the ice house and then bring so many into the house. Well, this one day, it was a hot spell in the summer. He came over to me and he said, "Fred, I want you to make me a very solemn and sincere promise. Will you do that?" And I was kind of half-scared, you know. And I said, "Yes, Mr. Leacock." "Well," he said, "I want you to promise me most solemnly and most sincerely that during this hot weather you will drink at least one large bottle of pop a day."

FRED PERIGO

NO COMPROMISE   Dr. Leacock hired my father to do some building, and Fred Perigo was taken on as a helper. They built the boathouse with a study on the upper floor where Leacock did his writing. Dr. Leacock and my father had a dispute, and although Leacock tried to smooth matters over, he never succeeded. My father refused to return to work for him.

M.D.

BUILDING THE BOATHOUSE IN 1917
The reason I was there is because I was hired to help the carpenter who was building him a boathouse which was going to have a study above it. This is about 1917. It was the study he wanted more than anything else. He wanted to get away from the house I guess, where he didn't have a place to write, because the house was small. And he went up there. And after he got it finished, it was something. It was lined with Georgia pine, little slips of Georgia pine. He hired a man called Malcolm Ball to do the rest of it. He was a carpenter. He actually was a handy man with wood, that's all.

I remember the building of the boathouse, I was there, and it was finished that fall, you know. I was there from the time I got out of school until it was time to go back to school. So then he had a nice study in which he could write; oh yes, he had the study up there later. He went up a stairway.

There was open water there. He could put his sailboats in there, under the study. He had two old sailboats and I don't know whether he ever put his sailboat in the boathouse, you know. But I'll tell you a story about one sailboat. He had two sailboats and he had one beached up here and he had all that shoreline there, you know, between there and the Ardagh house, across the other side of the bay. And then he had one sailboat down here and he wanted to move it further up the point. Two old sailboats and he wanted to move 'em up and they were full of water, see.

A poetic study of Stephen Leacock at his boat house, 1940. *Courtesy of the Stephen Leacock Memorial Home.*

128

I took Stephen and Mrs. Sydney Small out. She was the sister-in-law of Ambrose Small who disappeared in Toronto. He and Mrs. Small would argue all afternoon, they wouldn't do any fishing at all. And they'd get hot as the dickens—they'd get mad at each other. Oh, I don't remember now what they were arguing about. She was a smart woman, very smart.

They'd put their line in the water but they wouldn't pay any attention to the fishing at all.

HAROLD ROLAND

HE COULD SMELL THE FISH   Leacock was a great fisherman. He liked to catch anything that would bite. He had an old broken log with a piece of line with an ordinary hook tied on to it—nothing fancy about it. He'd put anything on it he could get hold of—generally worms.

Anyway, this time, this morning, Dr. McGillvray was visiting—he was married to one of the ladies from Mr. Kilgour's relations. They wanted to go fishing, so I said fine. So we left here at nine o'clock, went across and picked up the professor and Fred Pellatt, his brother-in-law. Mrs. Nelson, Dr. McGillvray's wife's mother, she had put up a big lunch.

So we started out in a motorboat, one of those hot blistering July mornings. Not a breath of air. So we fished all the way through, right down 'til about two o'clock in the afternoon and we didn't get a bloomin' bite, so we pulled in at Washago and we were going to have lunch.

There was about fifteen to twenty cord of wood piled up along the river

there. We went up and sat there because it was cool and had the lunch. Stephen had a bottle of porter—he liked his porter; it was homemade porter. I don't know where he got it but it was home brew. Anyway Dr. McGillvray and Fred Pellatt, they had a rye and water. So when we were having lunch, Leacock kind of looked at me and winked and said, "George them fellows don't know what they're missin', do they?" I says "No, Stephen, this is pretty nice drinkin', this is homemade porter." So anyway we had lunch and started out again and we had come back up the lake to Goat Island. This was getting on to seven o'clock in the evening and I had to come home to get the cows in to get them milked. Anyway Stephen said, "George, you see that leaning cedar tree? When I tell you drop the anchor, you drop it." Now we hadn't had anything over the size of a perch all day. Anyway, I dropped the anchor and we started fishing. You know we come out of there with four big bass and two big channel cats. Now those are big catfish, they're beautiful eating. So we got six big fish in less than half an hour. He knew where the fish were—I claim he could smell them.

If he dropped his hook in the washtub, he'd sit there and he was going to get a fish. That's the way he fished. An old broken-up rig, well, nobody'd use it, but he got fish on it. That evening there, I says, there's a whole day wasted—for me it was; and the other fellows wasn't enjoying it too much—but, my gosh, when we pulled in there and got those four big bass and those two big catfish in just about half an hour or more—and here we are, everybody happy!

He talked to Dr. McGillvray and those fellows. I was up running the boat; he was sitting back talking to them about anything at all. He was a great man for taking in the scenery. "Now, there's a beautiful tree over there," or "There's a beautiful island," he was that kind of a guy. He was always taking in the better things.

GEORGE MOASE

BIG BRAINS   We were getting Mr. Leacock's boat ready for a fishing trip. My brother and I—Valmont and I were taking the sandwiches and all the lunch and everything down to the boat. So Leacock was just ready to go and of course we had forgotten to get the ice. There was a little box especially for to put some ice in.

Leacock and his friends were just leaving for fishing. So, somehow or other, he just happened to look in the box, and no ice.

So he went back to the dock and he called us over and he didn't swear or anything, but you know, he was unhappy. So he says to my brother, "Valmont, get some ice; you forgot the ice." So my brother says, "How big a piece of ice do you want?" "Oh," he says, "as big as your brain!" So away we take off, my brother and I, and we brought the ice out, of course, we bring the biggest piece of ice we could carry between the two of us down to the boathouse and said, "Here you are, Mr. Leacock, this is how big our brains are." So they all roar in the boat, we laugh, and everybody laughs and we cut the piece of ice and we put it in the box.

ALBANIE PELLETIER

OUT ON THE WATER, DRINKING AND TALKING   If he was giving me a job, or he wanted me to do something, he'd say "Now." He always started by saying "Now." And he would write things down.

For instance, one day we were going fishing and he called me in to tell me that Dr. Ardagh wanted him to go fishing for brook trout. He didn't want to do that, so this is the reason he called me in to tell me about it and that I had said it would be an elegant day to go bass fishing. I didn't altogether agree with him, for the simple reason that it was a hot, still day, which was no day for bass fishing in the lake. But I had to say so. He didn't like me contradicting him. And he went on to say, "Now I'm calling Dr. Ardagh," which he did. And he said, "I have Aubrey Gaudaur here, he says it would be an elegant afternoon to go bass fishing." They argued about it.

And, finally, it was settled. Dr. Ardagh agreed to go along with the idea of bass fishing. He had no other way out of it. However, when Leacock was through, he got out his pad, which was always at hand, on his desk, and he said, "Now." And he wrote, "Now, Dr. Ardagh's fishing tackle is in the sun gallery, the professor's rods are in the boathouse, my spare anchor to the skiff is in the boathouse," and so on. And then the grub basket. I'd like to mention here that the grub basket consisted of liquor, with the exception of a sandwich for me with a soft drink.

And he wrote down, "Dr. Ardagh and Professor Leacock will arrive at McGuiness' Point at two o'clock. No Aubrey Gaudaur. What has happened? Boat has sprung a leak, or motor trouble?

They were sittin' on the land and they were just full of rainwater or anything else that was in there, you know, because he never took 'em out, or very seldom.

But he said to me, "Fred, I want you to go and bail that boat out, I'm going to move it." So I got a pail, and this was the one that was on the point, and I bailed 'er and I bailed 'er and I bailed 'er until I got her dry and then I went down and said, "I bailed the boat, there, Mr. Leacock." He said, "O.K. I'll be out."

And you know, you wouldn't believe what he looked like when he came out. He just had a one-piece bathing suit, which was cotton, with a little inch red band, and all the rest was blue. It had short sleeves and then it came down to his knees. And he had a flat straw hat on. And he said, "Now, look, you push her out you know, till we just get her so she's floating." And he said, "Jump in and grab the bowline, you know, over there," and he started to walk out. And, of course, he was up to his knees and then he kept walkin' out till he got to his armpits. And he had his hat on, and I kind of think he was smokin' a pipe, you know that! And that was the funniest thing. Here I was, a kid with the tiller, and he would go deeper and deeper and deeper, and eventually he came out and we beached her further up.

FRED PERIGO

HIS BOAT   He never did put boats in the boathouse, the boathouse didn't have a slip in it to put a boat in. Not the one I saw, anyway. He had a long dock at Brewery Bay and it was very, very shallow, just enough to float the boat, maybe two feet of water. You had to be very careful going

in. It was just a shack—the old boathouse.

In the winter, he just pulled them up on the shore. He had a sailboat and a rowboat—a skiff, with pointed ends. We called them rowboats then. He had a sailboat. There's a gaff rig which goes straight up to a point—that's the gaff rig, and I've forgotten the other. It had a gaff on it coming straight out, or at an angle, from the mast and a boom at the bottom. There was just the one sail.

He had a jib too. It was at the bow. That's what the bowspit was for. Just an old, old-fashioned sailboat.

HAROLD ROLAND

SIX GUYS PULLING A BOAT   There was a door, a double door that you could open, and drag the old sailboat in. It took about six guys to pull it in. We usually left it sometimes turned upside down and we would leave it on the shore. But it was a nice boathouse, a beautiful old place, and young Stevie sold it for a hundred dollars.

HENRY JANES

SWIMMING OFF THE BOATHOUSE
We swam off the boathouse because that's where the water's deep. I don't remember if Leacock swam. I can remember him having a lovely time one day throwing life preservers at us and shouting "Allez-oop, here comes the rope." And then he'd fling it.

ELIZABETH BURROWS LANGDON

THE MINISTER DROWNED   One day, there was a man out in the lake and he was a guest from the Ardagh cottage over there. I think he was a young minister.

And this young man went out and he got drowned. And they got a local boatman down there and he had a boathouse down there and they were huntin' for him.

Anyway, eventually, they found him. They dragged for him, and they found him and they put him in a bag in the boat. And they brought the boat in and Stephen was up at the boathouse and Mac Ball was there, and they brought the boat in there. They didn't bring it in to the dock then. But the boathouse was halfway up the point and they brought him in there.

And I went up there. I could see him and you know what a drowned man looks like, his skin is kind of white and blue, and they had him covered and everything else like that. And Stephen was there and he looked at it and he said, "Whoo, God, Mac, I think I need a drink, don't you?"

FRED PERIGO

BANGING AGAINST THE DOCK   He had three sailboats that I recall at different times. I don't remember the names. He never bailed one of them out. He'd come in from a sail and he'd just tie it up and, if it rained, it naturally would be half full of water and the sea would get up and would do quite a lot of damage.

That's where my father and I would come in. He would say, "Tom, go down and see what's the matter with that boat." Dad would go down and the dock was concrete, you might as well have taken a file and filed the side of the hull or the gunwale, whichever portion would be rubbing against it; the time of year would make a difference. You know, the height of the water.

Yes, he would just tie it up and walk away and leave it. They almost sank. Dad or I wouldn't go down unless we were told, you know. His boathouse was his workshop in most cases. He wouldn't put the boats in the boathouse, he didn't bother. Not until the fall. He'd just leave them tied, or if the wind was in the right direction, he'd probably moor them out. He had buoys and he would moor them out.

MORLEY YOUNG

BOAT BUNGLE   He always had his own ideas of how things should be done and instead of launching a boat one way, with the bottom of the boat floating in the water, he wanted them to carry the thing out and then tilt it over upright.

Well, they couldn't carry it, the thing dropped down so that the bottom of the boat was up in the air and the hulls were locked into the water and there was a kind of air lock on it and they couldn't do a thing with it.

They had to get a team of horses, I think, to pull it up on the bank. But I don't think those crazy things are very relevant about the whole picture of him. The thing, to me, was his remarkable ability to think, to help other people, and to try and get them to think.

HENRY JANES

THE LONER   He was always in the sailboat. He'd go out and get a little breeze and you'd see him sitting out there in the middle. The wind would go down and he'd still be sitting there. And, after a while, you'd see the paddle going. He'd paddle back home again. He was a great

But, evidently, Harold Roland went over and picked him off and whoever was with him and got into the boat before it sank, or before it filled, and shut the valve off. And that was the last for Leacock—no more damned boats. You just can't trust them.

He didn't sell it, he put it in the boathouse, which was down at the waterfront and he left it there for about three years.

And my father said to him one time, he said, "Mr. Leacock, do you want to sell that boat of yours?" "Yes, I'll sell it to you, Tom." And Dad said, "How much do you want?" And he said, "If you've got a hundred dollars or I'll take it out of your pay, so much a week"—and Dad said, "O.K."

He had no use for motorboats from then on and, as long as I can recall, he'd go out in a sailboat, or a rowboat. He'd fish from a rowboat. Just off this point, just locally at the time. He could fish from a sailboat too. And he used to trawl from behind. The sailboat was his favourite. He'd go out fishing with guides, at that time, either with Harold Roland or Jake Gaudaur. Gaudaur was a world's champion oarsman.

MORLEY YOUNG

WORMS AND GOOD FISHING TACKLE

My father, Jake Gaudaur, was a guide and he took the professor out quite regularly. And therefore Leacock got to know a lot of the famous fishing spots.

He'd say, "Now, Aubrey, take me to some of your father's favourite spots." I took it for granted that he should have some knowledge where they were.

Whether he had landmarks or not, I don't know but he had some idea as to just where to go. This is in the summer of 1933. That was the only summer I worked for him.

I wouldn't say that he had a lot of real good fishing tackle. He had a decent rod and it was well-geared and worms, of course, was one of the usual baits that he used. There are times of the year, of course, you go to crabs and you go to small frogs and that depends, too, on what you're fishing for. The fishing was good in those days. There were days that he went fishing with his sailboat. He and Dr. Ardagh.

And I didn't see his catches because he would come in late in an evening, around dusk, and I often wondered how he was going to get back, because the wind would go down and there was no breeze. And, of course, I never did know how good of a sailor he was, so I can only surmise that he had to have some knowledge of sailing or he wouldn't even have got in.

AUBREY GAUDAUR

FUSS, FUSS, FUSS   I had a twenty-six foot boat—utility boat—built for fishing. It had mahogany decks and transom, varnished transom and varnished decks. Oh, it was a beautiful boat. This is 1936. And Stephen called me up to come over to take them out fishing, he, and his two brothers, Charlie and George. They were standing on the dock at Old Brewery Bay, and I pulled in and Stephen says, "You'd better go and get my sailboat," which was in along the shore half filled with water, as usual.

And I said, "What do you want me to do that for?" He said, "I wouldn't get into your goddamn boat without something behind it." Well, my hair fairly stood on end when he said that and I said to him, right there in front of him and his two brothers, I said, "You don't have to get into this goddamn boat!" and I swung right around and come back to my boathouse. They just stood there with their mouths open.

I was only back to the boathouse about ten minutes or so, and he called up; he says, "Come on back Roland, you don't have to take my sailboat." But he didn't say anything else.

So I went back, and I pulled up at the dock with the motor still running and he said, "Now, go in and get my rowboat." It was in about the same condition as the sailboat. I said, "Now, lookit, if you want to go fishing, you're going in this boat without any tow on my new boat!" So they finally decided to come with me. They knew darned well that I meant what I said.

So I took them fishing and, as usual, Stephen got pretty high and one thing he did do was lose a minnow pail that my father had brought from Gananoque. I don't know what he was drinking—he was always drinking, to tell you the truth.

He lost the minnow pail, I couldn't get it up, and there we were, about eight miles away from Orillia with no minnows, no bait to fish with. I usually hung it on the side of the boat in the water to keep the minnows fresh. I went to get them out of the minnow pail and he says, "I'll do that," so he lifted the minnow pail up and untied it and then dropped the thing right

down into about thirty feet of water. The rope was on it but he had untied it from the side of the boat. That finished the fishing for the afternoon.

I tried to get it up but my pike pole was not long enough to reach it. It's still there. I've forgotten just what he said but I was so darned mad I turned around and come home. I certainly got paid for it. It would be fifteen dollars for the day and I supplied all the minnows and bait and cleaned their fish for them.

In Lake Couchiching, you couldn't go any more than about eight miles from Orillia.

We would stay no more than fifteen or twenty minutes in a spot. Then we'd have to keep moving till we find them. And when you did find them, you might get fifty in one spot. If they were biting, those fish would just bite, bite, bite. Some days they'd bite much better than other days. As long as you'd get the first, you'd stay there.

I'm talking about years ago now—thirty or thirty-five years ago, up to the 1940s and the 1950s too, until the traffic got very heavy on the lake. A good black bass was four to five pounds and the lunge—well, anywheres from fifteen to thirty-five pounds for a muskellunge. And the pickerel would average about six to seven pounds.

I never saw any decent tackle that Stephen Leacock ever had. He'd use worms. I never knew that he was a real fisherman. When he was out with me, he never seemed to get very many fish at all. To me, he didn't seem like a real fisherman at all. But he liked fishing, he was out in the boat practically all the time when he wasn't writing.

What do we do? We wait for one hour. Now Aubrey Gaudaur arrives at McGuiness' Point at two o'clock. What does he do? He waits for one hour. Then goes home."

I had picked up the grub basket, fishing rods, and the rest, and in tow with my boat, I struck off for McGuiness' point. In passing through the narrows, I stopped at my father's to get bait. This is something that he hadn't mentioned was bait. No bait. I spent half an hour talking to my father and therefore I'm a little late in arriving there.

The professor was down on the shoreline amongst the rocks and there's quite a steep bank there. The doctor was standing up on top and he's calling to me with his hands to his mouth as I approach, and I couldn't tell what he was saying through the noise of my motor.

So I got up close enough and shut off the motor and he called saying, "Oh, Aubrey what happened?" I said "Well, it took a little time for me to get bait." "Oh, oh, oh, did you hear that, professor," called Dr. Ardagh. "You forgot to tell him to get bait."

At that, I started up my motor and went around and picked them up at a little dock and he insisted that everything goes into the rowboat. That is, grub basket and fishing rods. So I was to take him in tow. This I didn't want to do. I was afraid of upsetting him—that's a poor thing, hauling anybody behind a motorboat, and that was the reason I didn't want to take him in tow.

But, nevertheless, this is what he wanted and I took him in tow. Well, after spending the afternoon, we didn't have

too good luck. They didn't catch nothing, it was just a dead, still, hot, uncomfortable afternoon. But they enjoyed themselves and that's what he went for. To sit in the boat and just drink and talk.

After putting in the day, I brought him back to the shore where the car was, and they took off for home.

And he would always say, "Now, Aubrey, the grub basket is yours." This is so I could have a drink if I wanted it. But he wouldn't let me drink while I was with them on the water. Dr. Ardagh—and Colonel Murphy was another I had taken fishing with them—they both thought that I should have a drink, but he'd tell them, "No, not while he's operating the boat." That basket was loaded. They had enough for a week, but I never touched it.

I would bring the basket back to the professor's and Kelly would take possession of it and I always figure Kelly got his share.

AUBREY GAUDAUR

ON AGAIN, OFF AGAIN   The first year I took him out fishing, we would go out and he would come in at his own time. Well, we charged seven dollars for a half day and ten for a day. But he would reserve me for a day and then he'd only stay out three or four hours, and I didn't know what to charge him, so I'd charge him seven. So that was that, and when the fall come, he said, "Now, Joe, you give me the bill and I'll pay it." So I went over and give Barbara Ulrichsen this bill and she took it in to Mr. Leacock and out come the cheque.

The next year, he come up. This was early in the spring. He said, "Joe, we're going to do a lot of fishing this summer." And he said "Now, I want to engage you for two days a week. What days would you be available? I don't want to interfere with your regular schedule." "Well," I said, "Saturday and Sunday are two regular days and I usually get a party for those two days. Mondays, sometimes, Tuesdays is slack, Wednesday afternoon the town has a holiday here and we usually get a trip there in the afternoon." "Well," he said, "how would Tuesdays and Fridays be?" "Well," I says, "that'll be good." So he said, "I'll take you for Tuesdays and Fridays." "Now," he said, "we got to get at the price. What are you going to charge me?" "Well," I says, "Mr. Leacock, you know the summer is short and I get ten dollars a day." He says, "Yes, I know, but you know what that means? That means a man coming up from Toronto, and there's usually three or four of them, and they'd split that. And that means about two-fifty apiece." "Yes," I said, "I know that, Mr. Leacock, but there's only so many days in the summer." "Well," he said, "that's true, but can't you do any better than ten dollars?" "Well," I said, "I can't see how I can." "Look," he said, "if I supply the gas and the bait and the oil, how would that be?" Well, I wasn't really good at figures but anyway, I was smart enough to know that that was better than the ten dollars. "Oh," I says, "that'll be fine." So anyway that was the arrangement. I come down to eight dollars a day, but he was going to supply the gas and the bait and the oil.

Well, Kelly was the fellow that was looking after it and he always made sure there was a five-gallon can of gas sittin' on the dock and there'd be a quart of oil and maybe one hundred worms and if there was frogs available, there'd be another couple of dollars worth of frogs there.

And Mr. Leacock would come down, "Joe, I'm sorry to disappoint you, I can't go fishing this morning." "Well, that's too bad Mr. Leacock." "Well, you just take that gas and that material and you go on home, and if I can find time, I'll call you." "Well, what if I get another trip when I go home?" "You go ahead and take it," he says, "I'll understand."

So I come home and, you know, the bait, I could sell it right off the bat. And the gasoline was five gallons of gas—I wouldn't burn three gallons a day with the boat I had.

So, anyway, no fishing that day. The next day we'd go down and he'd only want to fish for an hour or two, and take him back. Same damn thing. So this day, I come in and he said, "Joe I'm sorry I can't go fishing today. The hay's out and it looks like rain and we've got to get the hay in." "Well," I said, "maybe I can go up and help the boys there for a while." He says, "Would you do that?" And I said "Sure, I'd be happy to do it." "Well that's just fine," he says, "I appreciate that."

So I went up and met Lou and Jack Kelly and whoever was on the hay job that day, and we pitched in hay. Well, with that many fellows, you know, it only took about five minutes to throw a load of hay down. And we did more foolin' around and kiddin' back and forth than work. Well, after we finished the hay, he come over and gave Kelly five dollars. "I want you to take the boys over to Atherley and buy them a beer."

Well, this was 1934, and the Lakeview Hotel had just opened. So that when we got over there, Dominion #1 was a premium brand beer and it would run about eighteen percent, which is about equal to a wine. The other was equal to ten. So the beer sold for three quarts for a dollar—thirty-five cents a pint or three quarts for a dollar. So we ordered a quart apiece, and we were pretty well lit when I remember going out of there. We didn't know which way we were goin'.

He had designated spots that he wanted to fish, so far out from shore and all the landmarks that he had. Well, they weren't my usual locations to fish, but, anyway, he was the guy that was paying me and I'd stop where he said.

I had him one day, at the big rock at McCrae's Point. To my knowledge, at that time everybody in the area called McCrae's Point, Big Point, and it was him that put me onto the name, McCrae's Point.

So he wanted to go to McCrae's Point to fish at that big rock. And he used to think it was quite a marvellous thing that I could go in there and drop the anchor of the boat and swing around and he'd be right there on the big rock. But that was through crossmarks.

So, this day, it was exceptionally rough and that's where he wanted me to go. So we went over there and dropped the anchor and I got up on the deck of the boat and he and Captain du Roure were in the back. So Captain du Roure and Stephen were in the back and a wave come up and splashed over the deck and, of course, I went down into the water. And Stephen thought this was great. "Man overboard, man overboard!" Christ, I was just like a duck in the water anyway. So I swam around behind the boat and he had a round life-preserver that he insisted on

taking, with a line on it, each time we went fishing. So, he was going to throw me this and, I guess, probably he did, but I swam around. I didn't bother with it and I got onto the boat. And the first thing he starts to do is take off his pants and he says, "You've got to get these warm pants on." Oh, I says I'm all right. "No," he says, "you'll catch cold." So I had these big pants on and I remember they folded over.

He had a spot off Heron Island there that he liked to fish, at one time. I guess he must have caught a fish there. And he would line up certain landmarks and say, "Well, you're right on the right spot." And after he'd fish for a while, he'd say, "Joe, I guess the fish are taking the day off," and he'd want to come in.

He only seemed to have a limited amount of patience or time. I don't know which it was, when you'd take him out. Now if he had his friends with him, Captain du Roure and Colonel Murphy, they would keep him talking back and forth. And George Leacock used to come along too.

JOE GAUDAUR

OUT WENT THE PONDS He'd have these projects like a fishpond. He built two. One at Jack Drinkwater's on the 3rd Concession. It was an old mill pond, an old mill dam to be exact. My father and I and another man went out there and we built it.

The following spring, when the flood come on, the dam went out because there was nobody there to pull the logs. It just built up and built up and it'd run over and the first thing you know, it was washed out. And then he bought property out in Oro and we built a big pond out there. He had thirty acres.

And he put in, oh, I don't know whether it was 1,300 or 13,000 fingerlings, 1,300, I believe, fingerlings—trout, that is.

That pond stayed in for two years, and then the man that was supposed to pull the logs, who was the farmer who sold him the property, neglected to do so, or was told not to, I don't know. But it went out.

But Leacock, he used to come out there the second summer. He'd go wading. He'd have a pair of hip rubber boots on. Invariably, he'd go over the tops of them, he'd be up to his neck almost, casting.

Lots of times he'd step into holes. He was a fly fisherman. And he loved that. And the fingerlings grew and, for that year at least, he caught trout. He would catch them, they were about six to seven inches, which would be a nice little eating trout.

MORLEY YOUNG

IT BELONGS TO SOME OLD GUY
Stephen Leacock had a fish pond, a banked-up affair in one of the little freshwater streams. He had a whole little pond at Northbrook, which was about three and a half miles outside Orillia.

The dam he made to close the pond wasn't too secure, and it kept breaking out in the spring and the trout would all go down the river to everybody else's property. He had a man working for him, Kelly, and I presume Kelly would come over and do the work, hiring other people to help him. It never seemed to be done properly.

The pond was on the farm of John Drinkwater. I don't know what the ar-rangements were; but hearing stories, I'm sure there was no money that passed hands. I do remember hearing one thing. Stephen Leacock was wandering around his pond one day and he ran into two young boys who had been fishing. And Stephen asked the boys what they were doing and they said they were fishing, and he said whereabouts. They said in this pond. And Stephen said, "Did you get permission?" And they said, "No, we didn't. It belongs to some old guy, and I don't suppose he'd know the difference anyway." I don't know who the boys were and I don't think he did either, but he didn't let on that he owned the pond.

CATHERINE DRINKWATER
and NORAH BASTEDO

HE LOVED THE WATER   He loved sailing and fishing. He also had a fish pond over on the west side of Orillia, a private trout pond.

You usually started dinner with trout. He would go out and say, "We are going to have trout—we will start dinner with trout."

Then he would proceed to go out and catch the trout and bring them in an hour before dinner. I think he was quite a serious fisherman, and he went out with Jake Gaudaur a lot. And he'd catch bass in Couchiching and bass in Simcoe.

ELIZABETH BURROWS LANGDON

THE OLD SLOOP   Stephen was very interested in the sailing races. There was a small yacht club, it was pretty active. It was exclusive. He was very interested in Barbara Stephens, my sister, and Peggy

Shaw. They were very special and they were there all the time.

So he got the old *Peggy S*. It was an old sloop, a heavy, waterlogged old thing. And they got it fixed up so it held and he got old sails for it and they used to enter the sailing race. Well, they were never, ever going to win anything, but they had a beautiful time. A lot of boys who came from Princeton, and this sort of thing, used to come up in the summer here. There'd be two boys and Peggy and Barb. And they'd get a tub and Stephen made sure they had this tub and they'd fill it with ice and put beer bottles in it. They had a ball. Half the time, they didn't go around the whole course. But they had a lovely time and Stephen was just delighted with that.

The *Peggy S* was always in there. And it was in the famous storm of 1939, when the last play that Stephen wrote for the young people was put on in August, 1939. And it was done on the front lawn at Mrs. Shaw's place. They had a special stage built.

There had been a terrible, terrible thunder-storm. The races were on and there were about thirty-six sailboats in the race and there were only two sailboats that didn't tip or go over. One was the *Peggy S*—they always said it was too heavy—it couldn't possibly tip. And the other was a little one called *The Mug*. It belonged to Bill Moore and it was a little bitty thing, but he was an ex-Great Lakes sailor and he stayed afloat. He put out a sea anchor and he ended up away over up at Barnfield near the Tudhope Memorial Park.

Fortunately, everyone was safe, but, I tell you, the excitement, the people tearing around in cars, and they were up on shore and everywhere. It was really very lucky there wasn't anyone hurt.

Well, that night was the show, it was the last Stephen Leacock play. That was in August, 1939.

War was declared in September and none of those young people were back in Orillia.

JEAN CAIN

CHAPTER TEN

The Gentleman Farmer of Old Brewery Bay

A LARGE GARDEN   He used to plant quite a large garden. My Dad would plant some of it and Jones would plant some of it and Leacock would plant a little patch.

I know that he tried to have a good garden over there but it was almost impossible, because of the soil. Even today it isn't good soil after all the build-up my father put on it. He would say to Dad, "In the fall, you better plough that garden, Tom, and give it a good ploughing in the spring also." And Dad would say to him, "Don't you think that we should put something on there to kind of loosen that soil up?"

He would say to Dad, "Well, what do you suggest?" "Well," Dad said, "let's try peat moss. We'll go down into the swamp—that's in the bush. We'll haul as much as we can up and plough it in. There's not much nourishment in it, but it would loosen the soil."

That was the idea: to keep the soil from packing. "That's a good idea, Tom. You do that." But, of course, any manure from the horse would be put on in the spring and we'd plough it in. But we put load after load after load of this bog peat.

And if you didn't plough it under, why, it would dry out and blow away just like sawdust.

MORLEY YOUNG

THE TOMATOES ALWAYS FROZE
My husband was Bob Street and he was a florist and the firm was George Street & Sons Ltd. The shop was at the greenhouse first and the greenhouses were beside the house.

I saw him many times in our old store in the 1920s. He was a good customer of ours. He always wanted the first tomatoes in Orillia. I think there were several gentlemen—each tried to outdo the other with the first tomatoes and he was one of the main ones.

Anyways, in the greenhouse we grew tomato plants. You could get single tomato plants, which were more advanced, to put out, which he always wanted. Some of them would have small little tomatoes and that's the kind he wanted.

And he'd come in, and my husband would tell him, "Now don't put these out before the 24th of May." "Well,

I'll just take them over and maybe set them out in the sun in the daytime and take them in at night," Leacock would say. He'd buy quite a few—about a couple of dozen, sometimes more.

Anyway, my husband would lecture him on not putting them out—yes, every year he told him that. Then, there'd be a frost and he'd come in very sheepishly and he'd say, "I've had my tomato plants frozen," and, of course, this would be before the 24th of May. So we got used to this, because this happened every year. We knew he was sure to put them out before the 24th, so he could beat the other fellows in getting the first tomatoes, but they always froze.

My husband would just put some aside and have them for him when he came back in again. He was a great old customer, I'll tell you.

IVA STREET

RACKING PAINS   One morning he greeted me by saying, "Good morning. We're going down to the old carpenter's house, Aubrey, where I have a job for you." And it turned out that he had a load of one-by-twos piled up and he wanted me to make this rack for his tomatoes. And the rack was to be four foot wide and sixteen foot long with one foot apart, making one-foot squares in it.

And I was confused as to how he'd ever pick the tomatoes, so I interrupted him by saying, "Now, professor, how are you going to pick these tomatoes?" "Now Aubrey, please, my brother Charlie and I have grown some of the nicest tomatoes in the country." I said, "Well, I'm sure you have," and let him go on talking.

It turned out that I made up all these racks and, after they were made up, he had one of Kelly's men haul them up to the orchard, as we called it, where the garden was and to the tomato patch, naturally. I was to wait there until he came and instructed me how to put these on the tomatoes.

Now, Kelly had planted the tomatoes and he'd done a good job in planting them. They were nice-looking plants, about two foot apart, several rows. So I'm waitin' for the professor to come to show me what he was going to do here. And all the time I knew that it wouldn't work.

However, he arrived to instruct me, he said, "Well now, Aubrey, we'll drive a stake here." So I drove a stake in the ground and then he said, "We'll drive the next stake here." Then he paused and his face started to get red. "Oh, oh, oh," he said, "Aubrey, I see what you mean. How in the hell am I going to pick the tomatoes? The racks are so wide apart, how can you get in there to pick the tomatoes, the rack's going to be where there are no tomatoes." They were two feet apart. "So," he said, "Aubrey, I'll order more material of one-by-twos and leave it up to you. Kelly can have this as firewood." And that was the end of that.

That was good pine lumber, the very best—no knots in it or nothin'. The very best. You couldn't buy material today like it, I don't think.

AUBREY GAUDAUR

THE GREENHOUSE   When I was there, he built that greenhouse and Jack Kelly used to plant that in March, all the tomatoes. There were two greenhouses.

There was one behind the lodge. That was the house that he built for Jack and Tina. We'd start tomatoes and a lot of flowers. He used to grow a lot of flowers. We'd plant those in March.

I used to see him work in the garden. He used to pick a lot of the peas, or things like that. That's what he would have done, was picking tomatoes and the vegetables and getting them all ready for the market.

ALBANIE PELLETIER

THE INEPT COMMERCIAL GARDENER

He would go up to Hatley's and see about selling some of his produce, tomatoes by the millions. When you could buy tomatoes at five cents a basket, he was growing all kinds of them and he even had poor old Kelly taking them up to the market, and he'd cart them back home again and half of them were dug into the soil. It was just no use.

Instead of having a mixed garden, one year he'd have peas, another year it'd be corn, and another year it'd be tomatoes—he didn't have mixed vegetables. You either had a lot of everything or none.

And he did the same thing on his farm. He went into raising turkeys. He had turkeys there for, I guess it was two years, the turkey runs all built so the turkeys were never put on the ground. He didn't make a cent on it—not one cent! I don't think there was any doubt about it when it came to this sort of thing––fiddling around, canning peas—he had no idea what it was like.

JEAN CAIN

BREWERY BAY PEAS

I can remember my father coming home with a basket of peas which he had bought from Hatley's, and they had come from Stephen Leacock. He grew peas at Brewery Bay and sold them to Hatley, who sold them again to different people. And on this basket there was a little printed ticket, "Brewery Bay Peas."

DORA NOY

BY CAB, TO MARKET

I think his sense of the ridiculous is illustrated by his amateur gardening and farming establishment over here whereby he grew these root crops and peas and that sort of thing and went to the trouble of printing labels, hoping to market them at the Orillia market, and would send in a few cans of peas suitably labelled by cab to be sold at the market on Saturday morning. There's no possible way he'd make a profit on this. And I don't think he cared at all, I just think he enjoyed it.

JAY CODY

SOMEONE PINCHED THE PUMPKIN

He had a garden, as you know, back out at the lodge. And he had a gardener there, Michael Miller. And he had a certain good-sized pumpkin. They decided to feed the pumpkin and have a good pumpkin so he could put it in display at one of the grocery stores—at Hatley's. They would feed the pumpkin with milk.

See, they put a straw in it and they'd blow the milk in it and the pumpkin would grow. So, apparently, they did it for weeks and the pumpkin was huge.

So, Mr. Leacock decided that it was just about ready to take to the store to put on display. And they got up the next morning and the pumpkin was gone— somebody had stole the pumpkin. So that was quite a tiring morning to see who had got into the garden and stole the pumpkin. Leacock's hand was up in the air and he was carrying on about the pumpkin. But Michael was in the doghouse that day, for lettin' somebody steal the pumpkin, I know that.

HILDA ELSLIGER

THE GREENHOUSE, THE GARDEN, THE BELL, THE BULLETIN BOARD Jack Kelly was the boss of what you would call a small farm. He was the boss. Mr. Leacock would give the orders to Jack, and Jack would give the orders to the men to do whatever type of work they had to do. There were three working men, Sergeant Jones, who worked in the greenhouse and

In 1932, Leacock fired off this telegram to Ontario Premier George Henry. *Courtesy of the Stephen Leacock Memorial Home.*

he looked after the flowers around the house. That was his job. The other two were from outside of Orillia. There was a Mr. Rowe and his son. Mr. Rowe was an elderly man, quite old, and his son was in his thirties, anyway.

Jones was fairly old when I was there. He was a small man. He was short. He used to tell me all about the places he had been overseas and the battles. He was very active, not much hair, but he looked very distinguished to me. Always very well-dressed, very military, his work clothes, his overalls always bright and clean, very, very clean. He had a beautiful voice, he always used to whistle and sing in the garden. I enjoyed that. I used to go and work a bit with him and he'd tell me this and that and he'd start singing and whistling.

An angry Leacock offered a reward for the apprehension of the thief who filched his chickens. *Courtesy of the Stephen Leacock Memorial Home.*

Leacock brought Kelly there to build the farm buildings, more or less, and all that. Kelly was handy with the hammer and that's when they started to build the barnyard, as we called it. There were four buildings, one in each corner, like a fort.

One was the carpenter's shop, one was the workshop, one was a building for the grain for to feed the chickens, and one was the ice house. And in the centre, was the barn for the horses and the cows. They weren't very big. Jones had a beautiful greenhouse. The greenhouse was at the corner of the main house, which would be the east corner of the main house, and there was a garden there right beside it.

One of my jobs was to milk the cows. I had two cows to milk and he would have sometimes maybe three young heifers and the cows. The milk was separated—you would separate the milk, take the cream out, and that would be used for the kitchen. One cow was a fine Jersey and the other one was like a black; it wasn't a purebred, it was a mix.

Sometimes Leacock would have hundreds of chickens. He would sell eggs at the store—Hatley's, the big grocery store in Orillia. And he used to sell tomatoes and, of course, he sold a lot of vegetables too, which were picked by the helpers. At one time he had five or six pigs. He kept them outside in a pen. He would kill them in the fall. He would sell some, and Jack and his wife and myself, we stayed there all winter, so we had the meat for the winter.

At one time he had one horse, Silver, a fine horse, a beautiful animal and I used to work with that horse. I knew about horses from being from the farm in New Brunswick. In the summer, he used

to get a horse from a farm in Oro. There was a good friend of Mr. Leacock who had a farm there. Mr. Leacock bought a farm in Oro and Jack was there, and he was growing things and it was Jack's work. It was fifty acres. There would be wheat and potatoes—mostly wheat. He sold some and some was for the feed.

The horse, Silver, was a beautiful animal and I really loved that horse. I used to work with it in the field hoeing between the rows of the peas, and that. That was part of my job and I used to enjoy doing that. The other horse was to plough: you need two horses to plough the land, so they used to get the other horse to plough. The Rowes would do the ploughing.

Leacock loved tomatoes, a lot of tomatoes, and green beans and peas, but tomatoes was the main vegetable. There was corn for the family. And, of course, there was watermelons. He had an orchard. He must have had about at least seventy-five trees. The orchard was on towards the town of Orillia—west about 200 yards or so. He had apple trees—not so much peaches—there were a few pears, but it was mostly apples. Three or four kinds of apples. Tina used to make jelly— that was Tina's job—she made beautiful preserves. He had strawberries and raspberries and asparagus.

I was talking about the barnyard, the centre building was, more or less, in the centre of the yard. It had a bulletin board with a little window that you opened and there, in the morning, that's where you went to get your orders. All this was put on the bulletin board by Leacock.

Leacock would get up, I would say, about four o'clock to five o'clock in the morning, he was writing, or whatever, and then he would put that bulletin there. All our names were there: "Albanie, you do this," and "Mr. Jones, you do this," and so on and so on.

He had Jack Kelly put a bell up on the tower of that barn—there was like a bell-tower on top, and there was a bell inside and we all had our own numbers, and when he wanted one of us, he went there and he pressed that number. I believe mine was two rings. And Jack would do the same, if he wanted one of us, he would press that, for anyone that he needed. That didn't last too long, but it was fun! I believe it lasted one summer.

My job was looking after the cows. He had them in the field. There was no water in the field, so we had to put a line to a big trough for the water, a pipeline from a pump at the lake. Of course, in the summertime, the cows drink quite a bit and I wasn't always there to make sure that the water was in the trough. You had to turn the tap on, so Mr. Leacock used to give me a talking to.

So, one day, he said to Jack, "Kelly, we got to fix this, so that we know when the trough is empty." So he got Jack and the carpenter to build a gadget. It looked like a scarecrow. It was like a man with two arms, and the two arms would be straight out, and he had a float in the water, and when the water went down, the arms would drop down, and that's when I used to go and turn the tap on.

Leacock used to come in the garden quite often, come around when I was working. He would come around and check and make sure that I was doing the work right. He would talk to me just like a

friend. He was very good to me. I was there till 1942. I was born in 1923. I was there from age twelve to nineteen.

He wouldn't joke with me so much as he would with Mr. Jones. Him and Mr. Jones used to talk a lot and we would hear them laugh together.

ALBANIE PELLETIER

PAPER OUT OF CORNSTALKS They had a very good garden, but the stories about him wheeling wheelbarrows full of stuff into Hatley's store in Orillia and selling them, that would be very early, 1907 to 1910, maybe, when he didn't have very much money. He might had done it then.

But, as he began to get more successful he was too busy writing. And he'd

Leacock pinning up instructions on the bulletin board at the barn, circa 1940. *Courtesy of the Stephen Leacock Memorial Home.*

Leacock and young Stevie (r. and l.) with unknown man and boy. *Courtesy of the Stephen Leacock Memorial Home.*

write in the morning, starting early, and his way of doing that and having breakfast was really extraordinary.

Anyway, after a couple of hours of writing, why, he'd go out and take a walk in the garden with Sergeant Jones, and they'd take a look at the tomatoes and the grape vines and things like that. He had chickens there and I think he had a pony and a cow and quite an establishment.

He was very interested in the economic side of the utilization of agricultural waste. And I remember him telling me that he'd read somewhere that they could make paper out of cornstalks and instead of burning them, why, they could be making paper out of them. All this kind of thing interested him, as an economist.

HENRY JANES

THE WHITE PANTS THAT WEREN'T WHITE   A lot of people just saw Leacock as a person that always loved to go in the garden and, you know yourself, you wear old clothes. He always wore white pants. Well, when you're walking in the garden at four o'clock in the morning, or at daybreak, it's wet, and everything— well, you're gonna get all wet. He didn't mind that. That was his way. When you saw him maybe at seven or eight o'clock, he hadn't changed, so he looked like a bum. Well, you know, that's not a thing to say because he was never like a bum to me.

He had white ducks, thousands of pairs of those. My sister used to do the washing there and they would hang on the line—must have had about two dozen pairs. He wore white or blue shirts.

ALBANIE PELLETIER

WHITE FLANNELS AND RUBBER BOOTS   He wasn't particular in his dress but he did what other people thought was odd, like myself. He had knee rubber boots and we were going to go into the bush to do something there. As a matter of fact, he had me digging little willow trees and moving them up the shore and planting them there instead of throwing them in the bonfire. Little willow trees that were growing there.

But it didn't matter to him; he had rubber boots on and he also had white flannels on. You understand, dress didn't mean anything to him. He'd have white flannels on and knee rubber boots. The flannels were tucked into the rubber boots.

FRED PERIGO

BARRELS OF WATER   I heard later he planted fruit trees and I wasn't there then but Tom and Bill were down there. And he said, "I want you to give every one of those trees a barrel of water a day." And they thought that was nuts, you know. But they had to lug that water from the lake and pour it on those apple trees.

FRED PERIGO

THE PERAMBULATING HAWTHORNS
He wanted a hedgerow on his property. To us it's a hawthorn; I don't know what it is in England, but he called it a hedgerow. And Dad said, "Now let's get this straight, what's a hedgerow?" "Well," he said, "Tom, it's a bunch of hawthorns planted as close as you can get them together and then you keep trimmin' them." He said, "Nothin' will go through them, not even a rabbit. And you don't need fences. I want that around the garden."

The damned rabbits would come out of the little bush that he had there at the end of the point, and they'd eat all of his fresh lettuce and anything that they could, or anything that rabbits eat. And the groundhogs.

We planted it, my Dad and I, and I think it was about a hundred feet long. We let it grow for about two years and Leacock come out one day to my Dad—I wasn't there,—I didn't hear it—but Dad came home and he said, "Do you know what, Leacock wants me to move that

damned hedge, that hawthorn hedge—my Dad called it that. And I said, "Well, where does he want it moved to?" "Well," he said, "he just wants it moved to the opposite side, there's too much shade. It's shading his garden too much."

That was just an excuse. Of course, we went at it, and that's hard clay ground over there, and my Dad had a horse and he would plough two or three furrows up and down as deep as you could. But we had to dig deeper in order to plant and Leacock would come out and he'd lay it out for him— where he wanted it. It should have only taken twenty minutes but he'd have to have it just exactly in line with something. I don't know just what his idea was, but my Dad would stand there and wait till he got finished putting the stakes out.

And we planted it. By that time they were getting pretty high—they'd be at least five feet. I had a pair of long mitts and I'd leave my shirtsleeves down and I'd grab ahold of the tree and I'd pull it over, so my father could get his shovel underneath it and pull it out by the roots.

In the course of this, one of the limbs flew out and hit my father right in the ear and almost punctured his eardrum. It cut his ear right inside and he bled and bled. Leacock insisted that he go to the doctor's with it and he went to Dr. Ardagh, I think it was, and he had quite a time with that ear.

Leacock was quite concerned about it. He'd ask Dad about his ear because it would get cold very easily, I don't know why. But he took medication for that for some time. Eventually he recovered. There was never any results from that injury. Most of the hawthorns grew and we had to replace any that would die over the course of the years. I think they are all gone now from there—I'm not sure. Over something like that, Leacock was very fussy. I couldn't understand why he'd be so fussy.

MORLEY YOUNG

THE COW KICKED LEACOCK OFF THE STOOL   I was around him quite a bit. I was there just about the time he bought that black cow that kicked him. He bought this black cow and he had a gardener there at the time. He bought the cow off of Harve Barkley. This was a very quiet cow, I know. It was a Guernsey and was awful easy to milk, a dandy cow, quiet and nice. And I know, because Harve was my brother-in-law.

And Stephen come and bought this cow, and I don't know what he paid for it. At that time I was lumbering up north and I was down for a visit. So he bought the darned cow, he took it home, and he said to his gardener, "I'm going to milk that cow."

So he sat down to milk the cow and the cow kicked him. He wanted to know why that was. The gardener said "Do you know, Steve, you sat down on the wrong side of her you see. Now you should sit on that side."

The gardener told me he was laughing like heck. The cow just rolled him off the stool. He went and sat down on the other side and finished, and the cow was all right.

OSCAR OLIMER

MAKE-WORK PROJECTS   He was all the time trying to invent jobs to keep them busy. They were criticizing him, saying, "The silly old bugger, he doesn't know what the hell he's doing. What the hell's he doing this this way for?"

I remember, one time, taking down a board fence, we had to move it because he thought that the wind was west and it was northwest, and that's where his tomato plants were going to be.

So, after he got the fence up and painted and trimmed up, the fence wasn't right and it had to be moved. "Well," I said, "that's simple, we'll just loosen the fence in pieces and lift the posts and move it." "No, no," he said, "the boards have to be individually drove back, the nails drove out and straightened and put back in the keg, the lumber piled, the posts dug out, instead of pulling them out, and the new post holes put in, put the posts back, and then you start and you erect the fence."

Now, that was to give you work. That damned fence, it didn't make any difference whether it was there, or where it was. I did see that he was trying to help people, just by what he used to do for me. This was in the 1930s, in the Depression days. Things were tough.

JOE GAUDAUR

RELATIVES OF TINA'S   During the Depression, there were always a good many extra domestics around the house, both inside and outside. And I think probably they were all relatives and people who needed jobs, relatives of Tina's and also, perhaps, just other people he knew who needed jobs, who could earn a few dollars hoeing, or something.

He also had a very good garden. And he took great pride in the fact that when you went to dinner, everything came from his garden. He picked things and I think he acted in an advisory capacity quite a lot.

ELIZABETH BURROWS LANGDON

FREE CHICKENS, FREE CHICKEN HOUSE
He wanted me to come over and talk to him because he had a brooder house back there that had to have some repairs done. Now these were manufactured jobs that he had no interest in at all, but he wanted to give me a job; I know this. So, anyway, I went over and we went out to the barnyard and there is the brooder house. And now he said, "I want the lining taken off the inside here and all painted with creolin. I want the floor taken up and the joists all painted with creolin. Then the floor laid down with a new paper in between." And he says, "Then it will be fine!"

"Well," I says, "fine, Mr. Leacock, I can do that."

So, anyway, I worked on it there through the winter and had the job finished up when he come up at Eastertime. He came out and he complimented me that it was a fine job.

It must have been an early Easter, because we took the chicken house across the lake. So, anyway, he complimented me on the job and he said, "Well, Joe, you know, I've given it second thought. Those young birds can't take these strong creosote odours; it'll kill them." So he says, "Do you have a chicken house?" "No," I said, "I don't, Mr. Leacock." "Well, how about if you take this one?" "Well," I said, "that's all right, Mr. Leacock, but I can't afford it. You've already paid me for repair-

in' it." "No," he said, "I'm giving you the chicken house." "Well," I says, "that's different. But it's quite a piece away from my yard." "Well," he said, "we'll get Kelly and Lou and Old Silver and we can move it."

So we jacked up the chicken house and we put the sleigh under it and we took off down through the fields there and hit the ice and went acrost it and we come up the 6th Concession. And when coming up the 6th Concession, the sleighin' had gone. There wasn't enough snow there, so the thing got stuck, and Kelly went back to the lodge and he brought back the truck and we hooked on to it with the truck and the horse and we pulled it up into my yard and we blocked it up and there it sat.

And so, a little later on, see, Mr. Leacock would buy maybe 500 chicks in the spring and then raise them, and what he didn't need he'd have for layers. So over come Jack with the truck and he's got two chicken boxes on there with half-grown chickens and layin' mash and grit and scratch. He says, "Mr. Leacock said that you had to have stock in that chicken house and he says this is for you." "Oh Jesus, Jack," I says, "Jack, where in the hell am I going to get money to even pay for the feed?" "Well," he says, "I don't know. He'll probably look after it."

Mr. Leacock done that—just manufactured a job for me and paid me for it and then he give me the building that I repaired. Plus the chickens.

JOE GAUDAUR

FOUR O'CLOCK IN THE MORNING
John Drinkwater, my uncle, had a story that Stephen phoned him at four o'clock in the morning, he would quite often

phone at any hour of the morning. In those days the phone was way downstairs, you didn't have it beside your bed. Stephen wanted a place for his horse and he would bring some hay out and he wanted to bring it out in the morning. And Uncle Jack said, "Well, you know, Stephen, it's four o'clock in the morning," but Stephen wanted to clear the matter. The horse would be coming out.

I haven't any idea how the horse got out here, but he wanted to leave it for a short period of time and he was going to bring hay out.

Well, Uncle Jack said, the horse arrived out with, I think, two bales of hay or something, and he was going to be paid for it. But I don't think he ever got any money for it and I don't think he ever got any more hay.

But the horse remained there until it died, I guess.

CATHERINE DRINKWATER

THE IRISH BARNYARD   For some reason, he seemed to have a lot of pride in Kelly. And he was always talking about his barnyard, he wanted things fixed up. It was the stable where Leacock had the cow and a horse and chickens, the horse Silver, and he had a couple of pigs. I can't ever remember any ducks or geese.

This barnyard, he had it more or less fixed as an Irish barnyard, according to the professor. Well, everything was painted green and a house here and a house there, and so on—chicken houses.

Kelly was a character and Leacock liked that. Now, whether Leacock just liked Irishmen, or not, I don't know. If he took a liking to somebody, he liked him, and if he didn't, he didn't want him around.

I remember one time Kelly tellin' me that a hobo had come up to as far as their fence line and asked for something to eat. And Leacock wanted to know who he was and what did he want. And so Kelly said he was asking for something to eat. "Well," he said, "tell him to stay on that side of the fence and you go and ask Tina to get him a sandwich." So he wouldn't let him come in, but he gave him a sandwich.

Another time, there was an insurance agent who did business with him. Now his name was Davie Davidson, and he was a nice person, I knew him well, but Leacock took a disliking to him, for some reason, I don't know what was wrong, but he'd come there on business, of course, and he ordered him out.

Davidson was well known and well liked, and had a thriving business but, for some reason, something took Leacock the wrong way and he ordered him out.

AUBREY GAUDAUR

THEY TORE THE LODGE DOWN   It was too bad, after he died, the place went downhill. They finally just tore the lodge down. There was a lovely lodge there for the caretaker and they finally just tore it down. It was right at the entrance as you come in over the railroad tracks there. They tore that down. He used to have a nice stable. He always had a cow and a pony around there. One small horse.

GEORGE MOASE

CHAPTER ELEVEN

Stirring up a Small Town: Orillia, Leacock and *Sunshine Sketches*

SLEEPY LITTLE TOWN   Orillia in 1912 would be about one-quarter of the population it is today, around 6,000 at that time, probably. In those days there were no paved streets and practically all the sidewalks were wooden.

There was just one policeman and one night watchman, so the policeman could go home and sleep. Goodness gracious, you hardly ever heard of anybody doin' anything wrong.

REDVERS L. STUBLEY

...BUT IT COULD BE LIVELY
I would call it a lively town. We had sports people here and a skating rink, and a hockey rink, and we had championship lacrosse teams, championship hockey teams.

The Opera House was here as long as I can remember. Originally, there were just plays that came through on tours. Then they went to silent movies. I would say they had silent movies during the First World War.

REDVERS L. STUBLEY

The Orillia Cricket Club, 1902. Leacock is standing, second from left, wearing a battered fedora. *Courtesy of the Orillia Public Library.*

FROM SUTTON TO ORILLIA

Leacock's coming originally arose from the fact that his mother and her family moved from Sutton to Orillia in the late years of the last century . . . Stephen, already at McGill, came home for the long university vacations and became a loyal Orillian thoroughly identified with the town.

. . . Mrs. Leacock had reproached her gifted son for lampooning her rector, Canon Greene, easily the most beloved man who ever lived in Orillia, whose tolerant kindliness was demonstrated by the fact that he never resented the rather cruel exploitation of some of his idiosyncrasies . . .

HAROLD HALE

HE PLAYED CRICKET AND LACROSSE

He was a member of the Orillia Cricket Club. He was quite a good cricketer and he also played on the lacrosse team.

Around that time, you see, his mother was camping at our place. And he was a very, very great friend of Harold Hale, the editor of the *Orillia Packet*. And that friendship never wavered.

Harold Hale was the greatest teetotaller that ever walked on two feet. But he was a brilliant man. And he and Stephen just never talked liquor. Stephen was one of the greatest non-teetotallers. I always said he got a reputation for being a drunk because he made a point of attacking Prohibition in Ontario. He thought Prohibition was for the birds. And he wasn't going to speak unless he had a Scotch.

Fine, but that didn't mean that he drank from nine o'clock in the morning until nine the next morning. He couldn't have written what he did if he'd been drunk all the time.

JEAN CAIN

THAT OLD CODGER

He was an active member of the Orillia Cricket Club, and took part in the matches that used to be played with the surrounding towns when the good old English game still flourished in this district. Later, fishing became his favourite recreation and he owned several trout ponds in the neighbourhood, which sometimes provided more trouble than fish. He used to tell with gusto of meeting an urchin, who, in the course of the conversation, revealed that he was in the habit of fishing in one of the ponds. Asked if he wasn't afraid that the owner would catch him, the lad replied, "Oh, that old codger! He'd never catch anybody!"

ORILLIA PACKET & TIMES
(on Leacock's Death)

NOT A BRAIN IN HIS HEAD

As a person he just didn't impress you as being anyone great and I just thought of him as being Stephen Leacock, a friend of my father's, John Drinkwater.

Well, Stephen Leacock never tried to impress you. He did not ever say anything about himself and he wore these rather old scruffy clothes and you just thought of him as being an ordinary person that lived in Orillia.

This would be probably what made him very approachable to people; he didn't scare people. He probably walked around and they probably didn't even think he had a brain in his head. And this is probably where he got his stories from. If he'd come in all dolled up, everybody would have been afraid of him, perhaps.

CATHERINE DRINKWATER

BLACK DUCKS   I came to Orillia in 1898. Leacock used to come down to our boathouse, the original boathouse on the Grand Trunk Railway waterfront. He would come over to our boathouse and my dad owned it at the time, and he just tied up there to go uptown, do his shopping, and come back. He wouldn't ask permission but we didn't mind at all. I was pretty young at that time, about ten years old. It would be about 1905 when I first saw Leacock. Really early.

Any person knew what he looked like. He put on a pair of white ducks when he first came from Montreal, and he kept wearing those white ducks all summer without washing them at all. They were black ducks at the end of the summer.

HAROLD ROLAND

A TYPICAL SMALL TOWN   Orillia was a dry town when Stephen Leacock was in Orillia. Most people in Orillia, I get the feeling, being a native Orillian, they didn't think too much of him, partly, I suppose, because he was what you would call a "character."

Orillia has always had its share of characters. But he was probably a little more prominent one.

I always think of Orillia as being a fairly conservative town and I think when he brought the spotlight specifically on to certain Orillians, they didn't like it too well. These were old Orillians who lived fairly staid lives and, when he put them

Orillia, the early days on Mississaga Street, facing west. *Courtesy of the Stephen Leacock Memorial Home.*

into print, you could pretty well go by what he called them; you could easily tell who they were.

I'm sure most of the people who read his books kind of laugh at it now, where I don't think they did when it was first written.

You knew everybody a number of years ago, and these were families that had been here practically since Orillia was founded in 1867. It was just a typical small town. Orillia certainly was no different than any place else.

But there's so few of the old guard left now. Orillia is a changed town from twenty years ago even.

The Leacock home, I guess it certainly generates money—the home and his manuscripts and such like. There's been good response to his memorabilia that's been out around the country that's been returned to the home. That's the best collection I guess there is of his works.

FRED CARTER

HITTING THE NAIL ON THE HEAD

I would say, definitely, that *Sunshine Sketches of a Little Town* was so typical of Orillia that some of the people that were characters in his book wanted to sue him for the snide remarks he made in reference to their banking for instance—the banking incident where he went into the bank and how long it took to get his money deposited. He wasn't too far off.

Dean Drone was Canon Greene, and he had two sons that became missionaries and went out to the British Columbia coast mission and they came back on occasion and addressed our congregation and you'd just think for all the world that it was Dean Drone, Reverend Canon Greene, speaking again.

REDVERS L. STUBLEY

"WHO DIED ON THE POST?"

Well, Leacock did his banking in Orillia and he poked fun at the manager of the Toronto Dominion Bank. And the drugstore—it was Slaven's, he was in there. It was on the corner of Mississaga and Peter.

He went to the Anglican Church. I never remember him being in church, but I remember his brother Charlie being there—but that was years later. Then he'd go to Jeff Short to have his hair cut. Jeff was Thorpe in the *Sunshine Sketches*. It was a small town and it was easy to get to know the people. And then he'd go in to Hilda Outridge's father's to have his suits made and he probably sat around there and chatted. And of course, in those days, they always said, "Who died on the post?"

On the corner of Peter and Mississaga there was a wooden post and they just had a little door there and whoever died,

they had a notice up there. That was before we had a daily paper. And so, the saying was, "Well, who died on the post today?"

I think the fact that he had this gift for writing and this gift for being interested in people, that naturally, wherever he went, he was going to make a study of people, whether it was in Orillia or not.

BETH HATLEY and HILDA OUTRIDGE

POETIC LICENSE

I do not think that his portrayal of Orillia in his book, *Sunshine Sketches* had too much influence on my father's family living in the country, because he was not an Orillia town person. But I do recall my father-in-law, Tyson Bastedo, who was in the bank at the time in Orillia, got a terrific amount of humour out of *Sunshine Sketches* because he could practically pick out all the people.

I think there was a lot of antagonism—whether I heard it personally or not—by people whom he mentioned and the people whom he described in *Sunshine Sketches*, although he said there was no similarity to anybody living or dead. It was obvious that there was.

That program on CBL a few years ago called "Our Town" about Orillia! People were very incensed about it because they didn't think it depicted Orillia completely. That we were being laughed at, in a way.

I think people were peeved or upset about his writing because he did take a bit of poetic license, I would say. I don't think it was all fact, and yet he implied it was. I think now we're much more used to being exposed to the media. In those days that was quite unique.

154

I'm sure they thought that it was a little bit frilly. He'd exaggerate some incident that possibly happened. I read part of *Sunshine Sketches* again, which I do periodically, and of course I get a whole different outlook on it. I look at it in a much different light now probably than I did the first time. Maybe when I first read parts of it I was probably at home and living in a small community, and we're very community-minded and I wasn't worldly, I suppose I would be incensed by somebody poking fun at us and exaggerating things. Now I look at it as a wonderful way of showing the fun that can be seen out of every day happenings.

NORAH BASTEDO

TAKEN FOR GRANTED   We always had *Sunshine Sketches* around and I knew he had written that and it was about Orillia and that a lot of people were upset about it—people he had mentioned in the book. And I knew he was a professor at McGill. But I didn't know he was as famous as he was. We just sort of took him for granted. You know, we didn't see him that often.

BETH HATLEY

PROPHET WITHOUT HONOUR
There's a lot in town here that have never read even *Sunshine Sketches* or have been over to the home. There's always been that type of person that's not interested.

HILDA OUTRIDGE

NOT PART OF THE SAFARIS   I believe my father probably was critical of Stephen Leacock, but not of *Sunshine Sketches*. He was not part of Stephen Leacock's summer safaris at Brewery Bay, and I believe he probably knew more about what he thought was going on there—we never discussed it at home at all until many years later, and the CBC interviewed my father in our back yard about Stephen Leacock, and I think perhaps quite a bit of that tape wasn't used.

I believe that many of the people in Orillia thought that it was too wild out there at Old Brewery Bay—what they thought went on. And so the main reason that they would be critical probably was because they didn't know what was going on.

SUE MULCAHY

DON'T MENTION LEACOCK   (An excerpt from an article in the Orillia *Wednesday Nighter*, July 1, 1970 that gives tourists advice about how to find, identify, and deal with an Orillian. This piece was written by a certain "Martin the Scribbler," who, to a degree, had his tongue in his cheek:

Another thing, don't mention the word "Leacock." To the old inhabitants, he was a no-good, drunken, arrogant, loud-mouth trouble-maker who should have stayed in Montreal, or some other suitable location like hell.

Leacock may be Canada's greatest humourist, but to most Orillians he is just an overworked stunt. Of course, the celebration of his feast has become THE thing for a certain "in" group. But don't let that fool you. Most Orillians couldn't care less and the last place you are likely to meet an Orillian is at the Leacock home.

SOME PEOPLE WOULDN'T GO NEAR HIM   I wouldn't think there'd be any lingering resentment now because none of the family is left. I'm about the only member of the family that's left that was mentioned in that book. My uncle was the teller, Peter Pupkin, that rowed the boat and rode the bicycle downhill so fast.

Now, there was no hard feeling as far as my family were concerned at all, or Uncle Jack; he couldn't have cared less. There were a lot of people that didn't ever go near Stephen Leacock or have anything to do with him socially or otherwise on account of that book. But Leacock was very smart. He had nothing in common with most of them anyway, so he couldn't have cared whether he saw them socially or not. It didn't matter. Now old Canon Greene, who was Dean Drone, he loved it. It was right up his alley, he liked that sort of thing. And Stephen knew that, and he knew he could get away with it.

JEAN CAIN

I TALKED TO THE FELLOW   Jeff Short, who was Jefferson Thorpe in the book, used to say—he was Stephen's barber—"I talked to the fellow though I didn't know he was going to put all these things in the book."

HAROLD HALE

Geneva Park, Orillia, near the turn of the century, on a gala occasion. The man in the foreground with his hands in his pockets is believed to be Leacock. *Courtesy of Sue Mulcahy.*

THEY COULDN'T BEAR THOSE BARE FEET   He was an Anglican and he used to come to church. Both Leacock and Hale and I were Anglican; that's how I got to know him.

Stephen Leacock once entertained our choir over at his residence on Brewery Bay and, of course, "drinking" wasn't a favourite term with those people.

Nevertheless, they went and he was the perfect host, there was no doubt about that. And, of course, many of us individually have been over to his place—many citizens of Orillia have been over to his home and enjoyed it.

In the summertime Stephen Leacock would just get out of his boat and walk in his bare feet and he'd even come to church with his knee pants on and no socks—in his bare feet. Of course, some people held up their hands in holy horror. He was the only one in the church with bare feet. There would be plenty of people on the street with bare feet, but not in church.

He wasn't in church often, but he would come once or twice a summer likely.

REDVERS L. STUBLEY

FEW PEOPLE KNEW HE EXISTED
Personally I think right down in the area here where he lived that there was very few people that knew he existed. I for one didn't. I used to work the place right next to him. They had a market garden there, the Bay brothers and, Leacock's place there, you'd look at it from the road and it was all grown up with hawthorn trees and so forth. That's being English. They were planted in rows. They're not now. Possi-bly at that time they were about eight or nine feet, or something like that. I've seen the same type of farms over in England where they use the hawthorns for fences.

Leacock had grapes in there, they were planted in rows. They used to grow vegetables in between these rows. He grew tomatoes.

Actually, very few people, unless they had occasion to go in there during the summer, ever knew that this stuff was in there.

I personally never realized that the man was a writer. I never read anything

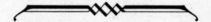

He wrote from McGill University on February 9, 1915, to his good friend, E.V. Lucas, the well known English writer. In part, he said:

I think that perhaps you are right about the greater freedom of satire allowed to writers on this side of the water from the editorial point of view – not however from the point of view of the public; as far as they are concerned you (that is one) may 'get away with it' or one may not. You can never tell whether they will say in a lazily amused fashion, 'how very true,' 'how extremely entertaining,' or whether all of a sudden there will descend on you a dense flock of clergymen, temperance workers, women-rights women, municipal purity people and all the whole battalion . . .

Courtesy of the Stephen Leacock Memorial Home.

that he ever wrote until after he died. I was up at the City Hall one time, they had a copy of *Sunshine Sketches* there and I read a little bit of it. It's quite a book.

BOB KILBY

HE CAME WITH ORILLIA   Possibly because I was quite young when I came to town, I had never heard of Stephen Leacock, and no one in the town seemed to refer to him as being a great writer, or what-have-you, at that time. As far as I could see, he was just part of the surroundings—he came with Orillia.

I was amazed, actually, how famous he became. After I met him, I had an entirely different picture of Stephen Leacock. I don't think it dawned on me until after he had passed away.

WILF VARLEY

THEY SHOULD HAVE LIVED IN MONTREAL   They should have lived in Montreal and they'd have realized what Stephen Leacock was. But in Orillia he was just an ordinary fellow, They had no idea of his fame. I knew what he was before I left Montreal—an important man.

JENNIE MACKENZIE SMITH

HOW THINGS CHANGE   A lot of solid, upstanding Orillians thought the baggy man who arrived each spring from McGill to pass the year's sunny hours in the secluded summer home at old Brewery Bay was a bit of a weirdo.

He was a college professor (political economy) who used to sail into town and walk through the town's main street in his bare feet, and there was a lot of talk about that.

In a community that was unyieldingly dry, he used to stock staggering quantities of liquor, though much of it was consumed by the guests who used to linger at the big house on the bright patch on Lake Couchiching.

It was there, too, in quieter hours that he wrote those gleaming sketches of a small Canadian town thinly disguised under the name of Mariposa. Some of the citizens were pretty irked by the book at the time.

But today the citizens cheerily refer to their town as Mariposa and everybody knows that Stephen Leacock was the golden ray that shone on Orillia.

THE TORONTO STAR, 1967

OPPOSITES ATTRACT   The one person that made Stephen Leacock famous in Orillia and supported him was Harold Hale, the editor of the *Packet and Times*, who was a firebrand temperance advocate where Leacock loved his booze. I think Harold Hale and Stephen Leacock got along very well because they had a love of people. Harold Hale recognized the fact that Stephen Leacock was a professor, a teacher, and that he had a lot in common mentally with himself.

Harold Hale never went to high school, only a couple of years, but he was recognized in Orillia as Orillia's man of the century before he died.

REDVERS L. STUBLEY

THE NONCONFORMIST   Harold and Russell were two brothers. There was J. Russell Hale and then there was C. Harold Hale and I worked for them all my life. I started workin' for them at the Orillia

Packet when I was goin' to high school. I think in my contact with the Hales they always made disparaging remarks about Leacock. He didn't dress properly, or he did this, or he didn't dress according to what they'd say. He'd come up to the Opera House to address a political meeting and he'd just as soon have his knee rubber boots on and his white flannels, you see. And he seemed to despise all the formalities that they expected of him. And they gave me that impression. I talked to Russell Hale a couple of times, and when you mentioned Leacock he always talked disparagingly, you know.

Harold Hale was a writer, but I don't think that Harold Hale would go to any kind of festivity, a family festivity, that belonged to Stephen Leacock. But I think in the later years, things improved because he gave them a lot of business. We printed books up there by Stephen Leacock.

The ones I remember, they were paperback books, you know, and there was one with a red cover and I think it was about the early history of Montreal, because I set some of that type and when I set that type I was astonished to find that he wrote about the slave market in Montreal and other things.

FRED PERIGO

HATLEY'S   My grandfather had the butcher and grocery store. It was just called Hatley's. I knew Leacock was in there and they'd be sort of chuckling over the things he said or did, but I couldn't tell you what they were.

I do remember seeing Leacock on the main street, with an old coon coat on, and with Stevie, who was, of course,

dwarfed. He used to sort of dress Stevie the same as he did himself, you know, in the big hat and all this.

He was a great man for organizing things and having lists of exactly how you were to do this, that, and the other thing. I think he was really rude to the clerks and looked down on the help in the stores, but I never heard of him being rude to the help in there. I don't remember that. My father and two uncles took over the store—they probably would look after him when he came in.

Hatley's was a large store; it had the first refrigeration plant north of Toronto, it was a huge thing. And it had a lot of rooms. And they had their meat in these rooms. There were about five of these rooms in the basement of the store.

And then there was the grocery store and you'd go in and write down and give your order. Everything was written down or you could phone and it would be delivered. And they delivered all around Lake Couchiching.

There were two stores and a doorway between them. The office was between them. One was the grocery store and one was the butcher store. There were long counters and people would go in and there'd be a big case with cheese in it and another barrel with pickles and, at the back, people were bringing the fish in and they'd clean them there.

And there were always a lot of squaws around, waiting for the train to go back to Rama Reserve on Saturday night. They'd be Ojibways. And they'd be down there with their baskets waiting to go back to Rama.

The deer hunters, in the fall, would

go up and then they'd come back with their catch and there was always animals hanging outside the store, rabbits and bear. And they would cut the meat up for them, they butchered it.

At Christmas, people would order their spiced beef and it would be just piled up. Then they had these butchers' blocks that they cut up the meat on. It was really a big, old store. I think in days gone by it was *the* grocery and butcher shop of Orillia—the important one. It was more expensive, mind you, than some places in town. It was around 1869 that Grandad started it and it was 1945, I think, when my last uncle sold it.

I used to hear stories of my grandfather going delivering groceries over to Leacock's. I don't know what he went for—whether it was to deliver groceries or to have a little nip when he went in with them.

I remember, probably in the 1930s, I was down at my uncle's for dinner one Sunday at noon and the phone rang and it was Stephen Leacock. Someone had run over one of his chickens and he wanted to bring it in, I suppose to have it drawn, so he could eat it, because he didn't want to waste his chicken.

I just kept hearing little things like that. He might want groceries at a peculiar hour of the day or on weekends. I think he was a real character and very demanding.

BETH HATLEY

OFF TO HATLEY'S   Leacock liked to have his own home-grown produce and I think part of the fun for him was to go to Hatley's in Orillia. They were a very old Orillia family. I think the Hatley's were all friends, too, of Stephen Leacock's.

He'd buy cheese for instance; they had beautiful cheese, coffee that was hand-ground, and lamb.

There was a very good butcher in Hatley's store. It was an old butcher shop with sawdust all over the floor and big barrels of all sorts of things which you sampled if you wanted something. Pickles in barrels and crackers. The butcher knew what everyone in town liked. Leacock liked lamb. Local lamb has always been very good in our area and that was one of the things he looked forward to when he came to Orillia.

We also had chicken a lot when we went to dinner. You would have some soup and you would have trout and you would have chicken. He liked fish. He enjoyed catching trout and serving it. I would imagine that Kelly's wife, Tina, she would be doing pies—fresh fruit pies, like blueberries. And he had raspberry canes, so there'd be raspberries.

I think one of the few places he ever went in town was Hatley's.

DODE SPENCER and
ELIZABETH BURROWS LANGDON

WALKING TO TOWN   He went into town. I remember walking along beside him on the Atherley Road. We walked to town together—more than once, anyway. If he wanted to go to town, he walked. I would say that would be going on for two miles from out there.

FRED PERIGO

BUYING VICK'S BREAD   My grandfather started a grocery store and a bake shop and the mill at the park. The store was called George Vick & Sons. He made the first loaf of baker's bread made in Orillia. And later he was in competition with Leslie Frost's grandfather or father, I'm not sure which.

They had a large window in the front of the store, of course, and that was full of this baking—buns and fruitcake and something called butterfly tarts with a little cream in it, and chocolate éclairs and cream puffs and pound cake and so on, and all kinds of bread, which was famous all over the countryside.

They took bread up to the resorts in Muskoka in the summer by truck and sent it by rail in big wooden boxes to various stores in the area. This started in 1852 and, eventually, my father was the only one left in the family and he sold out in 1929.

This period I'm talking about was about 1900 to 1925, I think. Right into the Leacock period. Oh, he would buy Vick's bread.

DORA NOY

THE UNKNOWN STEPHEN LEACOCK
He wasn't always recognized in Orillia. One day he was in the Bank of Montreal and my father was in there, Harry Outridge, and Leacock yelled at him. He said, "Harry, you come over and identify me. This chap at the bank here won't cash my cheque!" That's right. This was, I'd say, maybe about 1938 to 1940. Let's not forget that some of Leacock's cheques had bounced. I'm just suggesting that maybe this is why.

HILDA OUTRIDGE

THE HOBO AND THE LITTLE FRENCH GOVERNESS   I was working with Red Flannery. Mr. Heward used to own the point up there. We were trimming trees for him and the professor. That was Heward's Point. We were trimming the trees so the man could see off his verandah and see the boats there on the lake. He was, I believe, a retired sea captain, or something, from England. Used to come over here every, oh, maybe ten to fifteen years. He liked to see the water and we were using a horse and wagon to draw the brush away.

This was in the mid-1930s. Mr. Heward had a little French girl as governess—she came from France to look after his boy and girl. The children used to ride on the wagon with us and she had to travel everywhere they went. And we bumped into the professor when we were dumping a load of brush off. He was trying to persuade her to go to the corn roast and he wasn't succeeding, so he invited us to his corn roast too. So I informed him that I wasn't interested in going to any corn roast in a hobo jungle, because that's what he resembled as far as I was concerned. He had an old battered-up felt hat on, an old tattered coat, and so forth, and he just chuckled when I said that.

And he said that they were going to hold the corn roast on the lakeshore over at the Leacock place, Old Brewery Bay, and I said, "Well I don't imagine you'll get away with it because I don't think Professor Leacock would approve of you having a corn roast on his property." I still didn't know who I was talking to.

And after he had left, a fellow I was working with, he told me that it was Professor Leacock that I was talking to. He wanted the little French governess to come to the corn roast by herself. She was a real shapely little doll and her words in English were very few and far between.

Flannery, that I was working with, was having a big laugh about that too, about me telling Leacock that he wouldn't approve of having a corn roast in his own place. None of us attended it.

BOB KILBY

I HAVEN'T GOT A THING TO GIVE THIS POOR GUY   One time—this is some years ago, you mind, when the hoboes used to come around for a sandwich—we had just finished dinner. This chap was coming down the driveway and my wife looked up and said, "Oh, my gosh, lunch is all over and I haven't got a thing to give this poor guy!" Well, I kinda took a second look, and, why, that's Stephen Leacock!

So, anyway, I get out to the door and walked out the door and he says, "Hyah, George" and he put the hand out. And my wife thought, who in the world! Evidently he'd run outa gas and the boat was up along the shore. So he come in and wanted to see if there was any chance he could have a couple of gallons of gas. So I said, "Sure, I got a can, there's about two gallons, maybe better, in it." And he took it up to the boat.

"Now," he says, "I'll send this back to you in a couple of days." So I said, "Fine, Stephen, that's dandy." I called him Stephen when we were fishin' and that and he liked it. He got so much "professor" that he was kinda fed up on it, ya know.

Anyway, the can didn't come back for a week or so, and I happened to see

him one day and I said, "Say, drop that gas can of mine someday, will ya, I could use it." The gas can come back full right to the top—five gallons of gas!

My wife thought he was a hobo— the way he was dressed—come for a hand-out, the old shirt, sleeves rolled up, open down the front, and a tie for a belt. That was Stephen—always a good inch of whisker on him, ya know.

GEORGE MOASE

A GRACIOUS LETTER   My brother died in 1938 and Stephen Leacock wrote to my father and said:

H. Outridge, Esq.
Orillia

Dear Harry:

I have been deeply grieved to hear of your sad loss. Please accept the sympathy of one of your oldest friends and I am sure that at such a time, it means something to you to know that old friends are thinking of you and sympathizing in your sorrow.

Very sincerely,
Stephen Leacock.

HILDA OUTRIDGE

CHAPTER TWELVE

The Humourist: A Mingled Heritage of Tears and Laughter

MEETING G.K. CHESTERTON   Stephen and I played a game of billiards at the Cambridge Club in London in 1919 and were joined afterwards by G.K. Chesterton, the English writer of great distinction and humour, who wished to have a chat with Stephen and, of course, the game had to wait.

And this is what Stephen said then and G.K. Chesterton was most enthusiastic about it. He said that, in its larger aspect, humour is blended with pathos until the two are one, and represent, as they have in every age, the mingled heritage of tears and laughter, that is our lot on earth.

GLADSTONE MURRAY

HOW HIS FIRST BOOK GOT INTO PRINT   Stephen had written a great deal for different magazines—*Truth*, *Life*, and lots of those, and once in 1909, when I was in Montreal, he had all this stuff catalogued and piled up in the sitting room.

I think he and B.K. Sandwell had got it together, but they had never done anything about it. I said to Stephen, "Why don't you publish it?" "Publish it?" he said. I said, "I'll see what we can do about it."

So I went down to a news company in Montreal and I showed it to them and I said I would like to find out what it would cost. "Oh, well," the man said to me, "if we would publish it in a small book it wouldn't sell for more than thirty-five cents." Anyway, I said all right. And he said, "The most we could get out would be say 1,000 copies or maybe 2,000 copies—you'd be lucky. You'd have an outlay of say $500 to start with.

And I said, "What would it cost?" "Well," he said, "it'll cost you twenty-eight cents a copy" and that left a margin of seven cents, if it sold at thirty-five cents.

So I went back to Stephen and I said, "He'll publish it. It's going to cost us twenty-eight cents a book and that gives us a margin of seven cents. I will be responsible for that money and I will take five cents and you get two cents for the books." Which is fair enough.

Stephen said, "That's all right, George. I'll do that."

So I put in an order, and at that time I was travelling a great deal and I was away, and I got a letter from Stephen and he said, "Dear George: I don't think this thing will be much. Enclosed please find my cheque for $500 and I will take it over."

And he took it over and it was published, and the first 1,000 or 2,000 copies of *Literary Lapses* were sold almost immediately.

GEORGE LEACOCK

HE WROTE WHEREVER HE HAD A PEN
It was quite some time before Stephen really got into the big money, if you could call it big money. He did a lot of writing in his later years at his own summer home at Orillia. But, originally, most of his writing was done in Montreal in the Côte des

Staff at Upper Canada College, 1897. Leacock, with moustache, is standing at the back, seventh from the left, wearing a bow tie. *Courtesy of the Stephen Leacock Memorial Home.*

Neiges Road house. But then, Stephen wrote wherever he had a pen. He once said to me, "George, I am going down to Montreal this winter and I'm taking nothing but $200 dollars and my pen, and that will keep me very well through the winter."

I always thought that *Sunshine Sketches of a Little Town* was about all the little towns in Canada, and I think Stephen meant it to be and I don't find them changed very much.

GEORGE LEACOCK

THE HO-HUM DAYS AT UPPER CANADA COLLEGE   Stephen Leacock began teaching me French in the year 1891 at Upper Canada College. He was a good teacher, but I don't think he was very deeply interested in it. As a matter of fact, he was just trying to earn enough money to get his Ph.D. He was much more amusing out of school than he was in school. We boys all knew that he was writing for New York comic papers, and now and again we would get him to read us things that he was doing for them. But he never allowed that sort of thing to interfere with his classes.

B.K. SANDWELL

HE READ HIS WORK ALOUD   He got up around five or six o'clock, made his pot of tea—did a lot of writing. So, by the time we were all down and had sort of assembled, had our breakfast and coffee, he would have several manuscripts or piles of sheets of paper that he had been writing and he'd come in and say, "George, I want you to hear this. Mary, sit down, now, just sit down over there."

And he'd get up in front of the fire and start reading. Well, that was the best way, of course, to absorb anything he had written. He read in his lovely voice, using his hands a great deal, and walked up and down as he read it, laughing and enjoying his jokes.

"George, I want you to hear this. Isn't this priceless, now Mary, isn't this good?" And that's the way it went. And that really was an experience, to hear him read what he had written.

MRS. MARY LEACOCK,
(GEORGE LEACOCK'S WIFE)

DRIP, DRIP, DRIP   He used to write his books in the sun gallery at the back of the house at Old Brewery Bay. It was raining very hard and he discovered the gallery was leaking, so he sent Kelly to the hardware store to buy some pails. And I don't know how many pails Kelly arrived with. So he hung them all up under the drips to catch the water. Instead of fixing the roof, he left the pails there all summer.

AUBREY GAUDAUR

UP IN THE MORNING BEFORE DAY-LIGHT   He would go to bed very early when he was going to write. And then he would maybe get up by one o'clock or so in the middle of the night. We would never see him and lots of times we would be up early and he would still be writing. And then he would go for a walk. See Mrs. Shaw or whatever. Then he'd come back and have breakfast, maybe seven o'clock or eight. Lunchtime was at noon and dinner six-thirty to seven.

HILDA ELSLIGER

Stephen Leacock graduating as head boy at Upper Canada College, 1887. *Courtesy of the Orillia Public Library.*

WALKING AROUND THE DINNER TABLE, TALKING   You know his working habits—he used to get up every morning about five o'clock or five-thirty and start working, and by noon he was pretty well through the day's work and then he'd go fishing if the weather was right. And once in a while, though he didn't care much for golf, he might make a stab at it.

He likely put on dinner parties at night. And then he'd tell his stories. And often at night at dinner, he would tell us the stories that he was going to be writing the next morning and he'd be trying them out on us. And he'd walk around the dinner table and talk and talk and he was at his very best, really. And he'd probably have a couple of drinks but he certainly wasn't tight or drunk or anything. And he'd go to bed about nine o'clock or nine-thirty.

HENRY JANES

IN PRAISE OF *SUNSHINE SKETCHES*
Sunshine Sketches is the best and that's the only one that was sold internationally. *Nonsense Novels*, which isn't really that funny, is not in the same category. I knew instinctively when I read it that it wasn't as good as the first.

HAL LAWRENCE

WHAT'S PERFECT, ANYWAY?   The philosophy of that trip on the *Mariposa Belle* was magnificent. All the people on the shady side rushed over to the sunny side because they hadn't come to freeze, and the people on the sunny side rushed to the shady side because they hadn't come to be hot.

I think that's a perfect description of life, isn't it—in a very simple way?

NORAH BASTEDO

SPEEDY BICYCLE KING   My favourite Leacock episode, from *Sunshine Sketches of a Little Town* is the account of the young bank teller who was madly in love with the beautiful daughter of a local judge. The judge had a handsome house, halfway down a steep hill. The teller, wildly infatuated, bicycled down the hill in the frantic hope of catching a glimpse of the gorgeous damsel sitting on the porch. Unfortunately, he became so wrought up, and pedalled so furiously, that in his excitement he tore by the house in a

streak, hanging onto the handlebars for dear life, and the bicycle zoomed downhill at a breakneck speed.

It's a great anecdote and it has always amused me—the way in which life eludes us.

ALLAN ANDERSON

A GREAT DAY FOR MOTHER   I just loved his story about Mother's Day. The family decided that Mother had to be honoured on Mother's Day. They decided to have a picnic in honour of Mother. And Mother would have to cook the chicken and get the picnic all ready and pack it nicely so that the whole family could enjoy Mother's Day with Mother's picnic.

So, poor Mother worked so hard getting the picnic ready that she was too exhausted to go on the picnic. She was very glad to wave all the family good-bye and stay home and rest while they were at the picnic. And, I guess, Mother had to do the dishes.

I thought that was kind of a symbol of Stephen Leacock's humour and fun. And humanity, really.

PAUL PHELAN

A PRETTY LONG ROAD TO GO   I'd ask him about writing, you know, and things like that. Oh yeah, I asked him, I was kind of a mouthy kid, I guess.

And he'd tell me, "Oh," he said "that's a pretty long road to go; it's a long hard road before you get it." He told me he was writing for *Maclean's* and he was just beginning to make money.

"Yeah" he said, "that's a long hard road." But he'd talk to me and we'd chat.

And another thing he did, when I left—I

had to go back to school, you see—it'd be in September—he said, "Fred, I want to give you something. Now here's three books," he said, "I enjoyed them very much." One was called *Stalky and Company* and it was about three guys that went to an English public school, and then I think he gave me a book of Conan Doyle's called *The White Company*, and I can't think of the third book. I think this *White Company* is something about the Mormons or something. I don't know what it was now.

But he signed those books—he gave them to me. I read them. Oh, I read them, yes, sure; and I enjoyed them. I was a good reader then—I was only fourteen.

I put them in my mother's bookcase and had them for years, and then my father died and my mother was living alone and my nephew and his wife came in there. Towards the last seven years of my mother's life, she lived with my wife and myself—but my nephew and his wife, they got the bookcase with the books. I guess they threw all the books out, because the last time I saw that bookcase she had it painted white and she had dishes in it.

FRED PERIGO

SPECTACLES AND STORIES   He always read aloud his articles or his books, piece by piece, to any of us who happened to be around. There was a sort of exultation in his spirits then, as over a thing well done. "Fetch me that manuscript on my study table," he would ask me (I'd usually find it somewhere else), "and my spectacles—I don't know where." So many of his stories I've heard

him read as he stood before the fire, either in the living room in the Orillia house or in his study in Montreal. I can always hear his rich and full-toned voice as I read anything he has written. I can hear the laughter that went with it—can feel the pauses of emphasis. I remember especially well the night he read *My Remarkable Uncle* to us. A group of my young friends were gathered that evening around the fire. Uncle Stephen appeared about midnight, clad in dressing gown and slippers and smoking a pipe, after two or three hours of sleep. He liked going off to bed early, often just after dinner, with his book and spectacles—to reappear a few hours later if there was any one still up to talk to. If not, he'd cut himself a hunk of cheese and crackers at the sideboard and go off to bed again.

BARBARA NIMMO

HE'D SIZE YOU UP FAST   Stephen Leacock was a man of very high intelligence. He'd only need to meet a person once before he could size them up and write about them.

REDVERS L. STUBLEY

TEA AND BREAD   Professor Leacock always appeared to be a man with endless leisure time, which he generously and genially shared with all his students. But this time was purchased at a price. He used to rise at five o'clock or five-thirty in the morning, then he would seat himself at his desk, a little tea and bread at his elbow, and begin to write. Then about seven o'clock he would call me up and we would take a walk around the mountain. He'd wear whatever clothes were closest— generally the dinner jacket that he had worn the evening before—and then he'd go back to his writing until noon.

JOHN CULLITON

NEW HATS GALORE His agent in New York was Paul Reynolds and Leacock would get these telegrams; please send so many words as soon as possible. Dr. Leacock would say, "You'd think all you had to do was turn on the tap to write humourous stories."

In those days you could take a letter, which would be the short story, to the Windsor station and it would be delivered the next morning in New York.

Stephen Leacock wrote every morning. It would take him an hour and a half or two hours to write a short story. He had a big old table—he didn't use a desk—and he would sit down and write at this table. It was one clutter. He wrote in longhand all the time. I would read it, and I would type it and then I would take a taxi down to the Windsor station and put it in the mail, and it got delivered in New York the next day. Very often, this required typing at night to get it finished and get it down to the mail. Whenever I did this he would give me ten dollars or whatever, and he'd always say, "Buy yourself a hat." There were a lot of other things I would have liked to have had but if he said buy a hat, I bought a hat. In those days you could get quite a good-looking hat for around ten dollars. I had a cupboard full of hats.

GRACE REYNOLDS

NOT A WORKAHOLIC I certainly wouldn't regard him as a compulsive worker—far from a workaholic, to use the modern expression. It's true, that he had unusual work habits. He would do some of his best writing from 6:00 to 9:00 A.M., or something like that.

On the other hand, he treasured his relaxation. He didn't have to work as hard as most people to achieve what he achieved. He didn't really spend a lot of time preparing his lectures—he didn't stay up late nights working over tomorrow's lecture. Literally, he was quite correct when he said that his whole life was a preparation for his lectures. So, most of the things that he did he was able to do with relatively little effort and without the kind of effort that would have commanded so much from other people.

And even when he was writing, he didn't go to great lengths to make inductive research-type studies that would involve evening after evening in the library. His writings were the kind of things that, with his talent, he could do without the kind of effort that university people normally make. As a matter of fact, one of Leacock's favourite stories would be of the university professor who spent the first ten years of his career preparing to write learned pieces on a subject, the second ten years of his career writing the thing, and the third ten years revising it, you know. And finally a posthumous edition would appear and this was his life's work. I heard him tell that story many times.

He would quip about the kinds of things that university professors do in their writing. In fairness to an understanding of Leacock, one of his motivations was making enough money to provide financial security for his son. As a consequence of which, he did a lot of his writing very quickly. It shows; there's a certain amount of unevenness because he wrote quickly.

He didn't bother to polish it, or revise it or rewrite it, or put it away and come back to it later on. He dashed it off and maybe would make a few changes.

He would seldom rewrite anything. I've seen some of his manuscripts and you know, it was all done like that. There was very little editing or revision or anything else like that. But he had a very good command of the English language. He was quite articulate.

One thing in recollection that surprises me. He once told me that when he was an after-dinner speaker, he would never eat dinner—the chicken or steak that they were serving—because it would interfere with his ability to speak. And he always had a little nervousness or apprehension. Perhaps some people feel that you have to be nervous to be a good speaker, but you'd think somebody as accomplished as Leacock wouldn't worry about a thing like that.

I was quite surprised by that, because, in recollection, he seemed to be doing everything so casually and so easily.

But I would not rate him as a hard worker; he had too mellow and happy a philosophy of life to be a hard worker.

PHILIP VINEBERG

MRS. LEACOCK WENT HOME He would never let Mrs. Leacock be in the audience. He could sense that she was there and he used to make little scribbles on the cuff that didn't mean anything but it was part of his act. He'd make his apologies and then he would say to Mrs. Leacock, "Would you please leave."

GRACE REYNOLDS

AN ARDUOUS CONTRIVANCE
Leacock once said that, "There is no trouble in writing a scientific treatise on the folklore of Central China or a statistical enquiry into the declining population of Prince Edward Island, but to write something out of one's own mind, worth reading for its own sake, is an arduous contrivance only to be achieved in fortunate moments, few and far between."

He may have been fooling himself about this, because the whole bent of his mind was towards a whimsical view of the delicious foibles of life, and I think this kind of writing often came to him as easily as picking peas in his garden.

ALLAN ANDERSON

THE RIPPLING FOUNTAIN He wrote with such ease that he could turn out an enormous amount of stuff with little work. Writing wasn't the kind of job that it is for some people, where you might have to do fifty whacks at the first page or something. And I speak with some feeling. On one occasion I had to do a particular job and I wrote the first page fifty times and was almost in despair.

I don't think Leacock would ever be like that. It just rippled out of him—it was like a fountain.

SENATOR EUGENE FORSEY

DOGGEREL UNCHAINED Once Leacock received an invitation written by his hostess in doggerel verse:

If you are free,
For a sort of spree
At eight o'clock, April the seventh
There'll be some food

Gingerale and Vermouth
And possibly conversation
Maybe they'll sing; Maybe they'll play
We really can't tell at all
But a word in reply,
On which to rely,
Would considerably help the cook.

He replied in kind:

If I were free,
That kind of spree
Appeals to me.
Gin and Vermouth
Hits me at the root
In short, I am long
On Wine, Women and Song
But here is The Rub
The Graduates Club
Sherbrooke St. West
Have made me their guest
That night at a show
And I've got to go.
But if all of the graduates are tight enough,
soon enough,
And supposing you still have got gin enough,
room enough,
Still a drink, still a smile, still singing and
laughter,
Perhaps you'll allow me to come along after.

ARCHIVES
STEPHEN LEACOCK MEMORIAL HOME

HERE'S MR. LEAROYD   I don't know about my classmates, but I remember I read a great many of Leacock's books and enjoyed them. I still can chuckle over some of the episodes when he lectured in England, for example, in the parish church. Now if you go back to the book you may find I am not remembering accurately, but in his comments on being introduced there by the secretary of the society he said, "I'd be glad to receive your fees. You know these speakers are very expensive."

Then, whether it was in the book or one of his anecdotes, he tells about a person who introduced him to an audience and said, "Ladies and gentlemen, our speaker's name is a household word, I have much pleasure in introducing to you Mr. Learoyd."

MAYSIE MacSPORRAN

A SUPERB TALENT FOR FUN   I think he was interested in the human side of the thing, but I think had he wanted to, he could have done superb work simply as an abstract intellectual writer on either political science or economics. But I don't think he wanted to; I don't think he was prepared to do it.

He had this wonderful facility for speaking, he had this wonderful capacity for lecturing; he would seize in a moment the whole point of a large book and he had this amazing capacity to communicate. And he had this superb talent for fun. And so the easy thing was to let this superb talent for fun take over.

SENATOR EUGENE FORSEY

TOO MUCH WRITING TOO QUICKLY
I'm sure he read enormously and voraciously; I think he had such a lively turn of mind.

I would consider that his writing is uneven because it was often, I feel, turned out just on the spur of the moment, in answer to a plea and not particularly considered. He was a very convivial man. A great deal of the time he was enjoying life at the club with his buddies, and teaching is very exhausting and demanding and he didn't give up his teaching career when he discovered he had a fortune in his pen.

I think he said somewhere that when he was teaching at Upper Canada he discovered that he had no fortune in his face but he had a fortune in his head. I always enjoyed that: "My fortune was not in my face but in my head."

MAYSIE MacSPORRAN

IN THE GREAT TRADITION   Leacock belongs to the really great humourous writers of history. He is really in the train that began with Aristophanes, went on to Molière and then to Mark Twain.

GLADSTONE MURRAY

THE SIMPLICITY OF HIS SENTENCES
The thing he really taught me was how to use the English language. If you look at the simplicity of Leacock sentences, they're marvellous to read. Except for the vocabulary, they're as simple as the St. James version of the Bible. So I admired him for his language, for the breadth of his knowledge and the application of it, and the way he could simplify answers to people.

I remember he was talking about an era when people knew little about the planets and he said, in those days, people thought the world was simple. There was up for Heaven and down for Hell, and you were in between. And if people ask where is heaven, his answer was, "It isn't in 'a where."

HERBERT H. TEES

HIS AWFUL HANDWRITING   His handwriting was pretty awful. Here's one

letter I can read with ease. He was at the Royal Victoria Hospital—it was April 28, 1938. He was ill; I don't remember what it was. "Dear Carl. Best thanks for your note. I hope soon to be out of here as a reconditioned 1938 model of a professor—four cylinders. Good luck to your inter-provincial labours. Yours sincerely, Stephen Leacock."

A year before that, I had apparently sent him some documents and this is his acknowledgement: "Dear Goldenberg. Thank you ever so much. These look to be documents of extraordinary interest and value. I can take about one page of your economics, dilute it with twenty gallons of talk, and about sixty drops of pure humour, and sell it anywhere as extract of Canadian patriotism. Thank you. Very sincerely. Stephen Leacock."

SENATOR H. CARL GOLDENBERG

HE TAUGHT AT McGILL?   I've done a great deal of travelling and the American people whom I met in my travels had not heard of him as an economist. The world knew him, primarily, as a humourist, for the great number of books he had written, and not as an economist at all.

They were surprised to hear that he had taught at McGill University.

MARGARET STEPHEN

EXECUTIONS FOR SENILITY   I can't say that I read everything he ever wrote. I thought most of it was of a very high standard of its kind. One little thing he did that didn't strike me as particularly brilliant was *Hellements of Hickonomics*, which I thought was rather a failure. But most of his stuff I thought was extremely good.

And, of course, some of the things that he did privately, were even funnier. I don't know if there is a record anywhere of his description at the Political Economy Club of the executions for senility at McGill University. Oh, that was marvellous!

He came to a farewell dinner at the Political Economy Club and he read out a piece on the executions for senility at McGill University. There were thirteen senior professors, who, in December, 1935, received a letter which said, "Dear Professor So-and-So. Under the statutes of the university, members of the staff retire at sixty-five, the university reserving the right to retain the services of those it considers of sufficient value. You will retire June 1, 1936. Yours truly, So-and-So, Secretary, Board of Governors." Now that was all. These were men and women of international reputation—many, if not all of them. Sounds incredible, but you can find the text of it there in black and white. It is true it was in the statutes, but it hadn't been enforced for years.

Well, then he did this thing on the executions for senility at McGill University. And one professor after another was brought up before the court and charged. And he had the most enormous fun. He had Professor Walter, the professor of German, brought up and charged with senility. A particular charge was that he had put on a German play in German. The defence's plea that it was not really German was rejected out of hand by the court on sworn evidence of one of the audience that he had distinctly heard the words "Ein glass beer."

And he told it with the tears running down his face with laughter and just shaking from head to foot. And the rest of us who were listening were in exactly the same shape—we could hardly hold ourselves upright. It was the funniest thing I have ever heard. This was in 1936.

The retirements were absolutely ludicrous, beyond reason. And of course it held the governors up to the most awful ridicule. These were eminent people who were being fired simply because they reached a particular age and the charges against whom were, of course, obviously perfect nonsense.

What a way to do the thing—what a way to behave! What a letter to write! Good gracious!

SENATOR EUGENE FORSEY

THE $150 COMMISSION   One of the editors of *Fortune* called me just towards the end of the war, when it looked like peace was going to be coming soon, to ask if I could get Stephen Leacock to write about a thousand words for them on the world of the future. And they would pay him a dollar a word.

So I wrote to the doctor and I got a letter back from him saying he was too busy, he couldn't undertake to write this article, and thanking me very much for thinking of him and then suggesting that I come up and see him and go fishing.

So I went up to Old Brewery Bay and there was no help around, the place was cold and really run-down. Little Stevie was there but he was practically no use. The first thing I did when I got there was get an axe and a saw and wheelbarrow and go out and try and get some firewood to put on a great fire and warm the place. It was almost an impossible job to winterize it and he had his house in Montreal, you see.

But, anyway, he told me flatly that he couldn't do this article for the *Fortune* series. That night he stayed up late, the first time I knew him to do that. Well, I got up early in the morning, because the house was so cold, and when I got downstairs about five-thirty, he was already out in the back porch with a heavy coat on and hat and he was writing.

I didn't want to interrupt him, but I put on the stove in the kitchen and got some hot water and stuff. He already had his own invention for getting breakfast. He had a tea kettle with a couple of eggs in it on an old toaster and an alarm clock beside it. And when the alarm clock went off, he put the water on cold and he had it figured out that when the alarm clock went off, the eggs were hard-boiled, or boiled anyway, so he could eat them. And he'd break them on a couple pieces of bread. Or he might take a soup plate and break two or three slices of bread up in it and pour hot milk and water over it.

And the kettle that he boiled eggs in—he would make tea in it and he would keep working while he had a little breakfast. Tea rather than coffee.

Well, anyway, this morning he worked away and I kept the fire going. I was in the living room; he was out in the old back place where he used to write and the roof was leaking there.

About eleven o'clock he came in and he said, "There it is." And I wondered what he was talking about and here was the article for *Fortune*.

So I got it on its way to *Fortune* and I didn't think any more about it. But about three or four months later I was up there again and saw him and after he had greeted me he disappeared into his little study and

came out in a couple of minutes with a cheque for $150 made out to me, and I asked him what this was for. *Fortune* magazine had paid him a dollar and a half a word for the article that he had done the morning some months before. The $150 was supposed to be my literary commission on it.

HENRY JANES

TWO TOES TALES   He showed me an article—I think it was in the *Saturday Evening Post*—I looked at it and I would never say to Leacock that I didn't think anything he had written was not the best, but I seem to remember he thought I wasn't duly impressed and he said, "Look, all I have to do is put a pen between two toes and I'll be paid $500 for what results therefrom."

SENATOR H. CARL GOLDENBERG

UNTIL WE MEAT AGAIN   When Joan, my sister, was a volunteer worker at the Toronto General Hospital during the war, she used to help take meals up to the rooms. When they were being given the trays to carry around she was standing beside the girl who was supposed to take it up to Stephen Leacock, so she asked if she could switch. She said she would like to take his tray.

So she arrived in Stephen's room and introduced herself and Stephen chatted away, and she put the tray down and he lifted the little warming lid on the tray and there was a little cockroach running around, or some kind of creature, and Stephen just looked at it and he said, "Well, that's the first meat I've seen since I've got into this place!"

And that must have been not long before he died, I suppose.

CATHERINE DRINKWATER

CHAPTER THIRTEEN

Fond Memories

THE BLEURY STREET BOOKSHOP I was about fifteen when I first met Stephen Leacock in Montreal. This was around 1931. I had a second-hand bookshop on Bleury Street. My father was Joseph Melzack.

It was a typical second-hand bookshop—shelves from floor to ceiling, tables overflowing, not terribly small, one big room only. It was just below Dorchester. We had gone into that store in 1930; I had another store on Bleury Street, but that was a real firetrap and I was anxious to get out. We stayed in the second one until 1938.

My father put up the money—I was thirteen. Needless to say, I had no money. He had sold an insurance policy to get the money; he'd cashed it in. And with that $800 he opened the bookshop. The first few years were really rough.

He continued working in the factory; he was a factory worker until about 1934 or 1935, and then the two of us worked in the store.

There were shelves around the whole periphery of the shop and, in the centre, I think there were four tables, rather large tables to fill up the centre and all new arrivals went on those tables. We also had a stand outside where the books were ten cents, take your choice. And

when it rained, of course, we yanked them in in a hurry.

I drew fifty cents a week for the first three or four years and that was my salary. In fact, when I got married in 1939 I was drawing eighteen dollars a week, so you can see that it wasn't that terribly profitable. In those days, fifty cents, seventy-five cents, a dollar, was a lot of money for a book. Occasionally, if you found a nice binding, you'd mark it two or three dollars, depending on what I had to pay for it. Five dollars was way out. I mean, nobody would pay you that.

Stephen Leacock came in one Saturday and he didn't tell us who he was and I had a few nice bindings and he bought them all—the whole lot—and he said, "Call me if you ever get any more," and he gave me his card.

And I was very pleased to meet Professor Stephen Leacock. He was a very nice man. He wasn't tall, he had a big shock of hair, he had a moustache, and he was very kindly. He must have taken pity on me—here's this kid, fifteen years old, running a bookshop.

He asked me what I was reading. And I said, "Oh, well, I've finished all the Hentys—read 'em all." He said, "What else are you reading?" I said I was reading Bulwer-Lytton; I remember that. And he said, "Well, you can do better than that." I said, "What do you think I ought to read?" He said, "Have you tried Sherlock Holmes?" I hadn't—I hadn't even got it. He said, "I'll lend you a copy." And the next time he came in he lent me a copy and I read it and I loved it. And after that I went through all the Conan Doyle books.

Leacock came along and I guess he had pity on me; he could see the kind of store that it was and he helped me—he helped me a great deal. As I say, it's over fifty years ago, so my memories are not very vivid, but I do remember him as a very kind man and willing to help this poor sap running a bookshop who knew nothing about books. He came in almost every Saturday.

You see, I went into the store having just finished public school; that was the extent of my education. And that's why this education, this guidance I got from Leacock was so important to me.

I remember one Saturday morning he came because I phoned him. I'd bought a big collection of books from someone who died. I said, "I've got a lot of beautiful books here." And he said, "I'll be right down." He rushed down immediately and took almost all the books.

He had a car. I don't remember the kind of car, but I was impressed. It was a big, high car. He wasn't a rich man and he never dressed like a rich man. In fact, his dress was not very impressive. I never saw him in a gown, but I saw him in a coon coat when he used to come here in the winter. Montreal winters could be very cold.

He used to talk to me and I guess he liked to see a mind sort of opening, and he helped it to open by virtually telling me what to read and then asking me how I enjoyed them; why I liked them.

It was marvellous, I had a private teacher for awhile; for a very short while, of course. Generally he stayed around for about an hour.

He had very eclectic taste. When I'd get a collection, as I say, this one collection I remember—he bought almost half of them. And these were a couple of hundred books. So he bought 100 books that day. But that didn't occur very often.

You know the trouble with the second-hand bookshop in those days: you had to wait for somebody to die before you got a book. If anyone asked you for a dictionary, you didn't have it because nobody had died who'd had a dictionary. That's why I went into the new-book business. I realized that I couldn't stay in a business as indefinite and as uncertain as the second-hand book business.

Leacock was interested in fine books, handsome books. I know for sure that he bought hundreds of books from me, and I was not his only source of books. He bought many books from England as well. He used to love poring over catalogues. What happened to the books I don't know. Much of it I believe is at McGill—I hope it's at McGill—I know that his house was sold to some speculator, who then sold it again.

But my memories of Leacock are of the kindest variety and he was good to me. He tried to help me. There was no need for him to go out of his way to help this bookseller.

Everybody who met him in the store loved him. My father loved him. And also he was a wonderful customer.

You could call him and he'd come immediately and buy anything that was good. I never saw him after 1938, when I got out of the second-hand book business.

LOUIS MELZACK

OFF TO EUROPE   The doctor thought it would be good for young Stephen to have sea air and a trip abroad and they had Prohibition in the United States, so the whole kit and caboodle of us, Mr. and Mrs. Herbert Shaw and their little girl, and Dr. Leacock and young Stephen, and myself and what seemed like the whole of McGill University, all the professors were on a ship going to England. I went along primarily to look after young Stephen.

When we got to Plymouth, instead of taking the train with the rest of the people, we stayed at Plymouth. Dr. Leacock said to me, "This is your first trip to Europe, and I want you to be able to remember a lot of things that will never happen again in your life."

In Plymouth there was a winding road down to the sea, all flowers on either side, and we went down this path and when we got to the bottom Dr. Leacock said Drake was playing a rubber of bowls when the Great Armada came and Drake said "They must wait their turn, good souls," and stooped and finished the game. I didn't know what the Armada was, so this was the history lesson.

Then we went up to London and we stayed in the Cecil Hotel and Dr. Leacock arranged to take Mrs. Shaw to the theatre and Mr. Shaw and I went to a place where we could have dinner and dance. Then the four of us met up and had *langouste*. That's lobster.

Then we went to Paris and Biarritz. He took me to the casino in Biarritz and he said that I could stay as long as the money he gave me lasted. So I put my money on and I was pulling in the chips and the little wheel went spinning around. I had lots of chips. Then all of a sudden things went into reverse and it was the croupier that was pulling in my chips. Let's say it was the equivalent of ten dollars, it didn't last very long, and I had to go back to the hotel. Dr. Leacock said, "Now, I want this to be a lesson to you that you never win at gambling."

GRACE REYNOLDS

THE INTERVIEW THAT CLICKED   In 1928 I had a job on the *Toronto Star* and I covered all kinds of stories, but the first thing they did was send me out of town that first day to Barrie.

And I did a story there and it involved Professor Leacock a little bit. There was a scandal in the church and there was a story in the old *Globe* about the minister firing the choirmaster because he was playing around with the women in the choir.

So I wrote this story and I sent it on the night wire to the *Star* and I thought, well, gee, it's Friday night and I'm pretty close to home, why can't I get home to Orillia for the weekend. I called my mother and asked her if she'd get me an appointment—I knew the professor would be back at Old Brewery Bay. So I told the city editor I could get an appointment with Stephen Leacock for an interview and I went to Orillia for the weekend.

Leacock, of course, didn't trust reporters at all, particularly a green one like me. And he dictated it—an interview. He was talking about the world of the future, and prospects, and things like that. I don't remember very much because he rattled it off so fast. And it went slap into the *Star*. They were delighted.

He and Howard Ferguson were classmates, and Mackenzie King, he knew. When I was on the *Star*, I got my first break through Mackenzie King by mentioning that I was a student of Stephen Leacock's.

This is how it happened. I was walking up from the old *Star* building at 80 King Street West, through the university grounds, and I saw the lights on in University College. And I went in to see what was going on and there was only one old reporter from the *Globe* there.

So I spoke to Mr. King and I mentioned that I had studied under Stephen Leacock and he said, "You wait around until the dinner's over and I'll get Sir William Mulock (it was a dinner for him) and we'll take you around the college and you can get some reminiscences from Sir William." Mulock was a famous politician, born in 1844. As a young reporter, it was an idea that I wouldn't have thought of, but Mr. King did.

So I did that, and when the thing was over, I went back to the *Star* and worked till about three o'clock on the story. And when I got in in the morning, I found there was a great hullabaloo going on because the *Star* hadn't assigned anybody to this important meeting. And the managing editor was giving the city editor hell for missing this news break, so

I gave my story to the wire editor and he gave it to the managing editor and in a few minutes the managing editor, H.C. Hindmarsh, came out. He sat my story down in front of the city editor and they ran it on the front page with a byline, and I got a ten-dollar-a-week raise.

But it was all thanks to Stephen Leacock, being able to use the professor's name with Mackenzie King.

HENRY JANES

COLLAPSE OF THE FRENCH FRANC
When I graduated from McGill with my Arts degree in 1935 I was awarded the Guy Drummond Fellowship. This gave me a year in France and, in those days, it was a very generous scholarship—far more than the Rhodes Scholarship or others. It was very well-endowed. Of course, you received your M.A. credit from McGill on doing it, and it was customary to write a thesis, which would then be printed by the university. And Leacock took a great interest in it. He immediately took me in hand—what was I going to do, what was I going to write about—and most of this was done by correspondence from Brewery Bay. He proposed certain alternative subjects for my consideration. One of them was even La Scandale de Stavisky, which was a commercial swindle of the times. And various and sundry other subjects. But I preferred to write on some aspect of economics. Of course, it was the custom for somebody taking the fellowship to study at l'Ecole Science Libre des Politiques.

Leacock corresponded with me continuously before I left to discuss what subject I wanted to take, and he guided me and we had an exchange of correspondence.

I have here, for example, a four-page letter—no date on it—it would have been written in 1935—and he was kind enough to start off this four-page letter by saying, "Dear Vineberg. I am so glad that you have taken the gold franc. It is a great chance. With your brains, you can, if you get keen on it, make a great hit." Then he goes on to tell me what I should do, and I should understand the earlier doctrine, and he gives me a lecture on some of the literature on the subject that I should first read, and so forth in great detail.

And when *The French Franc and the Gold Standard* was finally published, Stephen Leacock wrote the preface to the first edition. He speaks of the fact that the present monograph appears under the auspices of the Department of Economics. I had predicted that the French franc was going to be devalued. Leacock, in his preface, questions that because he was a great believer in the gold standard and he concludes, "But in differing in some measure with Mr. Vineberg's conclusion, I am only too glad to have been associated with the work he has done and very proud to think that the last of such monographs, prepared under my direction at McGill, should be such an excellent piece of work."

I was right about the French franc: it did collapse.

I might tell you that, after this was published, McGill University sponsored a lecture, which was chaired by Stephen Leacock, at which I spoke. And I can still remember Stephen Leacock's introduction. He started off, at one stage, by saying,

"Mr. Vineberg wrote a book on the French franc and it collapsed." And then at another stage, in explaining the collapse of the French franc and with a twinkle in his eye and bearing in mind that I'm Jewish, he said, "When the calming Anglo-Saxon influence of Mr. Vineberg was removed from the French scene, the currency went to pieces."

PHILIP VINEBERG

THE END OF JOHN MAYNARD KEYNES

In my time the noted economist, Irving Fisher, began to apply mathematics to an understanding of economics and he really began the School of Mathematical Economics. Leacock just hated that. He hated these tables and graphs and symbols.

I remember he said one day that he's not surprised that Irving Fisher started this new fad because Irving Fisher was a teetotaller. Leacock had no respect for teetotallers. "After all, what can you expect from a teetotaller?" That's what he said.

Anyway, John Maynard Keynes, the noted economist, was not a mathematical economist. One of his great books was *The General Theory of Employment, Interest and Money*. I was walking up McGill College Avenue, and there used to be the Montreal Book Room there, and I saw Keynes's book in the window. I rushed in and bought it; I think it was a big book, it cost $3.50 at the time, which was a lot of money for a book in those days in the mid-thirties.

And I rushed up to the Arts Building, ran into Leacock, and I said, "Dr. Leacock, I've just bought Keynes's new book." He said, "Let me look at it." Unfortunately he opened it at a page where Keynes had a few graphs and figures—the only pages in the book where he had them. Leacock threw the book down on the floor, turned to me, and said, "That's the end of John Maynard Keynes," and he walked away.

I'd keep in touch with him and tell him what I was doing. I stopped lecturing in 1936, practised law, but my career became a public career. I became an advisor to the Rowell-Sirois Commission. And then I was appointed, when I was barely thirty, chairman of the Royal Commission on the Finances of Winnipeg. I'm told that I was the youngest Royal Commissioner ever appointed in Canada.

I advised Leacock and here is his reply: "My Dear Carl. Best thanks. You are developing into a sort of permanent institution sitting on anything that defies hatching."

SENATOR H. CARL GOLDENBERG

OLD-FASHIONED HANDWRITING   I got my M.A. in 1932 and you didn't get jobs very easily. The secretary of the University Club was leaving, so Leacock wrote me a very fancy recommendation, which didn't get me a job. I don't remember using it particularly; I didn't go around looking for one. Anyway, I didn't have a job for some time.

He wrote a book on Lincoln, *Lincoln Frees the Slaves*, he wrote another on Charles Dickens, and I typed those because I had the advantage of being able to read his handwriting. He wrote everything out in longhand, the things that I typed. It's an old-fashioned handwriting, I would say, and not very pointed, and free-flowing. It has a liveliness and a ruggedness about it.

Leacock gave me a letter of recommendation from Orillia, September 22, 1932. It was written to Dr. Marvin at the Royal Bank and it said, "Dear Marvin, Miss Jean Schwav, who graduated M.A. in Economics last May, writes to me that she is to see you about a possible opening in the bank. She is a charming girl of excellent manner and address and as a student is absolutely first class in both brains and industry. We all thought a lot of her at McGill and I do not know of any girl who could better fill a secretarial research position."

Then there is a real scrawl, I think it is, "Very truly, Stephen Leacock." There is no problem reading the Stephen Leacock.

I don't even remember seeing Dr. Marvin and it certainly didn't get me a job with the Royal Bank.

JEAN VAN VLIET

RARE BOOK   In 1932, Leacock edited and wrote an introduction to *Lahontan's Voyage*. Lahontan was a very early explorer who may or may not have made up some fancy tales about his travels. Graphic Press in Ottawa published it and while the book was on the press, Graphic went bankrupt. Only a few copies were printed and they were remaindered. I was browsing the book stalls in Morgan's, the Montreal department store, and picked up a copy for a quarter. I told Leacock this and he was astonished because he hadn't been able to find a copy and, in fact, never did. Young book collectors are a strange lot; it never occurred to me to give him my copy.

ALLAN ANDERSON

INTO THE FIERY FURNACE   Dr. Leacock had a small steamer trunk filled with newspaper and magazine clippings. He asked me if I would sort them and arrange them in a scrapbook, placing them in order as they were dated. This was a tedious job, but I finally got to the bottom of the trunk and there I found several manuscripts with rejection slips. I tied them together and when I told Dr. Leacock about them he wanted to see them. A few days later he brought the manuscripts and gave them to me with these instructions: when Enrico, the furnace man, came, I was to accompany him to the basement. The manuscripts were to be placed in the furnace and burned, and I was to stay and watch the proceedings to be sure of their destruction. I carried out his orders, but have always regretted that I did not read those manuscripts.

M.D.

THAT'S EXACTLY HOW I FEEL   He sat there looking at the portrait I had done of him with no expression and, actually, as he looked at it, I looked at him, and the silence in the studio was literally quite awful.

As I looked at him, gradually the colour began to rise from inside his collar, as it did habitually, and the flush spread up over his face and finally into his brow and up into his hair and then, suddenly, his eyes twinkled and what I had feared as the worst, I began to think might not be.

At any rate, he half stood up and then he sat down again and then he pounded his hands down on the arms of the chair and jumped to his feet and bellowed, "By God Taylor, that's exactly how I feel!"

FREDERICK TAYLOR

NOT QUITE FAST ENOUGH   One of my professors was Dr. Stephen Leacock. He was such a great man that I decided to try and make a friend of him, which I did, and started to collect his works. At the time of his death I had the world's greatest collection of them. He helped me immensely, aiding me wherever possible. Many a chat we had together, and at one of them he suddenly said, "Friedman, do you know my funniest story?" I said I didn't and he chuckled and began:

"When I received my Doctor of Philosophy degree I was mighty proud of it and on going on an ocean voyage I signed on the ship's register, 'Dr. Stephen Leacock.' A few minutes after sailing, there was a rap on my cabin door and the steward said: 'Captain's compliments, sir, will you come to see the stewardess' knee?' I rushed off to see the stewardess' knee, but was beaten to it by a Doctor of Divinity."

Dr. Leacock said that if it was not his funniest story, at least he got $500 for it.

NORMAN H. FRIEDMAN

TROUBLEMAKER   In 1909, he toured much of the British Empire, talking about imperial organization. Afterwards he told people how important these lectures were by saying, "When I tell you these lectures were followed almost immediately by the Union of South Africa, the Banana Riots in Trinidad, and the Turco-Italian War, I think you can form some idea of their importance."

HERBERT H. TEES

WAVING HIS HANDS, TALKING JAPANESE   In talking with him this day, he told me he had to get back to Montreal because he had these Japanese fellows coming and some form of reunion, and he had to make a speech in Japanese.

So I had to remark that I thought it was wonderful that he could speak Japanese. And he said, "Well, don't get me wrong, Aubrey, I don't." But he said, "I visited Japan a few years ago and I was asked to give a speech, so I had some knowledge of the language and I did some rehearsing, and I managed to get by and they thought that it was wonderful. So I have been asked to give this speech again."

So I says, "Well, I still think it's wonderful that you're able to talk and give a speech of that sort in Japanese. I'd like to hear that." So he went on to illustrate, and he talked in Japanese with his arms flailing around in the air, and his face got real red as he was doing it, and he had a big smile on his face and he walked away laughing.

AUBREY GAUDAUR

MAKING A FINE POINT   I remember once Uncle Stephen was fined nineteen dollars for allowing his truck to be driven without flares. He showed up the fallibility of the law in a letter he wrote accompanying the cheque, with a twist of humour to bring out his point. He could do this sort of thing well; it was hard to come up against him in an argument.

I desire to say that I am fined because I permitted my driver to drive my truck without flares. I never in my life heard of flares until now; neither did my driver, and I had no notion that a truck must carry flares — nobody told me. There is no obligation on the man who sold me the truck to tell me about flares, and there ought to be, but there isn't. Now what comes next? There may be a dozen more obligations and limitations. My driver speaks French. Shall I be fined in Ontario for that? My truck is painted green. Is that legal? Or is it too Irish?

BARBARA NIMMO

BACK UP, AND FAST   Leacock was a precise man. While he jovially accepted the fact that the world was imperfect, in that part of it over which he had control, he wanted things done exactly as he thought they should be done. So there would be, on a daily basis, bulletins containing specific instructions for the farm help, pinned up on one of the barns, long before the help was up.

What applied at Old Brewery Bay applied elsewhere, too. Leacock took a little train that chugged along from Orillia to Toronto, and then he caught the train from Toronto to Montreal, which would take him back to dear old McGill.

One wintry day, Leacock, bundled up in his disgraceful coon coat, was waiting in raw weather for the Orillia train at the small station near his place. The train pulled in, a few cars and a beat-up engine. The train stopped and the conductor appeared on the steps of one of the coaches. "Have the engineer back up the train," Leacock told him. "I always get on the coach ahead." The conductor looked at this rather scruffy-looking old man, pulled the cord, and the train took off.

Leacock wasted no time. He shuffled into the station and started tapping out a message to the CPR chief dispatcher in Toronto. Leacock was a good friend of Sir Edward Beatty, president of the CPR and chancellor of McGill. The chief dispatcher in Toronto knew full well they were pals.

In no time flat, the little train came puffing backwards and stopped with the doorway of Leacock's coach right in front of him. Leacock boarded the train, satisfied that the world was functioning as it should be, and to as great an extent as possible under his command.

ALLAN ANDERSON

ODD TWISTS   There are one or two very good examples of a little twist in the introductions to his books. For example, in the introduction to *Happy Stories*, he says, "There is no need to give the usual assurance that none of the characters in this book are real persons. Of course not! This is not real life—it is better." Again, in another of his publications he wrote, "Ten years ago the deficit on my farm was about $100 but by well-designed capital expenditure, by drainage and by greater attention to details, I've got it into the thousands."

DR. T.R. MATTHEWS

MOPING MILLIONAIRE   It was a great pleasure to accompany Leacock from the Arts Building at one o'clock, along Sherbrooke Street to his house on Côte des Neiges Road.

One day during the Depression we were walking along Sherbrooke Street, and a big Rolls Royce stopped on the side and Sir Herbert Holt got out. I don't have to tell you that Sir Herbert Holt was, probably, the wealthiest man in Canada at the time—president of the Royal Bank of Canada, Montreal Light, Heat and Power Consolidated, and a director of the CPR. He was a tycoon in every sense of the term. Empire Incorporated. He also carried his cane; he was a tall man.

He got out of the Rolls Royce and he saw Leacock and myself. And he said, "Hello Dr. Leacock," and Leacock replied, "How do you do, Sir Herbert, how are things?" Sir Herbert said, "Very bad, very bad." And he walked up the steps of the Mount Royal Club. Leacock and I walked on for a moment and Leacock turned to me in a very sad voice and he said, "Poor Sir Herbert, I only wish I could help him."

He wrote *Arcadian Adventures with the Idle Rich* and you recall the Mausoleum Club? The Mausoleum Club represented the Mount Royal Club. He liked being in the company of the rich, but he saw through their façade of power, he had sympathy for the common man.

SENATOR H. CARL GOLDENBERG

SOUL SURVIVOR   One evening I stood on one of the corners of Peel and St. Catherine streets and Stephen Leacock stood at another. We had been imbibing at the University Club. Somehow or other we had come into possession of Jehovah Witnesses' pamphlets and were handing them out to passers-by, with appropriate remarks. Stevie would have made a great evangelist!

A. GORDON NAIRN

A DICKENS OF A TIME   He was very interested in Dickens, among other things, and he was a speaker at the Dickens Fellowship one night, and my father-in-law was president of it then and Leacock was his usual dishevelled self. And he had written for the occasion a little sketch with Dickens's characters speaking and in Dickens's style, four or five parts. And he acted out the parts. He brought the house down. He was laughing far more than the audience; he was chuckling away and looking down at his own jokes you know. And it was great. He gave the script to my father-in-law and I wish I knew what had become of it. That would have been an unpublished work. My wife has looked for it, it has just disappeared.

THE HON. MR. JUSTICE ALLISON WALSH

FIFTY CENTS WORTH OF GAB
Stephen Leacock described to a McGill class in 1930 how he prepared for his famous speeches:

First you sit down and write out the speech in full. Then, you make a summary of this—which some people call the "executive summary." Then, you make a summary of the summary and put it on little three-by-five cards.

Then you tear up all these pieces of paper, throw them in the waste basket—gulp down a couple of Scotches, and stagger up to

the platform, laughing all the way at the big joke you have played on the audience, each of whom has paid out fifty cents for the privilege of hearing you talk.

FRED STONE

STAMP OF APPROVAL   I've got here a letter from Stephen Leacock and attached to it is one of those six cent stamps—the

From Stephen Leacock's *The Stamp-Album World, in Short Circuits*.

FIRST DAY OF ISSUE

STEPHEN LEACOCK COMMEMORATIVE

. . . Whenever a part of the earth contains a sufficient number of people to need stamps, the people all get together and join in forming a government, the purpose of which is to issue stamps. If the stamps are to have a man's head as the design, the country is placed under a king, the person selected for the king having the kind of features needed for a stamp. The British Royal family makes such excellent stamps that it is thought that they will be kept at the head of Great Britain for a long time to come. On the other hand, the Emperor of Brazil had to be deposed in 1889, his whiskers being too large to go through the Post . . .

From Stephen Leacock's
The Stamp-Album World, in Short Circuits

Below: The Stephen Leacock first-day-of-issue commemorative stamp.

Leacock stamp that was issued on November 12, 1969. That was the 100th anniversary, the centenary of his birth. And I bought that stamp.

I said, when I saw that stamp, wouldn't Leacock have chuckled had he known that twenty million Canadians were going to be licking his backside.

FRED STONE

THE MONOLOGUES   When I was at boarding school, there was a girl called Pamela Matthewson and she used to be very good at doing make-believe conversations. She just made up recitations that were very funny. We thought they were very funny, and she used to do this when we were doing darning on Friday nights at boarding school.

So, then, I came to McGill and one day I was walking out of the old McGill Union Building, and somebody came up to me and said to me, "Oh, Barbara, we wanted to get hold of you. We want you to arrange part of the entertainment for the Freshie party," or something they were having at Royal Victoria College about two or three nights afterwards. This was in 1936.

So I was kind of astounded and I didn't know what I was going to do and I walked along Sherbrooke Street wondering. I didn't know who to get to entertain and I thought, well, maybe I could do something like Pam Matthewson did. And I thought up one about a woman going to the hairdresser and leaving the hairdresser to use the phone all the time, because a lot of women do that.

And I made up this thing and I did

it that night and they seemed to think it was O.K. So, the next thing I know, they asked me to be in the McGill Red and White Revue. So I did this thing in the Red and White Revue in 1936.

Then I got a letter—I can't remember whether it was a letter or a phone call—from Stephen Leacock who said—he had seen the revue—and he said, "I have arranged with my friend Gladstone Murray for you to do a series of broadcasts over the CBC."

I don't think he asked me, I think he expected me to be delighted. And I was glad. I think it was a series of seven; it was a long time ago. I was in Dorval staying with my grandparents at the time and everybody was kind of interested and I did these things.

Stephen Leacock used to send them to me special delivery. And then he'd send me bits and pieces. He sometimes just tore the thing out of his books, or sometimes they were written in handwriting to insert, and sometimes he had somebody type them—all from Old Brewery Bay in Orillia.

And I went merrily off to CBC with my heart in my mouth, as I remember! I was scared to death the first time. I don't remember what the first one was, really, they were quite long—and I changed a lot of them, incidentally. I probably shouldn't have done it; it never occurred to me not to. But I practised them and when it didn't sound natural, I made it sound natural for me.

These were fifteen-minute little things and I think they gave them a name eventually on the CBC. I think they called them "Monologues of the Moment." Each time I'd get a very nice telegram phoned in to Dorval where I was staying. It would say: "That was fine, more material coming, hold Mrs. Newrich until I write a new ending" or something like that, you see. And I'd get all these very nice encouraging telegrams. Very punctilious—it was always within the hour.

I remember the first time, right after the show, I'd be back home and they'd phone from Dorval and I remember saying to my grandfather I got a telegram from Mr. Leacock and my grandfather was very impressed. And letters came and bits and things to put in.

So this is about five broadcasts and then, all of a sudden, he said to me "All right, now you're on your own, you do the last two yourself." And I nearly fainted because I had to write my own. Well, anyway, the first one I did was simply awful and the second one wasn't too bad. I don't remember what they were, but I think I have them at home in a box somewhere. But what always amused me was they still paid me the same amount when I wrote my own and they also paid him. I thought that was funny. The CBC paid me and they paid Mr. Leacock, but when I was writing my own they still paid Mr. Leacock.

I remember "Mrs. Newrich Sells Antiques"; this was one of his stories. They were some of his short things. They were women meant to be talking. He had done these in monologue form.

There was one about a woman whose husband worked so hard in the garden he employed fifty gardeners from Italy to come and make over the whole pool. And she kept saying he works so hard, "The poor man, you know, he brought all these people from Italy to do

the work." This is the sort of thing that was in it.

I got a lot of fan mail, "I heard you and I enjoyed your broadcast."

But I was kind of angry when Mr. Leacock left me with the last two to do because I didn't feel I was qualified. And I told Professor John Culliton this, and I said, "You know, he just chickened out—he just got lazy."

And Culliton said, "Oh, not at all, Barbara. He was encouraging you, don't you understand? He felt you could do it and he got you going and he arranged to put you on your own." Of course, I had never given the poor man credit for that, so I was embarrassed.

So from then on, I was on the CBC doing fifteen-minute monologues under the name "Monologues of the Moment" for about ten years, on and off, from about 1937 to 1945 or 1950.

I enjoy reading Leacock to this day, and I have the happiest memories of the way he launched me, as it were, and I am tremendously grateful. As a result of that, I met people who were interesting, and I had all kinds of new experiences that a great many of my friends never had. I loved being on the radio; it was fun.

People would keep saying to me, "Oh, I heard you the other day, you're still doing those Stephen Leacock monologues." And I kept saying, "I'm writing them myself now." But I basked in his reflected glory and I am really very grateful. He was extremely kind to me and I think I was too young to appreciate the degree of kindness he had.

Often, when I was at Peggy Shaw's, he would be there at a dinner party. I found him rather terrifying; I was scared to death of him. I had the funny feeling—I was probably wrong—that he expected me to be funny, to sound like my monologues, you see. And I never really could think of anything funny. It is hard to do that when you are sitting talking to Professor Leacock and he's just sitting there, slumping in a big chair in the corner with his hair hanging down over his face.

But he tried to be awfully nice and he used to call me Barberry. I think that was kind of a joke. I think it was an effort to put me at ease. It didn't put me at ease. I didn't know quite where he got it. He just said, "Barberry, here she comes, here's Barberry, come and sit and talk to me." I was speechless, tongue-tied. That was all I knew about him.

BARBARA WHITLEY

FOOLING THE FOLKS   It must have been early in 1921 and there was a big campaign to raise five million dollars for McGill—a lot of money in those days. There was a breakfast at the Windsor Hotel and a lot of pretty important people were there.

And Colonel Molson, I think, told us something about the campaign and was giving us the pep talk and Stevie was supposed to be the person who really sold us the job and set us about our work and sent us on our way.

I remember he got up and he said, well, he was delighted to be there and, he said, of course it was a wonderful thing to be able to have a connection with the university and especially a place like McGill.

He said it was a great place and wonderful people to deal with, fine students, good quarters, good pay, easy life, and he went on with this, and he raved on about all these things and most of the people at the head table were beginning to shuffle around in their chairs and they didn't know what in the world he was going to do.

They thought he was killing the whole campaign. And by this time, I think the chancellor had taken a little nap and two or three of the older people seemed to be slouching. And then there was dead silence. And everybody thought, "Well, now what's going to happen?"

And Leacock chuckled away—he had a little chuckle you know—and he said, "But ladies and gentlemen, I have to tell you, it's not that way at McGill."

That was the end of the pep talk.
BRIGADIER GENERAL JIMMY DE LALANNE

HE LIKED POLITICS   I think there is a letter in Leacock's home, in which he was asked to run on the Conservative ticket, and he didn't want to and that was the year that Dad ran on the Conservative ticket. Leacock recommended my father.

I do feel that Leacock must have had quite a political interest there some place. The political party would have meetings and get together at Northbrook Farm, my father's place. Perhaps once a year they'd have a great big meeting over there and I'm sure Leacock attended those.

My father, John Drinkwater, ran in the election in 1935 and was defeated by a very narrow margin. George McLean was the Liberal who defeated him.

My father liked Scotch, so he had that in common with Leacock. There wasn't much difference in their ages though. Leacock had been a very young Master at Upper Canada College when my father was a student there.

NORAH BASTEDO

HE WOULDN'T RUN   Basically, Leacock was very conservative in politics. And did you know that he was invited to stand for Parliament in Britain about 1911, which he declined. He frequently lectured in Britain, not only in the United States and Canada. And three times he was asked to be a candidate in Canada. R.B. Bennett asked him once.

LAURENCE TOMBS

NO POLITICAL AMBITIONS   I don't know if he was cut out for political life or not. I don't think he had any ambition, and that was probably the reason he resisted any attempts to get him to enter active political competition. He was interested in public questions, but I don't think he was interested in the humdrum work that a politician has to go through, both to get elected, and to stay elected after he is elected. And I don't think he had any ambition to exercise political power.

DOUGLAS C. ABBOTT

MAKING IT UP BY THE YARD
Leacock was explaining the 1911 election. He was speaking for the Conservative party and he used to get up on the platform and wave a piece of paper and say I have here a copy of the treaty or the letter that somebody wrote to Laurier by which the Liberals are going to sell out Canada.

And then he told us later, it was just a sheet of paper that he'd picked up off a paper pad. There wasn't a word on it. However, it was dramatic and effective.

SENATOR ALAN A. MACNAUGHTON

A RED TORY?   In his political beliefs he was a strong believer in some things which were going out-of-date. For example, one of his great enthusiasms was the British Empire and he used to give a course on the Economic History of the Empire. It's a course which involved so much that was disparate and unrelated. One day, you'd be talking about Australia and the next day about India and then you'd be speaking about Hong Kong. There wasn't any theme or central core to it.

Leacock was convinced that there was an economic entity known as the British Empire. He refused to recognize the evolving commonwealth. But he had a humourous way of putting even that. I remember one of his favourite sayings oft repeated: "There is no oil in the British Empire, therefore Persia is part of the British Empire." I wouldn't like to have to explain that to the Ayatollah at the present time!

But Leacock rounded everything out with that quick wit of his, which even then recognized some of the imperfections of his own opinion.

Then, in political partisanship, he was a very strong supporter of the Conservative party in its old Tory sense of the term of right-wing Conservative. But he had had exposure to many other different ideas, so that he was more cosmopolitan in his approach.

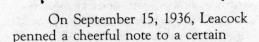

On September 15, 1936, Leacock penned a cheerful note to a certain Mr. Kon:

Dear Mr. Kon. I am immensely interested in knowing that there is to be a Russian edition of some of my work — pleased and flattered — Do tell me where to send & I'll gladly pay in rubles, or in bonds of the old Russian governm't of which I still hold 80,000 . . . When I get around to it I'll see what I can do in the way of making extremes meet by writing you a piece . . . I suppose humour is common ground. Stephen Leacock.

Reprinted courtesy of the Leacock Room, MacLennan Library, McGill University

He was very proud of the degree to which some of his writings, especially in political science, had been translated into many languages. And I recall one day his showing me, with great pride, a translated Russian copy of his *Elements of Political Science*. And the fact that it came from Soviet Russia didn't discourage him at all; he was very proud of that publication.

PHILIP VINEBERG

NO NONSENSE FROM STUFFY BRITS
Leacock was an imperialist and a Canadian nationalist in much the same way that Sam Hughes, Borden's Minister of Militia and Defence, was. Theoretically, he was a tremendous imperialist. But let some Englishman try to get the best of him in a la-di-da, upstaging performance, and he could light into him like a western bronco buster.

Hemmeon knew that, saw that one time. Leacock was to receive some eminent English journalist, Stephen Gwyn, I think it was. And Gwyn sort of called up at the last minute and said that it wasn't convenient for him to come. Hemmeon said Leacock opened up on him and he never heard a more furious denunciation in his life.

Sam Hughes was the same way. Sam was a tremendous imperialist. But when Kitchener ordered Sam to break up the Canadian Corps, Sam said I'll be damned if I will. He defied Kitchener and defied him successfully. So theoretically Sam was a tremendous imperialist, but he was also a very strong Canadian nationalist who wasn't going to be put upon by any Englishman whatsoever.

SENATOR EUGENE FORSEY

THE ONLY GOOD TORY IS A DEAD ONE? During his tour of Western Canada in 1936, Leacock addressed a joint meeting of the Canadian Club and the McGill Alumnae Society. At that time, Social Credit, under Premier William Aberhart, had taken over Alberta.

Nationally, R.B. Bennett and his Tories had been defeated and King and the Liberals were back in power in Ottawa. Leacock was a Conservative.

While Bennett was in power, from 1930 to 1935, he made a practice of winding up his speeches by dedicating himself to the preservation of peace, order and good government. Leacock told the Edmonton gathering, "When I arrived in Alberta, I made enquiries of my old Tory friends. I was told there were no more

Tories. They were all dead. Being like the man from Missouri, I determined to find out for myself—so I went out to the cemetery and, sure enough, I found them all there, lying row on row, enjoying the full benefits of peace, order and good government."

He began a lecture in Alberta by saying that there wasn't room in Alberta for Aberhart and him at the same time. And so he said, "By previous arrangement"—which of course was a fabrication, but it just happened to be true—"by previous arrangement, Mr. Aberhart today is in Vancouver and I am in Edmonton." But he said, "Tomorrow Mr. Aberhart will be back in Edmonton and I'll be in Vancouver."

His trip out West, I think, was sponsored financially by some people on St. James Street and, as far as I could see, the only thing that he did for the bankers on that trip was to advocate that they reduce the interest rates on the farmers' mortgages.

FRED STONE

CHANGING HIS MIND ABOUT FORSEY
One illustration of his emotionalism was that he was, I think, very much disappointed and upset by my forsaking conservatism and going socialist and he told Hemmeon he'd like to see me shot or words to that effect. He hadn't been notably unfriendly, but I knew he was disgusted and disappointed with me.

But after the governors sent him that letter saying he was out, his whole attitude changed completely. And I have the feeling that he was saying to himself, "Well, anyway, whatever he is, he doesn't like the governors. Well, I don't like the governors either. They don't like me and they don't like him; there's probably something good about him after all. One point in his favour." I think I went right back up for no reason whatever except that we were both disliked by the governors.

I was taking a very active part in the CCF, the League for Social Reconstruction, and making speeches all over the place. I was a sessional lecturer at McGill. I never had tenure, I was twelve years as a sessional lecturer. I was turned down four times for promotion after being recommended by the head of the department.

When I made enquiries as to why, I was told by the then Dean Hendel that I was injudicious. "Well," I said, "could you give me some examples?" Well, he gave me four. The choicest one was, and this is the way he said it, "You have been heard in this building speaking in an excited tone of voice." "Well," I said, "that about takes the cake! What am I supposed to have said?" Oh, the dean could not tell me that. Hendel, in conversation, always referred to himself in the third person, as if he were Queen Victoria. "The dean could not tell you that. It was told to the dean in confidence. Besides, it wasn't what you said—it was the tone of voice."

Well, I went upstairs to Hemmeon and said, "I've got a story for you Hemmeon and I don't expect you to believe it because it's too preposterous— nobody could believe it." And I told him. He said, "I have no difficulty in believing it. The damned fool put it in writing over his own signature." And he pulled out the desk drawer and here was a letter from the dean—a typed letter, signed, that I had been heard in this building speaking in an excited tone of voice.

Anyway, I was there for twelve years without tenure.

Of course, you must remember that, in those days at McGill, it was very easy to get a reputation for being ideologically a disparate character. And the first time I ever got into trouble, politically, was for an article in 1926 in *The McGill Fortnightly*, in praise of Arthur Meighen, the Conservative leader. And on the strength of that article I was accused—and this was the word used—of being "a Bolshevik."

I sent the article up to Meighen, whom I knew even then, and got to know later, very well indeed. And he wrote back and said, "Well, Eugene, I can't see any trace of Bolshevism in it," and I said, "No, I can't either." But that's what I was accused of on the strength of that article.

SENATOR EUGENE FORSEY

ALL UP IN THE AIR We used to live at Toronto Island. The family had a big old-fashioned house over there and we grew up at the Island. My mom and dad had ten children and the house was always full of guests and excitement and fun, but the island slowly became unfashionable. This was 1930 or 1932, and people started giving up the big old homes and moving off to places like Muskoka and Lake Simcoe and Jackson's Point and the Briars and all those nice homes along the eastern shore of Lake Ontario.

We used to go to dances at all these places and we all used to get very formally dressed and it was a very romantic time.My father had a beautiful old motor launch and the girls just loved going to the dances in that. Of course, we loved it too—in the moonlight, and all.

Well, anyway, the war came along and I had just come home from a trip around the world. Dad gave me $1,000 for not drinking or smoking until I was twenty-one. And, in truth, I honoured the commitment, which I had made as a little boy.

I took the money and bought a ticket from Toronto to Toronto, around the world, and it cost me $925 and I went to the Toronto Dominion bank and borrowed $3,000 on my dad's note and I took off around the world and it was a great magnificent journey.

I was in Germany in May and the war started in September and so I came home after the war started on the beautiful *Aquitania* across the Atlantic.

When I got home in 1939, my two younger brothers and I joined the air force. And we explained to the recruiting officer that obviously we were officers and gentlemen and therefore officer material and so, sure enough, he made us officers.

I was stationed at Camp Borden teaching flying and we would get these forty-eight hour leaves and we'd either go down to Toronto or, in good weather, we would go over to visit our friends around all the shores of Lake Simcoe. I got to be good friends with the two beautiful Tudhope girls from Orillia. I remember them as being very warm-hearted girls. One was Dode—Dorothy—and the other was Marge. Anyway, they were very elegant, handsome girls, warmhearted and full of fun. And the Tudhope family is a famous old family.

Up in my barn in Collingwood, I have an original Tudhope sleigh, a beautiful sleigh which I still use, and it's a hundred years old. They made carriages and sleighs. Then they actually made the Tudhope automobile. It was well-known.

Jack Spencer was in the air force with me and I think he got to know the Tudhope girls a little later than I did, or maybe he introduced me to them, I don't know. Eventually, he married Dode.

And the Tudhope girls, well, we got to be good friends and we'd go over to Lake Couchiching for dinner. They had a home near Stephen Leacock's. That's where we used to go for dinner—a nice barbecue. In fact, they wanted me to meet Stephen Leacock.

He had a study in an old boathouse, and, of course, as a sailor and yachtsman and a flyer, I just love boathouses and the ripple of water and the wind. And it was a very beautiful old boathouse and study.

I remember him as a very charming, tousle-haired, grey-haired, very rumpled old man. I think he wore old sort of nondescript trousers and a nice old grey cardigan sweater. And I think he smoked a pipe and the stains were all over the shoulders—the ashes and the burns from his pipe.

The girls asked me to go to see him, and I think it was after dinner and I went over to the boathouse and ambled upstairs to his study up over the boathouse. And he had a nice bottle of something there—I guess it was Scotch. But anyway, he gave me a bit of Scotch and we started to chat and he asked very penetrating questions. And you know, I just fell in love with this tousle-haired old man.

I think he wanted to talk to a flyer. I was wet behind the ears as a flyer, even though I was teaching flying; but we got into flying and, you know, are you frightened of flying, and all this business. Well, we didn't know fear in those days. I guess I was a typical youngster.

I was shy and it was a bit awkward. He was immensely interested—you could see how a writer would be interested in this—he was interested from a fuel-range point of view. If you're flying from point A to B, he wanted to know about the point of no return and what a pilot thought when he reached it—where he didn't have enought fuel to go back to his base, how would a flyer cope with this situation, if he ran into bad weather, and so on.

I didn't know much about that myself because we always had enough fuel for an hour's continuous flying; then we got back to our base. But he wanted to know about a transatlantic flyer reaching the point of no return and indeed what that man felt when he reached the point of no return. Well, I tried to explain to him, as best I could. I suppose I had had a couple of Scotches by then and I'd be pretty loose-tongued.

We had a wonderful time. I think I stayed until midnight. I arrived after dinner, say eight-thirty to nine o'clock, and I think I stayed until midnight.

I remember a very comfortable, very pleasant room. The rafters were open and he sat sort of with his back towards the shore and looking out over the water. I think it was a lovely moonlit night and it was a beautiful scene. And so, while he was interrogating me, he was also enjoying the beauty of the night and nature. I found him a genius. I instantly fell in love with him. I've always admired older gentlemen anyway, and I've always been good friends with them.

PAUL PHELAN

THE SICK LITTLE GIRL AND THE KIND OLD GENTLEMAN   I was eleven years old when I met Stephen Leacock, and I met him because I had a very infectious disease that required me to be in a state of isolation. It was erysipelas. My father was Leon Ladner, M.P. for Vancouver South, and my mother's name was Jeanne. She came from the north of France and she was expecting her fourth child and, for that reason, although it was very difficult in those days for members of Parliament to bring their whole family from Vancouver to Ottawa, we came to Ottawa in February of 1925 because the baby was expected in May.

I had, as a result of the measles, a very bad case of mastoids in both ears. I needed to have the attention of a doctor and, in the course of that treatment from the doctor here in Ottawa, I caught erysipelas. I was unable to be admitted to the Ottawa Civic Hospital because it was just about to be opened, or had just opened, and they didn't want an infectious disease in there. Through good fortune I was able to get into the Ross Memorial Hospital in Montreal.

My father took me to Montreal and I was in the Ross Memorial Hospital for about six weeks. I was in a special room at the end of a long corridor and it so happened that Stephen Leacock's wife,

Trix, was in the room adjoining. Nobody told me what she had, but they told me that she was dying.

Only one nurse was allowed to come into the room and I couldn't have any other visitors. So, of course, I was there all alone, and I wasn't allowed to have anything that could spread the infection anywhere, so I couldn't have any kind of toys. I was only eleven.

It was hard. And my parents were in Ottawa, my father was very busy and my mother was pregnant and so, of course, my family could only come down very intermittently.

I had a nurse all the time because I had to be looked after by only one person, and she had to make all sorts of precautions to come into the room. You had to be, you know, completely sterile, going in and out, so that it wasn't transmitted to anybody else in the hospital. In those days it was a very dangerous disease. And, in fact, I nearly died. I had a temperature of 106.

I remember I had a very nice, bright room. It was a well-situated room and I was prepared to accept what came along. In any case, all of a sudden, I was cheered up on a sort of daily basis by this man who used to come to the door and, of course, being eleven years old I didn't really know who he was.

I don't know how he knew I was there but he did. Coming to visit his wife every day, he must have found out that I was there.

One day, I guess the door was semi-open and he spoke to me, and I don't think he even told me who he was. He started to chat with me—the way you would to a child—and I responded. And he asked me if I needed anything. He tried to find out what I was doing. And I said that I liked those English comic papers that they had. They were called *Puck*, or *Tiny Tim*, or whatever. So he brought me those papers. Of course, they were the type of paper that could be destroyed.

And then he discovered that I was interested in stamps, so sometimes he would bring me some stamps. But mainly, it was just the fact that he came to the door and would talk to me. He just chatted in a pleasant way and he knew that he wasn't supposed to go into the room. He never came in close to the bed; he just stayed at the door for a few minutes. And he always had something to say.

But what I appreciated was the fact that he took the trouble, on a sort of regular basis, to say hello to me and make a few remarks and then he told me that he came to see his wife and that he had a little boy about the same age. And then one day he brought the boy to the door. The boy just stood at the door, Stevie.

I naturally discovered who he was because he introduced himself shortly after he became a regular visitor and, of course, it didn't mean very much to me. I think what really happened was that I told my father that Stephen Leacock had come to see me.

I think he probably came in to see me almost the same number of days that he came to see his wife, while I was in the hospital. He would go to see his wife and he would just pop his head in the door and say something to me.

He brought me presents almost every day. I looked forward to his visit very much because I had no other person visit me and it was, as you can imagine, a great treat to have somebody who was humourous and who made nice remarks and who was interested in me. And, of course he made me laugh.

We live on Mariposa Avenue in Ottawa—in Rockcliffe Park, actually. When I write down my address, many times I think about Stephen Leacock and his connection with Mariposa; it's very fitting that I should live here.

HÉLÈNE TOLMIE

CHAPTER FOURTEEN

Saving the Leacock Home: An Incredible Story

THE MANUSCRIPTS WERE COVERED WITH WOOD ASHES   I leased Old Brewery Bay in the summers of about 1949 to 1951 and I tried to clean up the place. The manuscripts down in the basement were covered with wood ash and we had a hell of a time saving them. Somebody had just dumped them down there and somebody was shovelling out the old furnaces and, oh, it was an impossible mess. I've got photographs of the place. Young Stevie asked me to come up and help. And I tried to help him.

People bust into the place and took books and manuscripts and everything under the sun. It was awful. For two or three years I went up there and we did try to put the place in shape, but I finally found that I had a family to look after and a business to look after and I couldn't cope with little Stevie. He just made difficulties.

His manuscripts were to go to McGill. The place had been looted and what happened to it would just have appalled Leacock. I saw to it that the manuscripts were cleaned up and spread out on the billiard table to dry. They were wet as well as covered with ashes. They were mildewy—books all over the place, manuscripts in the basement. Some I collected; some of them were scattered around just as if a bunch of squirrels had been in there.

I did pull out a good many, particularly *Sunshine Sketches of a Little Town*; I took that out. They were so wet that I asked some librarian what to do with some of them—Miss Coates, I think, in Orillia.

We had to sort of interpage them with dry paper and soak it up. I should have stuck right with it, but I had a family here and two businesses. I worked about two years, every summer. I'd be all summer up there.

Young Stevie had been messing around there and he was very untidy. A lot of furniture was stolen. He sold stuff off like he sold the boathouse for $100, and he sold the barn and stables for another $100.

HENRY JANES

MANSION LIKE A GHOST STORY

Stephen Leacock died in 1944. For more than a decade the big house stood like the mansion of a ghost story; white and stark in the moonlight, weeds choking the gardens, the lawn a hayfield. I saw it first in the summer of 1949, two years after my arrival as a copywriter and sometime reporter at CFOR, the Orillia radio station. My first reporting assignment had been the first ever Leacock Medal dinner in June, 1947, and from that I carried away a feeling that Orillia was not doing justice to the man who had immortalized the town.

Henry Janes, a one-time Leacock student had leased Old Brewery Bay for the summer, dreaming of converting it into a centre for seminars on the literary arts. Sadly, the idea interested almost no one, least of all the government agencies and private foundations who might have provided the funds. But it did impress a neophyte broadcaster sharing many a beer with Henry Janes that summer on the wide verandah.

That interest led me inevitably into the orbit of Charles Harold Hale (C.H.), a tall, spare man in his seventies whose whole life, like those of his father and uncle before him, was devoted to advancing the town in the sunshine. He had one dream left . . . he wanted Old Brewery Bay to become a literary shrine.

Harold Hale's attitude towards Leacock was an appreciation of his position in the world of literature, his political views. He was very much in line with Leacock's feeling about conservatism and Empire and all of those things. He regarded Leacock as at least a nominal Anglican. If there was any parting of the ways, it was over the question of alcohol. The Hales were notoriously teetotallers, Prohibitionists really.

I confess I found Harold Hale's attitude toward Stephen pretty ambivalent. On one hand, he was full of his praise and he wanted this shrine, and I think he used the word "shrine," at one point, to come into being. On the other hand, for a hundred years that family had been rock-ribbed on the subject of booze. They were totally anti-drinking and they had a world reputation—they wrote temperance papers and that sort of thing the world over.

There were two Hales, Harold and his brother Russell, who was Hustle, in *Sunshine Sketches*, Hustle of the *Newspacket*. But Harold is the dominating figure. He was the rightful heir of the Hale mission. His father and his uncle felt they had to bring Orillia into some sort of national position. They had a vision of a Golden Age for Orillia and they brought a good deal of it about—that is, instilling local pride into the history and institutions of the community, encouraging an industrial base, founding cultural groups such as the Canadian Club.

Harold Hale recruited me—I forget where we first got together—but it happened. A public meeting was called and on a night in October, 1954, at the town hall, the mayor, John McIsaac, a very good man, conducted the meeting; but Harold did most of the talking. He outlined the desirability of having the home of this world figure restored and to that end wanted a committee formed that would include town council.

At that point I knew a great deal about Stephen Leacock. I had been a devotee from my public school days, and had read most of his humourous books. My father, William, had lived in Orillia in 1905 briefly.

I remember Dad telling me about contacts with Stephen Leacock at the time when I was reading Leacock in school. He thought he was a pretty down-to-earth and good man.

I came to Orillia in 1947 and I attended and reported on the very first Leacock dinner, in June of that year. It was my first outside assignment from a radio station. It was the most marvellous occasion I had ever encountered, then or since. It was an explosion of humour from people like B.K. Sandwell and Louis Blake Duff and Harry Symons, who won the medal, and George Leacock, who was in his prime. They just topped one another in their remarks. That really spurred my interest in Leacock and in his town. But it was another two years before I found out where Old Brewery Bay was.

Apart from the Hales, and apart from the loyal group of friends that Leacock had in Orillia—John Drinkwater and the Tudhopes and the Ardaghs and people like this—there was really no Leacock movement in Orillia.

By 1954, as I began my second year as an Orillia alderman, Harold Hale and I were close friends, despite a half-century difference in age, and a wider difference still in political loyalties. We shared a belief Orillians were eager to do honour to their famous fellow-citizen.

We were to learn soon enough how misplaced was our confidence. In September, 1954, Stephen Leacock, Jr. put the property on the market. The price was $50,000 for the home and

28.8 acres of land. At the next council meeting I proposed the town purchase it, and was promptly rebuffed. I was reminded of the sewers, sidewalks, and streetlights $50,000 would buy. I was also reminded (by one elderly unforgiving council colleague) of what a reprobate and eccentric the late professor had been, with his well-known fondness for the bottle and his unkempt appearance occasionally on the main street . . . scarf dragging, in need of a haircut. Honour Leacock? Sooner honour the devil!

Stephen Leacock, Jr., was stung by the comment, and informed me by letter the home would NOT be available to the town for purchase, under any circumstances.

I wrote him right away and said I was sorry this happened, but I hoped he would keep the door open because, as I said in the letter, "I'm still looking for a buyer and please stay in touch." Well, we did stay in touch for a couple of years.

The house was somewhat rundown but it was a very solid structure. There had been some vandalism. The grounds were overgrown. The gardens were gone. It didn't look too presentable but, basically, everything was there. The house wasn't falling down and the rain hadn't done too much damage and, inside the house, scattered around, there were something in the order of 33,000 items— books and manuscripts, various things like this. There was no damage to the items upstairs; those in the basement may have been waterlogged.

The contents were a prize beyond price, manuscripts, business records, photographs, and books, including scores of autographed and dedicated volumes.

Left: The Leacock home at Orillia in a state of disrepair, in the early 1950s. *Courtesy of the Stephen Leacock Memorial Home.*

Below: The living room at Old Brewery Bay before renovations. The area in front of the bay window is where Leacock staged his plays. *Courtesy of the Stephen Leacock Memorial Home.*

The boathouse was still there at that time, and the lodge. Stephen, Jr., was living in the lodge in those years.

Then the property was listed with A.E. LePage in Toronto, and thrown on the national market. It was first of all optioned by a fellow named Wansborough. I never did meet him. We toasted him one night as the guy that now owned the property, and we hoped we could deal with him and have the home restored and so forth. But he let the option lapse and did nothing about it. A few weeks after that it was bought for $50,000 by Louis Ruby, who was the publisher of *Flash* magazine.

So then we started all over again. We met Mr. Ruby, who turned out to be a colourful character. He had no plans at all. It was strictly a property development, a good buy. He'd turn it over in time. The home and Leacock meant nothing to him, until he began to realize after the publicity started, how important that purchase was.

So I went to him, and what we worked out after a number of meetings was that he would give me a year to come up with a buyer for the home. He gave me a letter which said that if we did this, he would turn over to me all the contents of the home. We shook hands on it and that was it. So I took it back to the council and his price was $50,000, which would be for the home and the area for parking, a bare acre.

We didn't think that was unreasonable, considering the value of what was in the house alone. I found Ruby a very forthright and honest guy and I had no problems with him at all and I kept saying, "We are hopeful," but all we had was hope.

We're now into 1956. I had asked the council, when I got this offer, if they would go for it and they told me the same thing they did in 1954. But I was very confident we were going to get the home and, since it belonged to Ruby, I told him we were going to provide some security out there. So we assembled most of the materials, the manuscripts and so forth, and got them at least in closets and out of harm's way. There was still the problem of vandalism and nothing we could do about that, though we had police checking more regularly. We did replace some windows, too, that had been smashed. We did that on our own, but with Ruby's permission.

We were elated. But by the late fall of 1956 we were in the trough of despair again. Appeals to both town council and Queen's Park had fallen on deaf ears. The foundations were sympathetic, but committed no hard cash.

Then one of those ironies that would have sent the good professor racing for his pen occurred. At that time I was reeve of Orillia (my political life, unlike the Leacock movement, was an unqualified success), but on nomination night in November I declared my intention of retiring from council to devote my efforts full time to finding the money for the home purchase. My colleagues regretted my departure and wished me well.

It wasn't until the following morning that something like panic set in among them. I hadn't given any indication whether or not I was also withdrawing my nomination for alderman. If I did, it meant election by acclamation for the six candidates standing—something definitely not to council's liking. I had the power to prevent this. I also had until 8 P.M. to decide.

By dinner hour, a mad scheme had taken shape in my mind. What if I campaigned solely on the proposition that Orillia should purchase the home? And, if I got a good vote (maybe placed first or second) would my fellow councillors take it as a vote of public approval for the project?

I put the question to them, one by one in the next hour, and with one exception, they agreed. Moments before 8 P.M. I signed my nomination papers and the campaign was on.

I spoke and wrote of nothing else in the next two weeks but the marvellous possibilities if Orillia bought the Leacock estate and developed it as a tourist attraction. Orillia was a tourist town, and that message registered. On election day, for the fourth year running, I topped the polls.

A motion authorizing purchase of the Leacock home was unanimously passed by Orillia town council on December 10, 1956, less than a week after voting day. A second motion was the frosting on the cake—a $5,000 grant to allow the Parks Board to begin the restoration work.

We approached the provincial government for help immediately because of the Les Frost connection. He was an Orillian, born here, and always took an interest in these things. We felt we had that going for us, but it bombed out. There was no support at all from Queen's Park. We went to Ottawa. The Liberals were in and Jean Lesage was minister of northern affairs. We approached him through Bill Robinson, the local M.P. and

Deputy Speaker. We got a good reception from him; we felt sure they would help us. When we were preparing our brief, the government was tossed out, and the Tories were in, and the new minister in that portfolio was Alvin Hamilton.

I made a presentation before the National Historic Sites and Monuments Board. I felt I made a good presentation. They asked a lot of questions. We showed them our pictures and told them what we planned to do. We asked them for $15,000, and went home and waited and waited and waited and nothing happened.

One day, Jim Lamb, the publisher and managing editor of the *Packet and Times* of Orillia, and a great supporter, wrote an editorial which scalded the federal government for its inaction and inattention to this great national literary figure. He said we made this application months ago and never heard a bloody word and what the heck's going on.

He sent a copy off to Hamilton's office. Hamilton's office was on the phone in a rage the next day to my office saying, this is terrible, get down here, we want an explanation. They were really frothing. So Bill Greer, one of my co-workers on council, and I flew down. We met with P.B. Rynard, the sitting member, and he got George Doucette, and John Hamilton, the member for York-West and they joined me for moral support and we went into Hamilton's office. He was chewing a cigar and stomping back and forth and he had this paper in his hand and he said, "No two-bit local journal is going to make a fool out of me! You knew damn well, you were told by the board that we do not support home restoration, and what the hell is the point of dragging this all up again?" So I told him that we hadn't been informed of that, we had no communication from the board whatsoever, and he still insisted we had. But he went to the phone and he called the board office and they called back in a few minutes to say that, by error, we had not been informed.

He did a complete switch-around. From being belligerent and hostile, he became very accommodating, very agreeable and he said he would get the $15,000. He had no idea where he'd get it at the moment, but we could count on it and go home and restore the home.

What they did, because they don't have funds for restoring homes, they gave us a plaque and $15,000 to maintain the plaque in perpetuity. It took some genius in their department to work this out.

Then after Hamilton told us that he was going to give us the money, he turned around and began to tell us how much Leacock had meant to him in his life. Leacock had influenced him in many ways; he worshipped at his feet. He'd gone to his lectures. He'd taught and quoted Leacock all over the map, and he says that to this day.

The following June, Northern Affairs Minister Alvin Hamilton forwarded a cheque for $15,000 to complete the restoration. Showcases and shelving were built, the verandah reinforced, the grounds brought back to their former glory.

On July 5, 1958, the doors of Stephen Leacock's dream home on Old Brewery Bay were opened again, with a golden key. Fittingly, it was Charles Harold Hale who turned it, joined by the Honourable Alvin Hamilton. Premier Leslie Frost, Louis Ruby, and a bevy of Leacock's friends of former years witnessed the ceremony.

The day meant a lot to me, but one moment stands out in particular. A flamboyant politician, inspired by the crowd, and carried away by the emotion of the occasion, swept an arm towards the calm waters of Brewery Bay . . . "The very waters," he told us, "that Champlain trod."

Mariposa was alive once more and in his mystic home, Leacock was laughing.

J.A. "PETE" McGARVEY

A NEATER HOME NOW? I think, in the restoration of The Leacock Home, we must always strive for authenticity and resist the temptation to include fine furnishings merely to please the visiting public.

The house, in Leacock's time, was simply and sparsely furnished and I suspect that his housekeepers fought a losing battle against untidiness. We should try to portray it as it was. I think that today it may be overfurnished and too neat.

JAY CODY

NEW SHINGLES Somebody later put asphalt shingles on. They didn't take the cedar off and they put the asphalt on. It wasn't that bad, there was holes in it, they were curling in different areas. It's amazing how they curl so badly underneath where there's a tree or on the shady side of the roof. It just curls right up. We just put on the cedar in 1982, and it's back to the original.

It's what you'd call a large, rambling two-storey house, with numerous dormers out over each window. A dormer is a window that projects out into your roof. Back in Oscar's time they called them Gothics, and in our time they call them dormers. There's pretty well at least two on every side of the house. It is not a square house, it's not even rectangular. It's almost like two rectangular houses on each end and a rectangular house in the middle. Like an H almost.

I think it's in excellent condition. I think they were very wise in what they just did to the roof because they did it before they got into a lot of problems. The outside is stucco now. The stucco must have been on for many, many years.

The roof is a very steep-pitched roof, very steep. There's one big chimney on each end and there's a flat portion on the roof on top. It's eight feet wide and about sixty-one feet long. And then in the centre of that, there's two chimneys that would be about three and a half feet square, so there are very large chimneys coming up through the middle of the house as well. There's four chimneys altogether. The total length of the house is over eighty feet.

It's a very attractive house, and it's very different from anything else along the shoreline, more uniquely constructed in every aspect.

JIM NICHOL

Postcard of Old Brewery Bay. *Courtesy of Senator H. Carl Goldenberg.*

OLD BREWERY BAY, LAKE COUCHICHING, 1928

CHAPTER FIFTEEN

I Think of
Him Still . . .

I THINK OF HIM STILL   My association with Stephen Leacock, of course, was around his home in Orillia.

I think of him still. I think of him as out in the boat fishing. I think of him walking around the grounds, looking very tatty. I think of him, the odd time when he had a dinner party, coming in, supposedly all dressed up, with a black string tie, and a nice jacket and shirt, but he'd have on the wrong pants—nothing matched.

He was a most gracious host: nothing was too good for you, always beautiful food and lots to drink, very sociable, but he didn't spend any time with you, very rarely. I never had a long conversation with him.

The last I saw of him socially—and it was very beautiful—he proposed the toast at my sister's wedding in 1942. He made a very definite point, he hadn't been in a church in years and years and years, and yet he attended my sister's wedding. That was the last time that I saw Stephen Leacock, and of course, he died in 1944.

JEAN CAIN

THE MOST INTERESTING FIGURE, THEN AND NOW   His hair was thick and bushy, unruly. He paid less attention to his personal appearance than almost

Stephen Leacock toasts another bride, at Peggy Shaw's wedding on May 30, 1942. *Courtesy of the Stephen Leacock Memorial Home.*

anyone else on the campus.

Stephen Leacock was, without any question, or doubt, the most interesting figure on the campus in his day and probably to this day. He is truly a vivid and unforgettable man and my memories of him are as vivid today as if he were still living and sitting in this room with me.

TRUEMAN SEELY

NEVER MET ANYONE LIKE HIM   I've never met any other person like him. And both John Pemberton and I have been in contact with, and have known, many prominent Canadians over the years. He's absolutely unique. Everytime I go into the University Club and look at that picture of Leacock, it all comes back.

FRED STONE

A GREAT VISION OF THE FUTURE
I think he had a great vision of the future. He foresaw so many things long before they happened. I remember one thing he was very strong on. Back in the 1930s, he was always talking about the rising tide of colour in Africa. He said how the underdeveloped countries in Africa would some day rule the world, or, at least, would cause all sorts of problems. He discussed the problems of the Negro in the United States. And so he was tremendously interested in all that—and I don't say he was the only one, other people were concerned, too—but there wasn't the same emphasis on it that there is now.

He got me working on a fourth-year thesis on the St. Lawrence Seaway and its effect on the economic future of Canada. It hadn't been built—it wasn't officially opened until 1959. So this was twenty or twenty-five years ahead of time, though I don't think he was the first one that had ever contemplated it. And he said, "Now, you go down to the shipping people and the marine architects and so forth and find out what their forecast is as to the maximum size the ships can attain and what their draught will be, and so on. And try and get some figures on what it would cost to build the canal and locks to carry ships through the Great Lakes and then what cargoes they can carry." They didn't have the iron ore mines down the North Shore then, but he was thinking

largely of wheat. But he wanted to know what the maximum size of ocean shipping would be that could be conveniently brought up to the head of the Great Lakes.

He went into that in considerable depth and was tremendously interested in how that would affect the trade and commerce and the employment in Canada and in the northern States, and this was twenty-five years before it was built, so he was a man with a vision of the future.

THE HON. MR. JUSTICE ALLISON WALSH

A RARE BIRD   He was a lovable, colourful, wonderful teacher and friend. But there's no doubt about it, Leacock was a rare bird. He had very unique, exceptional qualities. And of course, he'll be long remembered by anybody who was ever exposed to him. He had a great impact on his students. Not always the kind of impact that he might have wanted, of course, but they were very much influenced by him without sharing his views. Many of the students reacted against his views and adopted the opposite political stance and the like. They didn't always respect his doctrinal background in economics or even his knowledge of the subject. But we all found him a fascinating and colourful personality and wonderfully interesting to have as a professor.

PHILIP VINEBERG

HIS KINDLY PHILOSOPHY   I remember Stephen Leacock as someone who played a very important role in my education. I think it's a little difficult to express, but I have the feeling that I got a great deal from Leacock. I think he taught not only about economics and political science and that sort of thing, but something of the man and his kindly philosophy and his humourous approach toward serious problems rubbed off.

I've always been grateful for the fact that I decided to go to McGill and study under him.

JOHN PEMBERTON

HIS UNIQUELY WARM PERSONALITY
Summing it up, Leacock is one of the great experiences of my intellectual life. I would say that Leacock is unique in his own warm personality; he was unique in his invigorating approach and his stimulating effect on other people, despite the fact that perhaps he was not such a great scholar as many of his colleagues.

Unfortunately, sometimes scholarship becomes synonymous with pedantry and a certain tedium that comes with excessive thoroughness. A story is told about him that he wasn't very cheerful about correcting papers, and that kind of dull thing, and that sometimes he honoured a young professor at another university by asking him to correct the papers. That young man usually was thrilled to be singled out by Leacock.

As I look back over the years, I can feel very much that vividness that was part of what I knew, even though it's close to sixty years ago. In 1982, I had my fifty-fifth reunion at McGill and it is very extraordinary the vitality of the man and the impression that he made upon not only me, but upon his students at large.

MAYSIE MacSPORRAN

HIS LOVE OF LIFE   I remember
Stephen Leacock as a very gentle man, a very great teacher who had a very profound influence on all of his students, in fact on everybody who came in contact with him.

Even a very minor student of Leacock's, as I was, was affected by his demeanor, his presence, his laughter, his love of life.

D. LORNE GALES

EXTRAORDINARY BRILLIANCE OF MIND   He could have done absolutely anything he chose. He could have been prime minister if he'd wanted to.

The only thing I could say about him is that he was so extraordinarily brilliant that he was able to put a considerable part of his mind on the shelf and do a superb job with what remained. Most of us have to use all the brains we've got. Leacock didn't. Accordingly, I don't think he ever produced the kind of serious work that he was evidently capable of doing. Of course, he did magnificent humourous work and perhaps that's enough.

But, on the other hand, a great many of his gifts, I think, simply went to waste. The gifts that you saw when he was giving introductory courses, for example, which he did superbly. Nobody could have done a better introductory course to political economy or political science than Leacock did. He opened up people's minds in a perfectly marvellous fashion.

He could have done so much more than he did. He could do the humourous work almost in his sleep, as indeed he proved in his last years, when he was doing excellent work of this sort.

But by all accounts that I heard, his last years as a lecturer were not his best. From people whose acounts I have some confidence in, he was becoming very rambly indeed.

SENATOR EUGENE FORSEY

HE PUT UP MY PICTURE   I admired Leacock enormously. I was an enthusiastic young man and a fairly good student, but I wasn't one of the most extraordinary students that Leacock ever had.

I was very sad when I heard that he had gone, I really was sad. He did have, somehow, an affectionate interest in his students and he was interested in their possible future.

For example, Sydney Pierce was a very distinguished Canadian diplomat, an ambassador to several countries, and an assistant under-secretary of state for external affairs. Soon after he graduated, Leacock had him appointed to a lectureship. He recommended him for a lectureship in political science at Dalhousie, but Pierce had other ambitions. I don't think he stayed very long in Dalhousie.

Leacock wasn't ambiguous about his students. He did encourage them. He didn't forget them, and they didn't forget him. I thought he was great. Maybe as a personality he was even greater than as a humourist. I sent him a picture of myself in graduation garb, and at least a dozen people who have visited his house said "We saw your picture, along with a few others, you must have been very close to Leacock." Well, I wasn't, but at least he put the picture up in one of his rooms.

LAURENCE TOMBS

I DIDN'T LEARN ANYTHING   My recollection of Stephen Leacock is a very favourable one, with one reservation, and that is that I didn't learn anything. Well, I shouldn't say I didn't learn anything, but, with a man with his reputation, I would have expected that I should have accomplished more than I did although I did very well in my results. It was my fault I guess.

But I really considered it a great honour and privilege to have been in his classroom because he was Stephen Leacock, and I revered him for himself, for the ability he had for inspiring students to think and to realize the importance of education, what it had done for him, what it could do for them.

MARGARET STEPHEN

STABBING PEOPLE'S MINDS   A genius *manqué*, a genius who might have done anything. A very inspiring teacher. He was inspiring deliberately, and I don't mean that as a simply hackneyed term. He did actually inspire, stimulate, arouse, awake, stab people's minds broad awake, and he was a very kindly, generous friend.

SENATOR EUGENE FORSEY

THE YOUNG WERE CATALYSTS   I would say that he had an enquiring mind, I think that's obvious. I'd say he had a highly disciplined, reasoning mind. He was interested in the stimulus which he got from his new classes. I find, in my old age, that the ideas of younger people set off all sorts of chain results in my own brain. So I think that was sort of a catalyst for him.

I would never have amounted to anything without the stimulus of Stephen Leacock. It's a big statement but it's true.

He stimulated me to study and work. Otherwise I might have ended up a social drifter.

SENATOR ALAN A. MACNAUGHTON

CHECK YOUR BRIEFCASE, SIR?
    I was training at Royal Victoria Hospital, between 1936 and 1939, and he was a patient there for a time. It must have been in the latter period of my training. I didn't see too much of him. I don't know what he was in for, and he was not a bed-ridden patient. He came and went. You were never too sure that when you went into his room that he was actually going to be there but there was a general check when he did come back that he didn't have too much liquid in his briefcase.

    He wasn't a genial or talkative patient when he was in the hospital. He sort of got about his business; he did seem to be doing writing—whether it was school work, I would have no idea.

    He was not a neat man. He was actually the absolute epitome of what I thought Aislin would have drawn, with the scruffy hair, and the pipe on the side of the table or wherever; he wasn't very good about keeping that tucked away.

MARJORIE FISHER

REALLY FURIOUS   I remember, one day, when he was very much enraged with somebody—and this must have been quite on toward the end of his life, and I haven't heard anyone else use this expression, or of anyone who had heard this expression of his—but he ended a discussion with this person with, "I invite you to my funeral!"

and he turned around. In other words, he did not care to see the person until then.

ELIZABETH BURROWS LANGDON

EASY TO WORK FOR   I liked Mr. Leacock very much. He was an easy man to work for and he was good to his help, because he was good to my father up until my father had to retire.

    He would pay him the going rate at that time, which was thirty-five cents an hour for his type of work. And I think Dad got a dollar and a half a day for the horse—that would be over and above his thirty-five cents an hour. As a boy, I got twenty-five cents an hour.

    He was very friendly, especially if he had a glass in his hand. He was always cheerful.

MORLEY YOUNG

TINGE OF SADNESS   There was a tinge of sadness that never left him after he left McGill. He was never quite the same. It wasn't a matter so much of his health, but he was uprooted. His departure from McGill aged him in the sense that it took away a good deal of his *raison d'être*, his reason for living. And made him a little bitter. But of course, he still preserved his mellow attitude about many things, but he wasn't quite the same and he wasn't as happy—he couldn't be as happy because of his severance from McGill against his wishes.

PHILIP VINEBERG

THIS SAD, RETROSPECTIVE AIR   I think that Stephen Leacock had many lonely periods. He had a lot of people around him, but sometimes that can be the loneliest existence on earth. And I really think he was basically a lonely man, particularly after his wife Trixie died.

Every once in a while that would come through. You'd see a look on his face and I think it was for Trixie. And it would, all of a sudden, at the very oddest moments come over him, and all of a sudden he'd have this sad retrospective air about him.

JEAN CAIN

NOT ENJOYING HIMSELF   My recollection of the last time I saw him, he had on his white ducks and this rather sloppy tweed jacket, slouched and rather a scowl on his face, but when you spoke to him, his face lit up. He almost looked as if he wasn't enjoying himself and he was rather thin through his face from the cheekbones on down. You wouldn't say gaunt at this point, this would be 1943.

NORAH BASTEDO

Christmas greetings, 1942. *Courtesy of the Leacock Room, MacLennan Library, McGill University.*

NOT WITHOUT PAYNE   Before we were married, I hadn't been in contact with Stephen for quite some while, and the phone rang one night and someone was on the phone and asked for me and I spoke to him and he said Stephen Leacock wanted to talk to me, and I thought "Sure." But it was. It was Stephen and he asked if he could come to the wedding. He knew about it; it was in the paper.

I had thought, no, I am not going to ask him, I haven't seen him for ages, I'm not going to ride on his coattail, you know. He was well known then.

I was marrying John Stewart Ross Payne. My husband had graduated from McGill as a Bachelor of Commerce and he had also become a chartered accountant.

When I got the phone message, I said you must be kidding, or you must be fooling. It was young Stephen that had called—his father asked him to call. So he put me on to his father and I spoke to him. Of course I was delighted.

The wedding was at Trinity Memorial Church in Montreal and the reception was at the Ritz Carleton Hotel in Montreal. At the reception after the ceremony, the minister informed us that he had been called away and he wouldn't be able to come and make a toast. So I didn't know what to do.

Stephen overheard all this and he said he would make a toast, which he did. He had on a blue suit and it was rumpled, but it was clean and he was fine. He was very cheerful. Always a twinkle in his eye. This was the 19th of December, 1942. I was very proud of him. He didn't even know my husband. He said that I was changing my name but not without Payne. I'll always remember.

I believe that was about the last semi-public appearance, with any number of people around, that he made. Certainly the last in Montreal. After that he went up to Toronto.

He was at the church and around after, but of course we went off, we weren't there, so I don't know. He was a great success and everyone thought the world of him. For me it was a wonderful experience to have him there and also to have him, in such an impromptu way, speak the way he did.

For a wedding present, Stephen gave us several of his books that he had appropriately autographed, and I was very happy to have them then and now. He gave me one of his books, *My Remarkable Uncle* about my grandfather, and on the flyleaf he wrote "To Lena Ross Leacock from her cousin Stephen Leacock, December 19, 1942," which was my wedding date.

That was a very happy occasion for me in many ways and unfortunately the last time I ever saw Stephen Leacock.

DOVIE PAYNE (LEACOCK)

NO WAY TO MAKE A WILL   My first job was working in a law office in Orillia for Mr. A.B. Thompson. This was early in 1941. Mr. Thompson was the city solicitor for Orillia and he was very well-known. Everybody that wanted good honest service came to Mr. Thompson.

One of his clients was a gentleman that I had never seen as far as I could remember. I had been there a very short time and I was on the counter at the front door of the office. This was in the morning and it was very cold weather, so I believe that it was March or April. The door opened and this gentleman asked if A.B. was in. Mr. Thompson was known as A.B. to his friends—the name was Arthur Boyd Thompson.

This man, at that time of the year, had on a white hat that was all pushed in—dinted in at the sides, he had on white ducks and I call them ducks, because, at that time, in our family, that's what the boys were wearing. And I can't remember the jacket particularly, but I know that he had on white ducks and a white hat and it was still winter as far as we were concerned. It looked odd. There were a lot of old farmers that used to come in to the office that looked a lot better than this man did. So I just thought that he was another old farmer.

When he asked for A.B., and I told him that he was busy, he plunked a piece of paper down on the desk. He said to me, "Sign this." And I looked at it, and he had pulled a page out of what I call a scribbler—the kind that I used to use at school that had lines on it—not even little eyelets for looseleaf, but it was obviously pulled out of a scribbler. And I looked at it and he said, "Sign this." So I signed it, and that was all. I was the only one that signed it. So he said, "Well, give it to A.B." Then he left. He didn't say who he was or what he was there for or anything else—just give this to A.B. I was so new at it that I didn't look to see what I was signing, of course; nor did I know what I should have done, if I had.

So I took it in to my boss when he was free and he said, "Where did this come from?" And I said, "Well, this gentleman brought it in." He looked at me and said, "Do you know what this is?" and I said "No, but I signed it." He said, "Did you see him sign it?" I said "No, he just told me to sign it and I did."

Well, I'll tell you, I nearly lost my job because of that. It turned out that this was, in fact, Stephen Leacock, whose signature I was supposedly witnessing. To begin with, I did not see him sign it; it was all signed before he brought it into the office and all I did was sign it as he told me.

Mr. Thompson looked at it and he said, "This is terrible." He said, "You can't sign something unless you see them sign it." Mr. Thompson said, "This is Stephen Leacock's will and it's all wrong because you did not witness it." It was written in pencil on the scribbler page, there were not two witnesses who were witnessing it at the same time as he had signed it.

Everything was wrong, so Mr. Thompson was really upset. He looked at me and he said, "You have to find Mr. Leacock and get him back in here." I had to take a taxi and went out to Stephen Leacock's home on Old Brewery Bay, and I told Stephen Leacock that Mr. Thompson wanted to see him right away. I couldn't tell him what had happened about all this; Mr. Thompson was so upset that he just said, "Get Mr. Leacock back in here fast." I think he thought he was going to die before we got a proper will. At any rate, he did come back in with me, willingly, because Mr. Thompson insisted that he come. So he came in and the office prepared—it certainly wasn't me—the office prepared a new will for Stephen. And it was properly witnessed, it was properly drawn up and typed. I was not a witness to the new will.

SUE MULCAHY

SURVIVAL OF THE FITTEST   I don't think he had too much sympathy during the Depression for the poor. I remember him chuckling one day and saying, "The poor are not only with us, they're on top of us," which was a rather unsympathetic statement to make, and he meant it.

ALLAN ANDERSON

HE HAD HUMAN WARMTH   One of the things that has concerned me in later life has been that, when reading various biographies of his life, I've never found anyone reaching in and talking about the sympathetic nature of the man, the deepness of his feeling, the love of his fellow man. "Human warmth" are the perfect words for what I'm trying to say. Leacock had that.

He was a kind, sensitive man, and a man who loved people and who loved life and who had the God-given gift of seeing and being able to relate the humourous side of life, the funny things that went on all around us.

WILSON BECKET

A COMPASSIONATE MAN   Stephen Leacock was a very gentle person and very emotional and felt things I think very deeply. My mother was one of the first casualties of the war—she was lost at sea. When I came back to Canada he wanted to talk to me about it. I was over at Old Brewery Bay and he couldn't talk—all he could do was cry.

This was a few weeks after France had fallen and his very good friend René du Roure had given up and was drinking heavily. I think Dr. Leacock was just generally very depressed and my appear-ance brought to mind one more awful thing. Of course he was a very compas-sionate man.

ELIZABETH BURROWS LANGDON

WISDOM AND HUMOUR   You never got tired of him because he wasn't just a funny man. It was wisdom that was garbed with humour. Indeed, there were very few things he said that didn't have some touch of wisdom in them, and that was the thing. People weren't so much attracted to his humour as such, as by his wisdom, which was portrayed through humour.

GLADSTONE MURRAY

THE LAUGHING EYES   He had a large craggy face, broad-beamed and with fine eyes. The eyes were a terribly important part of him. He had laughing eyes, and despite the fact that he had a rather sad life, he brought great happiness through his humour to many, many people.

CHARLIE PETERS

A COMFORTABLE, RAMBLING, HUM-OUROUS MAN   I think of a comfortable, rambling, humourous man who played a very important part, unknowingly then for me, in my develop-ing years. He had a marvellous, natural, lovely relationship with all age groups, that was the thing.

You had a feeling of excitement with him, that something was going to happen, something pleasant.

DODE SPENCER AND MARGE CARTER

HIS GENTLE HUMOUR   I love his humour; I think it's gentle, it's so real. The more you read it, the more you know the world he's talking about. He loves people; it comes right through in everything he did. I always get very angry when I see people making mock of what he was being gentle about. For instance, Mavor Moore's interpretation of Dean Drone, the way it was acted at His Majesty's in Montreal. It made Dean Drone into a kind of clown who was yelping away from the box, and jumping on it. And that was unfair because that wasn't what he meant Dean Drone to be like at all.

I enjoy reading him to this day.
BARBARA WHITLEY

THAT INNATE KINDNESS   I look back to Leacock very, very fondly. I feel that I owe him a great deal. I've had an interesting career. A number of people influenced that career, Leacock was one of them who influenced it at an age where I was more subject to influence, influence in the best sense of the term.

He broadened my outlook by his lectures, by his manner of teaching, by the reading which he encouraged, and by his broad-mindedness in his teaching.

I'm not suggesting that he was a broad-minded man naturally. I mean he had his political prejudices, he was a great imperialist, not the greatest economist, but a very good political scientist. He would not tell us to read one side of the story; he would tell us to read Karl Marx as he would ask us to read Adam Smith. He felt that one should see both sides, even though he was convinced that one of those sides was wrong.

I would put it this way: I admired, respected and loved Stephen Leacock. He

was unique in his personality, the variety of his interests and his innate kindness.
SENATOR H. CARL GOLDENBERG

WHAT IN THE WORLD IS WINE AND CHEESE?   On December 30, 1969, there was a party in Orillia to celebrate the 100th anniversary of the birth of Stephen Leacock. It was a wine and cheese party and my father, John Drinkwater, who was eighty-five at that time, was there. And he said, "I doubt if Leacock would have known what a wine and cheese party was. I believe he would have preferred a bottle of good rye whisky and water but he would have enjoyed himself—after a couple of drinks."
NORAH BASTEDO

HIS REPUTATION GROWS   I think outside of his standard book on political economy, I've read his *Sunshine Sketches of a Little Town* and some of his humourous books. I read more out of a feeling of loyalty to Leacock, because you hear so much about him.

If you mentioned his name to almost anybody, almost any age, in the last fifty or sixty years, in my experience, they'd say, "Of course, Leacock, the great humourist," even if they had never read a word of his writings. He has achieved an international reputation—and it's strange, it grows with the passage of time.
JUDGE HAROLD B. LANDE

A VERY GREAT CANADIAN WRITER
I think Leacock is a very great Canadian writer because he is one of the first writers to have understood the particular culture

of Canada and to have expressed that in literature. That culture had to do with the British inheritance in Canada and the fact of Canada being part of the North American continent. And it was that dual nature of what a Canadian is that I think Leacock assimilated into his own mind and it inspired him to look at things in a particular way. It is this way of looking at things which I see as particularly Canadian. And that is Leacock's achievement.

The particular Leacockian vision is what I think is the secret of Leacock's art and it is that which I relate to the dual way of looking at things which is particularly Canadian. And what that is, for Leacock at any rate, is to be able to analyze something intellectually but, at the same time, to withhold judgement. That is the secret of Leacock's art. It is to see clearly but not to judge too harshly.

He does not have a reformer's zeal. He sees what is wrong, but he does not have a clear idea as to what is right, or at least he does not show that in his writing. He takes delight in all aspects of human behaviour, the good as well as the bad. It is not that Leacock does not have preferences or doesn't see room for improvement, but his vision is such that he realized that people would, more or less, always be the way they were and perfection is not possible. It's hard to call him a pessimist, though he was certainly not an optimist. His vision is in between. This is the essence of the man, that he avoided complaint and had a quality of vision to see imperfection.

But he had other qualities—compassion, natural kindliness, perhaps just the good sense to realize that life spent complaining was not particularly a good way of living and perhaps that is the reason why he accepted the limitations of things as he saw them and tried to enjoy them. And we see that in his writing. To be alive was to be imperfect, and it made one more human, and it was funny, and that was the way people were and that was how one lived with people.

Mark Twain was a frontier writer—he wrote of rather rougher social values. Leacock, as I think various writers have pointed out, was in a more genteel tradition, British middle-class. He was a direct literary descendant of Susanna Moodie. Leacock grew up in a type of middle-class family different from that of Mark Twain, who had a rougher kind of experience.

Leacock has written a vast amount about his recollections of people, his comments on British people visiting North America, and about Americans and these are very interesting and funny. But the book on which Leacock's reputation rests is *Sunshine Sketches of a Little Town*. That is the book which will make Leacock's literary reputation live for a long time because in that book Leacock expresses his peculiar vision in the best possible way. We see kindliness, perception and compassion. The characters are perfectly suited to be called Leacockian.

He's a great Canadian and a great human being. He doesn't have any solutions to offer but to read *Sunshine Sketches* and other works by Leacock is to be inspired and to enjoy life. It is to lift one's spirits, and that is the work of a great man.

FRANK BIRBALSINGH

Epilogue: Leacock on College Life

Stephen Leacock usually had the last word, and this book will continue the tradition. Up to this point, people have been talking about Leacock and telling stories about him. Now, here is the flavour of the man himself. Only one of these pieces has appeared in a book. They showed up, mostly, in McGill publications. They all have a common theme that Leacock returned to again and again—college life, both during and after graduation. They're a splendid sampling of Leacock in full flight.

The Oldest Living Graduate

I find him wherever I go among the colleges—the Oldest Living Graduate. At every college reunion, there he is; at each Commencement Day you may expect to find him among the first—a trifle bent he is and leans, one cannot but note it, somewhat heavily upon his stick; and there is something in his eye, a dimness, a far-away look as of one to whom already a further horizon is opening.

Yet, frail or not, he is there among the graduates at the earliest call. The younger men may hesitate about a hundred mile journey to attend the annual dinner of the alumni—not he. The younger man may grudge the time or count the cost—not so the Oldest Living Graduate.

See, it is Commencement Day. There sits the Oldest Living Graduate in the foremost row of seats in the College Hall. His hand is bent to his ear as he listens to the President's farewell address to the graduates. But he hears no word of it. His mind is back on a bright day in June—can it be sixty years ago?—when he first heard the like of it.

Easy and careless he was then, the Youngest Living Graduate, happy in his escape from the halls of the Temple of Learning. A butterfly he was, hatched from his skeins and glorying in the sunshine.

The gaze of the Youngest Living Graduate was turned forward, not back. He was looking out upon life, eagerly, expectantly. For the time being the sights and sounds of the campus had faded from his eye and ear. His mind was bent, his strength was braced, to meet the struggle of the coming years. It is the law of life. He had no time, as yet, for retrospect, and in his very eagerness was over-careless of the thing that lay behind.

But as the years slipped past, the ties of memory began to tighten their hold. There was a time, here and there, in the struggle of life, for a fleeting glance into the past. And lo! how soft the colours that began to lie on the pictured vision of his college days. The professoriate, once derided, how wise they seemed. It is ever their sad lot to be honoured only when they are dead; but all the greater is the honour. The glory of the campus, the football game played in the November dusk—how the shouts of it will linger in the ear of memory when half a century has gone. Nay, even the Lamp of Learning, itself, how softly now does it illuminate the long-neglected page: and the brave lettering of the degree, what a fine pride of forgotten knowledge does it now contain!

My friends, you and I and each of us were once the Youngest, or at least the Latest Living Graduate. The time is coming, if we stay to see it, when we shall be the Oldest. The time is coming when you and I, and an ancient group that we still call our "class" will walk the green grass of the campus on Commencement Day with the yearning regret for all that we might have done; with the longing for lost opportunity that is the chief regret of age.

While there is time, let us be up and doing. Before we are yet the Oldest Living Graduate, let us borrow something of the spirit that inspires him. Let us discount a note against the future with Father Time and receive its value in glowing coin of a present affection. While our class yet lives let us realize what a splendid group they are; let us find the opportunity to tell the professors how much we owe to them before we write our gratitude upon their tombstones.

And if our college wants our support, our help and our enthusiasm, let us bring it forth with all the affection of the Oldest Living Graduate and with all the power and eagerness of the Youngest.

Courtesy McGILL ANNUAL, 1922

Some Anecdotes of McGill

My recollection of McGill goes back so many years that there are a number of the distinguished men of their time at college who are living memories to me, though to most people now only a record and a legend. Those of us who look back to such men like to recall them not only for their achievement but also for those little eccentricities of character which keep affection alive in the softened light of retrospect. I am thinking here especially of the admirable "Pat" Johnson, Professor of Mathematics and Dean of the Faculty of Arts, as the old century ran out into the new. His specialty was exactitude, the full rigour of the rules. He looked on the rules of the Arts Faculty, as formulated in the calendar, as comparable to the propositions of Euclid. I remember he once reprimanded the professors on the ground that "various blanks" had been removed from the calendar and he wanted them put back. As to what he meant,—ask Euclid, who was suffering something of the same treatment at that very time.

I came in for a reprimand from the Dean before I had been a month at McGill. I had invited a distinguished American visitor, an authority on immigration (the topic of the hour) to come and talk to my class. As a matter of academic interest and common sense, I got permission beforehand from Principal Peterson. The lecture was a great success. But the next Monday, Dean Johnson sent for me. "You had a stranger in your classroom on Thursday?" he said. I admitted it. "He gave a lecture," said the Dean, "and don't you know that no person is permitted to give a lecture in a McGill classroom without the consent of

214

Corporation?" "It was all right," I said, "I got leave from Dr. Peterson." "Hoot!" said Pat, "and what would he know about the rules? And him only here seven years?" That was the back kick he wanted, so he let me go, kindly enough.

At the time I thought his "seven years" very funny. Later I came to share his opinion entirely, and to feel that no opinion at McGill should be taken except from people there at least twenty years on the spot.

Contemporary but younger than Dean Johnson was Dean Moyse, who succeeded him, and served till after the Great War, leaving behind him a record of scholarship and devotion second to none of our time. Dean Moyse had a quick and nimble intelligence,—sometimes too nimble, as it had in it the flaw that he talked to so many people about so many things that he didn't always remember who had said what. I remember I came in just for a minute, to his inner office one day in the busy hour of the morning (this was during the Great War), to tell him that a rumour had come up from down town that the Russians had made a complete collapse and signed a peace (Brest-Litovsk). Two hours later I came into the outer room and the Dean called me into his private office, closing the door, as if for secrecy. "A most extraordinary rumour has come from down town," he said, "they say that it's all over with Russia—one better perhaps keep quiet about it till we hear.—A man came in here this morning," he continued, "and told me about it,—respectable looking man, too,—seemed quite honest."—I let it go at that.

But the anecdote of McGill that will never die is the story of the Professor, the Gold-Fish and the Policeman. One of our professors of physiology (I mustn't mention his name as he is still alive and might be kicking) was out visiting one winter night, and the people at the house showed him a gold-fish that had died because the water that it was in had frozen. The professor looked at the fish and said, "Let me take it home and I think that tomorrow I can treat it in the laboratory and revive it."

So when he started for home they wrapped the gold-fish in a bit of tissue paper and the professor put it in his overcoat pocket. It was a cold night, very late and with lots of deep snow along the street. On the way home he put his hand into his coat pocket and accidentally flipped out the gold-fish and it fell into the snow.

The professor knelt down to pick it up, but he couldn't find it and stayed there on his knees groping for it. Just then a policeman came along on his beat and stopped and said, "What are you doing there?"

Professors hate to be questioned. He just looked over his shoulder and said, "I am trying to find a gold-fish."

The policeman then understood that he was dealing with a mental case, and he said, coaxingly, "Now you just come along with me and I'll take you to a place where we've a whole lot of gold-fish—all you want."

"All right," the professor said, "only just help me to get this one first."

To humour him the policeman knelt down and began groping in the snow and, first thing he knew, out came a gold-fish! He was absolutely flabbergasted.

"Great heavens!" he said. "Are there any more?"

"Maybe a whole lot," said the professor. As he started off for home again, the policeman was still on his knees looking for gold-fish.

Courtesy of THE McGILL NEWS, 1943

How to Pass Exams Without Trying

A Leacockian treasure of high hilarity and fanciful nonsense is tucked away in time-worn copies of *Old McGill*, 1935. That was the student annual, and Leacock sometimes contributed to it. This is a gem, this one, and you can hear Leacock chuckling—if you listen hard enough!—as you read through it. Apparently, it was never published in any of his collections. He called it "Ars Examinandi."

"The Editor
Dear Sir:

You were kind enough to refer to certain of my writings in regard to the difficulties and fallacies of written examinations. You ask me if there is any way,—if I have your phrases right,—to "get by." I think there is.

Every student should train himself to be like the conjurer Houdini. Tie him as you would, lock him in as you might, he got loose. A student should acquire this looseness.

For the rudiments of education, there is no way round. The multiplication table has got to be learned. They say Abraham Lincoln knew it all. So too the parts of speech must be committed to memory, and left there. The names of the Wessex kings from Alfred (better Ael-frydd) to his Danish successor Half-Knut should be learned and carefully distinguished from the branches of the Amazon.

But these rudiments once passed, education gets easier and easier as it goes on. When one reaches the stage of being what is called a ripe scholar it is so easy as to verge on imbecility.

Now for college examinations, once the student is let into college, there are a great number of methods of evasion. Much can always be done by sheer illegibility of hand writing, by smearing ink all over the answer paper, and then crumpling it up in a ball.

But apart from this, each academic subject can be found on its own ground. Let me give one or two examples.

Here, first, is the case of Latin Translation,—the list of extracts from Caesar, Cicero, etc., the origin of each always indicated by having the word Caesar, etc., under it. On this we seize as our opportunity. The student doesn't need to know one word of Latin. He learns by heart a piece of translated Caesar, selecting a typical extract and he writes that down. The examiner merely sees a faultless piece of translation and notices nothing,—or at best thinks the candidate was given the wrong paper. He lets him pass.

Here is the piece of Caesar as required:

'These things being thus this way, Caesar although not yet he did not know neither the copiousness of the enemy nor whether they had frumentum, having sent on Labienus with an impediment he himself on the first day before the third day, ambassadors having been sent to Vercingetorix lest who might which, all having been done, set out.

Caesar, Bum Gallicum. Op. cit.'

Cicero also is easily distinguished by the cold-biting logic of his invective. Try this:—

'How how which what, O Catiline, Infected, infracted, disducted, shall you still perfrage us? To what expunction shall we not subsect you? To what bonds, to what vinculation, to how great a hyphen? I speak. Does he? No.

Cicero. In (and Through) Catiline.'

The summation of what is called the Liberal Arts course is reached with such subjects as political theory, philosophy, etc. Here the air is rarer and clearer and vision easy. There is no trouble at all in circling around the examiner at will. The best device is found in the use of quotations from learned authors of whom he has perhaps,—indeed, very likely never heard, and the use of languages which he either doesn't know or can't read in blurred writing. We take for granted that the examiner is a conceited, pedantic man, as they all are,—and is in a hurry to finish his work and get back to a saloon.

Now let me illustrate. Here is a question from the last Princeton examination in Modern Philosophy. I think I have it correct or nearly so.

Discuss Descartes' proposition 'Cogito ergo sum' as a valid basis of epistemology.

Answer: Something of the apparent originality of Descartes' dictum 'cogito ergo sum' disappears when we recall that long before him Globulus had written 'Testudo ergo crepito' and the great Arab scholar, Alhelallover, writing about 200 Fahrenheit, had said, 'Indigo ergo gum.'' But we have only to turn to Descartes' own brilliant contemporary, the Abbe Pate de Fois Grasse, to find him writing,—Dimanche lundi mardi, mercredi jeudi vendredi samedi,—which means as

much, or more, than Descartes's assertion. It is quite likely that the Abbe was himself acquainted with the works of Pretzel, Weiner Schnitzel and Schnierkase: even more likely still he knew the treatise of the low german, Fisch von Gestern who had already set together a definite system or scheme. He writes Wo ist mein Bruder? Er ist in dem Hause. Habi ich den Vogel geschen? Dies ist ein gules Messer. Holen sie Karl und Fritz und wir werder alle in's Theater gehen. Danke Bestens.

There, one can see how easy it is. I know it from my own experience. I remember in my fourth year in Toronto (1891), going into the exam room and picking up a paper which I carelessly took for English Philology; I wrote on it, passed on it and was pleasantly surprised two weeks later when they gave me a degree in Ethnology. I had answered the wrong paper. This story, oddly enough is true."

Courtesy OLD McGILL, 1935

Recovery After Graduation
Thoughts For The Class Of 1935

It is very commonly supposed, or taken for granted, that a man comes out of college with his mind hopelessly impaired. I do not think that this is so. I have known a great many cases of recovery, which, if not absolutely complete, seemed at least permanent.

More than that. If a man will set himself to preserve what he had gained at college, he will find that as he grows old, he is able in his leisure to fall back upon his education as a delightful *reductio ad absurdum*.

I know a case in point. Most boys at school have at some time learned all the dates of the Saxon and Norman kings. But as a rule they fail to keep this up, and lose all the good of it. I have an old friend, a college graduate, who has carefully kept this knowledge alive. He is now able in his old age to get great enjoyment from saying over these dates to himself. His keepers tell me that he shows many other signs of mental activity, and often recites for them lists of genitive plurals and verbs that take the dative.

How different with most of us! We all remember that the prepositions ad, ante, con, in and inter govern something—but just what, eludes us. We are, therefore, unable to apply the knowledge gained. You and I perhaps once knew that the genitive of supellex (furniture) was supellectilis. But later on when we came to furnish a house and could have used this information, it had slipped away. Horace puts it very well in his usual wistful way—but I forget just how.

I am not referring to the classics alone. The difficulty seems to appear all along the line. How much our college mathematics ought to mean to us, if we only kept them clean and bright, like a sword ready to be drawn from the scabbard. Take the logarithm. I suppose no more powerful implement of human advance was ever fashioned than when Montesquieu discovered the logarithm—I think it was Montesquieu. "The logarithms of a number to a given base is the index of the power to which the base must be raised to produce the given number." The old fellow hit the mark right in the centre first time.

But for most of us this bright instrument is useless. We have forgotten how to raise the base. Had we kept any reasonable recollection of second year

hydraulics the thing would be easy. But no! There is the base and we can't lift it.

Yet it pleased me, I must say, at my country place last summer when there was some mathematical difficulty about marking the tennis court to find one of my guests, a student in my classes at McGill, offer to work out the measurement of the court with a logarithm. He said it was quite simple. He needed, in short, nothing but a hypotenuse and two acute angles, all of which luckily were found round the place. It was very interesting to watch the boy calculating, at first. I am certain that he would have got his solution, only while he was preparing to mark the court by means of his logarithm the chauffeur marked it with whitewash.

It may be said that mathematics is, for most of us, a thing apart. Not all of us have the knack of my McGill student. But where we all feel the greatest shortcoming in our education is in the matter of our studies in English literature—the very language and thought of our nation. Here I am afraid it is only too true that our college methods fall short of what one could wish.

I am thinking especially of poetry. I fear it is an undeniable fact that poetry is dealt with by our literature teachers in exactly the same way as a compound of gases is treated in the chemistry department. It is broken up, analysed, labelled, examined, and finally reduced to the form of solid matter.

Let me take as an example a well-known stanza of which the melody and the pathos, even after a professor has done his worst with it, still linger in the mind.

The boast of heraldry, the pomp of power,
   And all that beauty, all that wealth, ere gave
Awaits alike th'inevitable hour:—
   The paths of glory lead but to the grave.

Now follows the professorial analysis:
Boast. How do you distinguish boast from boost? Would it be an improvement to say "The boost of heraldry?" If so, why?
Heraldry. What is the Greek for this?
All that beauty. Question—all what beauty?
Awaits. What is the predicate and what is predicated? *Lead but to.* What is the difference between *but to* and *but in?* Which is preferable here?
Final Question. Write out the life of the poet Gray, being particular to remember that his grandfather was born in Fareham Hants, or possibly in Epsom, Salts.

Somehow one feels that this is not quite satisfying. For many of us indeed a number of the greatest masterpieces of literature are forever hopelessly damaged by our having studied them in a literature class. I recall here particularly Tennyson's wonderful verses, written just at the close of his life, waiting to "cross the bar"—his wearied eyes looking out already from his seaside home in the Isle of Wight to horizons infinitely far.

Twilight and evening star,
And one clear call for me,
And may there be no moaning of the bar
When I put out to sea.
But such a flood as, moving, seems asleep,
Too full for sound and foam,
When that which drew from out the boundless deep,
Turns again home.

These verses seem to me the last word in poetry, the absolute proof of the sublimity of its reach—beyond prose; our measured life is pictured in the moving flood, moving never to return. But I have never felt that my appreciation of the poem—which appeared in my college days—was heightened by the notes I took on it in class. I have them still. They read:—
Twilight. At what time is it twilight in Hampshire in June?
Evening Star. Explain this phenomenon and show there is nothing in it.
Moaning of the bar. How was the bar regulated in Tennyson's time?

But yet all this doesn't mean that education is futile and thrown away. What happens really depends upon a man's self. If, after graduation, he sits down and broods over his education, why naturally it will impair his mind. But it is his duty to be up and doing when he leaves college, forget all about his education, act as if he never had any, cultivate bright thoughts and cheerful ideas and he will soon find himself on the level of those about him.

Then as time goes on, more and more he will acquire that comfortable feeling that after all he has got in his education a *pons asinorum* that no one is going to take away from him.

Courtesy OLD McGILL, 1935

Acknowledgements

First and foremost, I owe an immense debt of gratitude to my wonderful wife, Betty Tomlinson Anderson. She worked constantly, intelligently and enthusiastically on this book. I ran around recording people. She was, for many years, a well-known CBC broadcaster and, as such, picked up a flawless ability to edit tapes. She has worked strenuously on all my books, but she really saved my skin on this one. She logged all the material, edited the tapes, picked out the best stories and then we discussed them. She read the manuscript fastidiously and, over and over again, caught errors I had missed. Oral histories demand a great deal of hard work and minute checking. You are my companion, my love and my co-author, Betty.

Tina de Savoye typed all but a small fraction of the original transcript and then, very quickly, did the manuscript after we had done some final editing. Tina was endlessly cheerful, always excited by the continuing flow of Leacock stories, and more than willing to work and work and work. I was way behind schedule with the publisher, so thank you very much, Tina, for putting up with all that frantic hustle.

Jay Cody, the curator of the Stephen Leacock Memorial Home in Orillia helped me in the field more than any other person. He combed Orillia for people who had known Leacock and he kept coming up with new ones until I thought I would end up interviewing a quarter of the citizens of Orillia. Thank you, Jay, for your unbounding friendly co-operation.

Dovie Payne lent me a priceless early journal, kept by one of Leacock's ancestors, and she assisted me in other ways, as well. She is a descendant of E.P. Leacock, about whom Stephen Leacock wrote so fascinatingly in *My Remarkable Uncle*.

Jay Cody lent me a horde of pictures from the Stephen Leacock Memorial Home, from which prints were made at the Simcoe County Archives. I want to thank Peter Moran and the others at the Archives who did work in a hurry for me.

I want also to thank Mrs. Elizabeth Lewis of the Leacock Room at the MacLennan Library at McGill for allowing me to obtain copies of Leacock letters and a few pictures.

The Orillia Public Library very obligingly provided me with pictures and Leacock material.

I am grateful to McGill for the use of some material from various issues of *Old McGill* and the *McGill News*.

I thank McClelland and Stewart for the use of some paragraphs from Barbara Nimmo's excellent preface to Leacock's *Last Leaves*.

Edgar Andrew Collard graciously permitted me to use various recollections of Leacock from his book *The McGill You Knew*. These were stories told by people I simply couldn't reach or who are deceased.

This book started out, one morning, in the office of broadcaster Peter McGarvey, the man who single-handedly saved the Leacock home in Orillia. Pete and I decided that, before it was too late, an oral history of Stephen Leacock should be done. Later, Pete came up with a rare tape, made years and years ago, which contained the voices of people such as B.K. Sandwell, George Leacock, and others, talking about Leacock. That was really something!

Betty Jane Corson did the final editing of the manuscript. She is a charming, gracious woman. Her editing is subtle and discreet and adds greatly to the quality of the book.

Oral histories are expensive to do, and without the assistance of the Ontario Arts Council, I would have had to abandon the project. I had to raise more money than I was able to get from grants, though. The Stephen Leacock Associates got me under way with an initial loan. My sister, Jean, who has helped me so often in the past, came to my aid again, as, in the same helpful manner, did Hilda Tomlinson.

And finally, what is oral history without the storytellers who make up the body of the book? I have never before done an oral history where I found the people I was interviewing so overwhelmingly helpful, so articulate and so pleased that their beloved Stephen Leacock would be remembered in a personal way and they would be a part of that remembering. To all of you, my warmest thanks!

The Storytellers and Their Stories

Douglas C. Abbott

Connoisseur
An old country Frenchman
The Ladies' Department
A great raconteur
A Leacock
No political ambitions

Allan Anderson

Liquor loosens the tongue
Hang on to your pants
Now, look and see
Play up, play up, and play the game
Ask and ye shall be told
My great mistake
The wandering tie
Somebody has got to start and re-unite Canada
Slow learner
Speedy bicycle king
An arduous contrivance
Rare book
Back up, and fast
Survival of the fittest

Grace Annesley

He taught her Greek

Mrs. Alice Baldwin

The debonair René du Roure

Norah Bastedo

Like Mussolini after Hitler
Cheque it out

It belongs to some old guy
Poetic license
What's perfect, anyway?
He liked politics
Not enjoying himself
What in the world is wine and cheese?

Wilson Becket

You've got a girl, haven't you?
He had human warmth

Frank Birbalsingh

A very great Canadian writer

F. Munroe Bourne

Sable for a wife

Bob Bowman

McGill was a real fraternity

Jean Cain

A rugged man
Pants to spare
Tiny and chirpy
The brothers
Trixie was handsome
A domineering mother-in-law
A helping hand
Just cousin Stephen
The biggest cigar, the biggest drink
The lively and tempestuous Fitzie
I want a place of my own
At least she could bake bread

Like a valet
He got along with kids
Set destroyer
The funny old car and Bresso's hack
Red bow in the sunset
The old sloop
The inept commercial gardener
He played cricket and lacrosse
Some people wouldn't go near him
I think of him still
This sad, retrospective air

Bob Campbell

Don't watch the spider

Fred Carter

A typical small town

Marge Carter (Tudhope)

A Santa Claus face
Sense of the ridiculous
The plays
Too late!
A comfortable, rambling, humourous man

Jay Cody

By cab, to market
A neater home now?

Prof. John Culliton

This, that and the other thing
Tea and bread

Garner Currie

A delightful old gentleman
Roars of laughter
Asking Barbara
Back and forth, back and forth

M.D.

Icebound
A small piece of romance
The chores were endless
A basket case?
Eating him out of house and home
Only for the dogs
No compromise
Into the fiery furnace

Brigadier-General Jimmy de Lalanne

Too much lecturing
Checking out Viner
Brevity paid off
A certain little truth to it
Not delinquent
Fooling the folks

Catherine Drinkwater

Little furniture, lots of books
Distracted
Lady Godiva
It belongs to some old guy
Four o'clock in the morning
Not a brain in his head
Until we meat again

John Drinkwater

A con job

Hilda Elsliger

Hats off
Tina
Red as a beet
Someone pinched the pumpkin
Up in the morning before daylight

Charles Fisher

The University Club
The big armchair at the University Club
The University Club's best-liked character

Marjorie Fisher

Check your briefcase, sir?

Eileen Flanagan

Class memories, 1917

Senator Eugene Forsey

The key to it all
One way to dress for dinner
Never foggy
Mostly, he gave them a break
One-upmanship
The German student
Doing the donkey work
All eternity
The rippling fountain
A superb talent for fun
Executions for senility
No nonsense from stuffy Brits
Changing his mind about Forsey
Extraordinary brilliance of mind
Stabbing people's minds

Norman H. Friedman

Not quite fast enough

D. Lorne Gales

Dilly of a temper
An icy response
One good turn deserves another
A lice way of doing things
His love of life

Aubrey Gaudaur

Charlie and the wheelbarrow
Chaos at Christmas
Worms and good fishing tackle
Out on the water, drinking and talking
Racking pains
The Irish barnyard
Drip, drip, drip
Waving his hands, talking Japanese

Joe Gaudaur

Tragedy
Don't drink her straight
On again, off again
Make-work projects
Free chickens, free chicken house

Senator H. Carl Goldenberg

Tap, tap, tap
Passing the buck
He was heartbroken
Stevie Jr.'s progress
The pea-shooter
Trying to cope with Stevie, Jr.
A French monarchist
Water was her downfall
Read this, read that
Jumping the gun
Hounded into it
Senator Leacock?
My you're ignorant Goldenberg!
Morgan enforced the rule
His awful handwriting
Two toes tales
The end of John Maynard Keynes
Moping millionaire
That innate kindness

Harold Hale

From Sutton to Orillia
I talked to the fellow

Beth Hatley

"Who died on the post?"
Taken for granted
Hatley's

The Hon. Mr. Justice G. Miller Hyde

A bare pass

Henry Janes

Hat in the stacks
"Look after Stevie Jr."
There's nothing like them
On the end of a hoe
The gypsies and the mushrooms
Sun over the yard-arm
They were for thinking, not drinking
Six guys pulling a boat
Boat bungle
Paper out of cornstalks
Walking around the dinner table, talking
The $150 commission
The interview that clicked
The manuscripts were covered with wood ashes

Col. H. Wyatt Johnston

Ham on wry

Bob Kilby

The moustache vibrated when he laughed
A really wild temper
Sneaking a few
Few people knew he existed
The hobo and the little French governess

Judge Harold B. Lande

Right off the farm
The old coon coat
The black band slipped
The aristocrat
Tea in his salon
On the wavelength
He was a great attraction
Hemmeon would sort of smile
Unusual qualities, universal appeal
An unbiased view
A one-man show
Not prejudiced against women students
His reputation grows

Elizabeth Burrows Langdon

A sense of the ridiculous
A very happy marriage
The scent of phlox
A lovely billiard table
Tina, Kelly and Sergeant Jones
The plays
Changing his mind
Burn that shed!
Swimming off the boathouse
He loved the water
Relatives of Tina's
Off to Hatley's
Really furious
A compassionate man

Hal Lawrence

Write fiction
In praise of Sunshine Sketches

George Leacock

How his first book got into print
He wrote wherever he had a pen

Mary Leacock

He read his work aloud

Senator Alan A. Macnaughton

He looked straight at you
A little bit of an actor
Coming to the rye
A stupid thing to do
Making it up by the yard
The young were catalysts

Maysie MacSporran

A large, cuddly, woolly bear
Under a terrible cloud
He laughed like Santa Claus
Gentle handling
I got your letter from some God-forsaken place
Here's Mr. Learoyd
Too much writing too quickly

Dr. T.R. Matthews

Odd twists

Joe McDougall

Woman of mystery?
No friends?
The great radio caper

Bill McGill

Does this guy bathe in booze?

Pete McGarvey

Promise unfulfilled
Mansion like a ghost story

Karen McKee

The Shaw house was very like Leacock's

Louis Melzack

The Bleury Street bookshop

George Moase

High style
The loner
That was his life
He could smell the fish
They tore the lodge down
I haven't got a thing to give this poor guy

S. Morgan-Powell

The dramatic struggle

Sue Mulcahy

Stealing his stuff
Jackson's Brewery
Not part of the safaris
No way to make a will

Gladstone Murray

The handout
Meeting G.K. Chesterton
In the great tradition
Wisdom and humour

A. Gordon Nairn

Soul survivor

Jim Nichol

New shingles

Barbara Nimmo (Ulrichsen)

George Leacock, storyteller
One story after another
By October, he headed for Montreal
His parties were famous
Students all spoke to him

A hard taskmaster
How's the gas supply?
Spectacles and stories
Making a fine point

Frank Nobbs

Always in a hurry
He kept her ashes
The Côte des Neiges house
A dickensian character
No kidding
We can all stand on Bermuda
The other professors got turned off
Nobody but Leacock sat there
Thirsty in Nevada

Dora Noy (Vick)

Brewery Bay peas
Buying Vick's bread

Oscar Olimer

Homely without a moustache
The rush to build the new house
The cow kicked Leacock off the stool

Hilda Outridge

The knight of the road
Peekaboo
"Who died on the post?"
Prophet without honour
The unknown Stephen Leacock
A gracious letter

Dovie Payne (Leacock)

The Leacock traits
The old journal
That "Remarkable Uncle"
Not without Payne

Albanie Pelletier

The old homestead
Neat and tidy
Lots of screens
The Pelletiers
Free movies
The DeSoto
The Leacock place
Booze in the basement
Big brains
The greenhouse
The greenhouse, the garden, the bell,
    the bulletin board
The white pants that weren't white

John Pemberton

Safety pins and a collar stud
Part of the picture
He'd listen
A really trained mind
Home away from home
They were both poor billiard players
The only honorary member
His kindly philosophy

Fred Perigo

Charlie was odd
The blowup
Choo choo choo
Seventy-five dollars in his cap
Pop it down
Building the boathouse in 1917
The minister drowned
White flannels and rubber boots
Barrels of water
The nonconformist
Walking to town
A pretty long road to go

Col. Charles Petch

Remember this
He liked athletes
Rah, rah, rah, McGill!

Charlie Peters

Trouble at the University Club
Wrong way snow storm
The old fob watch
It's a tossup
Morgan was a bad choice
He was the University Club
The laughing eyes

Paul Phelan

A great day for mother
All up in the air

William H. Pugsley

Time waits for no man? Wrong!
The impact of a bomb

Grace Reynolds

Pipe dream
Don't ask for my flask
The ten dollars
Like a Spanish dancer
The death of Trix
Roughing it on the porch
We dressed for dinner every night
An unforgivable affront
New hats galore
Mrs. Leacock went home
Off to Europe

Harold Roland

Men in white coats
A problem collecting

His boat
Find Stephen
Fuss, fuss, fuss
Black ducks

G. Meredith Rountree

He slept in it?
Bunglers all
Mind your own business

B.K. Sandwell

The ho-hum days at Upper Canada College

Phobe Gutelius Seely

Very haphazard

Trueman Seely

His lectures were more entertaining than
    his books
The most interesting figure, then and now

Jennie Mackenzie Smith

Summer of 1924
A nice little boy
The maid met a man
Very plain cooking
They should have lived in Montreal

Dode Spencer (Tudhope)

Looked like a sack
Aftermath
Ambling around
Shrieking around
The plays
Off to Hatley's
A comfortable, rambling, humourous man

Margaret Stephen

Foxy Grandpa
And a watch-chain
The jazzy stockings
He taught at McGill?
I didn't learn anything

Fred Stone

You kept alert
A dazzling mosaic of ideas
Haw, haw!
Fifty cents worth of gab
Stamp of approval
The only good Tory is a dead one?
Never met anyone like him

Iva Street

The tomatoes always froze

Redvers L. Stubley

Sleepy little town
. . . But it could be lively
Hitting the nail on the head
They couldn't bear those bare feet
Opposites attract
He'd size you up fast

Bob Tait

Paper routed

Frederick Taylor

Shaggy Stevie, or Leaky Steamcock
That's exactly how I feel

Herbert H. Tees

A restless man
The fingernail treatment
Silver in India

Catastrophe
Half and Half
One day isn't as good as the next
Telling them apart
The simplicity of his sentences
Troublemaker

Hélène Tolmie

The sick little girl and the kind old gentleman

Laurence Tombs

Something of a ploy?
Grace Reynolds
He wouldn't run
He put up my picture

Jean Van Vliet

Barbara was very good to me
Bang went the drum
Old-fashioned handwriting

Wilf Varley

I'll take them
He came with Orillia

Philip Vineberg

It went back to Riel
He could hold his liquor
Questioning the questionnaire
He slaved to provide for young Stevie
French to the tips of his fingers
He'd start right in
Some whimsical theories
The unknown Greta Garbo
His fairness sometimes rebounded
Upping the marks
He gobbled up books
Teacher and friend
The messy office

Mad at everybody
Not a workaholic
Collapse of the French franc
A red Tory?
A rare bird
Tinge of sadness

The Hon. Mr. Justice Allison Walsh

He burst into tears
Nobody fell asleep
Rolling in the aisles
A Dickens of a time
A great vision of the future

Barbara Whitley

The Shaws
The monologues
His gentle humour

Morley Young

I thought he was kinda queer
The redhead fired him
A big time in Midland
Bill Jones
The crash of 1929
The fabulous trip to the football game
A drink when the door was slammed
Banging against the dock
Sailing was his greatest hobby
The absent-minded professor
Out went the ponds
A large garden
The perambulating hawthorns
Easy to work for